HAMMARSKJÖLD

HAMMARSKJÖLD

by Emery Kelen

G. P. Putnam's Sons   New York

*To my former colleagues in the United
Nations Secretariat who thought he was
"the best in us."*

ACKNOWLEDGMENTS

My thanks are due to my colleagues in the United Nations Secretariat and to Hammarskjöld's Swedish friends who have taken the time to reminisce with me about the Secretary-General.

I should also like to thank my wife, Betty Kelen, for her editorial help.

Contents

HAMMARSKJÖLD

I

The Empty Chair

THE news of the Secretary-General's death came over the radio on the morning of September 18, 1961, and it streamed through the glass house from the Third Basement to the 38th Floor in a dwindling lament. It left girls weeping in front of their typewriters and men staring with moist eyes through the windows. By and by they began to drift out of their offices to loiter in the corridors or knot together in silent groups.

"Never before has this house been so full of quiet sadness," wrote the *Secretariat News*, "and never before have we had so little to say to each other."

Pauline Frederick recorded her broadcast for the NBC radio network. "Dag Hammarskjöld lived—and died," she said, "in the belief, as he expressed it, that 'He who fears God will no longer fear man.'" Then her voice broke and she began to cry. Somberly the engineers edited her tears out of the tape.

"Did you cry when Hammarskjöld died?" I asked his executive assistant Andrew Cordier. He shot an amazed glance at me for this outlandish question, but perhaps because I am a caricaturist, he accepted it and replied in an uneasy voice, "Tears were shed on the 38th Floor."

"Why do you think so many people wept at the death of

Hammarskjöld?" I asked a young woman member of the Secretariat, and she replied, "Because he was the best in us."

Later in the morning of September 18, George Ivan Smith, from the Secretary-General's office, held a press conference. He told us that "sometime last night" the Secretary-General's plane had crashed near Ndola, Southern Rhodesia. "There is one survivor," he said. "His name is not known."

A muted voice was heard: "Could it be the Secretary-General?"

"I am sorry to say," replied Smith, "that the Secretary-General is not the survivor. His body was positively identified by the United States Air Attaché, Colonel Benjamin Matlick."

At 4:00 P.M. the Security Council met in an informal session and issued a statement: "Mr. Hammarskjöld's death is a great loss to the Secretariat, the United Nations and to all the member states. Secretary-General Hammarskjöld was an outstanding leader in recent years in strengthening world peace. His extraordinary diplomatic skill has helped carry the United Nations through many crises and has developed the organization into an important instrument for building a peaceful world community."

Valerian A. Zorin, the head of the Soviet delegation, did not associate himself with these remarks, though he joined in sending condolences to the Hammarskjöld family. His position was made clear: ". . . that the Soviet Union is known not to have recognized Mr. Hammarskjöld as an official of the United Nations and does not share the appraisal of his political activities contained in the communiqué." *

Another press conference, held in the afternoon, divulged the name of the lone survivor: Sergeant Harold M. Julien, a Security Officer. In Malden, Massachusetts, his parents told the newspapers that their son was always lucky, that he had frequently won lotteries, turkeys, and other prizes; and he had

* *New York Times,* September 19, 1961.

survived both World War II and the Korean War. In Miami, his Cuban wife gave thanks for his survival, and indeed we all did, not only because out of sixteen people one life was saved, but because his testimony might be all-important in laying to rest the many questions, conjectures, and suspicions that from the beginning had jumbled in our minds.

But a few days later we learned that Harold M. Julien was dead. The name of this young man, who had been born in Brooklyn, was among those names of several nations Mr. Cordier noted in the *Secretariat News:* "In life, Heinz, Vladimir, Bill, Alice, Harry, and Francis were selfless in their interests, devoted to their tasks and dedicated to the noble cause of peace . . . they died with their chief in the line of duty."

On September 19, the 16th Session of the General Assembly opened. The outgoing president, Frederick H. Boland, invited the delegates to stand for one minute of silent prayer. On the left of the president was Andrew Cordier, and on his right was the Secretary-General's empty chair. The delegates rose with their aides and advisers and all who were in the vast hall; the nations, races, religions, and ideologies of men arose and stood with their heads bent. Never was a minute so long, or silence so silent, or a chair so empty.

Commissions of Investigation were set up. Two were from the Federation of Rhodesia and Nyasaland. Another Commission was sent out by the United Nations, and the Swedish government also despatched observers. In due course, the reports of these gentlemen wended their way to the Headquarters Building, and they were studied attentively by the members of the Secretariat. None of us could believe that such a man as the Secretary-General was, could have been obliterated in a simple accident.

The hand of officialdom had borne heavily on these documents. One of the Rhodesian reports was addressed to "His Excellency Simon, Earl of Dalhousie, Knight Grand Cross of the Most Excellent Order of the British Empire, upon whom has been conferred the Decoration of the Military Cross, Governor-General and Commander-in-Chief in and over the Federation of Rhodesia and Nyasaland."

That is how Englishmen talk to one another when they investigate death in the bush.

All the documents were written in solid bureaucratese, made even more abstruse by the cabbalistic slang of aeronauts; and they were jammed with initials, dashes, and annexes marked with Roman numerals. In them no Bill, Alice, or Harry met their deaths; only Body No. 1, No. 2, and No. 3 were lost somewhere between Distresfa (Distress Phase) and Incerfa (Uncertainty Phase). Cold and heartlessly objective, the words had no penumbra of shock or grief, but were like the Latin name of an illness that carries away the head of a family.

Yet, somewhere in the catacomb of words were the palpable clues whereby the human mind could touch upon catastrophe. We had known the dead. It meant something to us that six colleagues were laid waste upon the ground and that all of them wore seatbelts as if they had expected to land in a few minutes; that four watches were found in the wreckage, which "stopped within less than two minutes of each other, indicating the time of the crash."

Among the documents we found the statement made by the sole temporary survivor, Harold Julien. A Rhodesian policeman named Allen had talked with him on the evening of September 18th. The conversation did not take place exactly as it was recorded, for Sergeant Julien was incoherent, and Inspector Allen often had to repeat his questions:

Allen: "The last we heard from you you were over Ndola runway. What happened?"
Julien: "It blew up."
Allen: "Was this over the runway?"
Julien: "Yes."

Allen: "What happened then?"
Julien: "There was great speed. Great speed."
Allen: "What happened then?"
Julien: "Then there was the crash."
Allen: "What happened then?"
Julien: "There were lots of little explosions all around."
Allen: "How did you get out?"
Julien: "I pulled the emergency tab and ran out."
Allen: "What about the others?"
Julien: "They were just trapped."

Inspector Allen was inclined to believe that Julien understood the questions that were being put to him. Later in the evening, a nurse heard Julien say, "We were on the runway and there was an explosion ... We were on the runway when Mr. Hammarskjöld said, 'Go back,' then there was an explosion ... I was the only one that got out, all the others were trapped."

The doctors nevertheless warned that these statements were unreliable because the patient was delirious and that some of his remarks might even be taken as describing his own shocked condition. During the last twenty-four hours of his life, he spoke of sparks in the sky; again the doctors pointed out that he was uremic and that part of the picture of this disease is spots and flashes of light before the eyes.

The question uppermost in our minds was whether the Southern Rhodesians had killed Sergeant Julien in order to keep him from telling the real story of the aircrash in Ndola. I asked a member of the United Nations Commission what he thought of the matter. He replied, "When Julien was found, a policeman put his own coat over him and carried him in his jeep to the hospital. Four doctors and eighteen nurses took care of him. You can't kill a man in the presence of eighteen nurses."

We read the last living words that came from the Secretary-

General's plane. The conversation was with Air Traffic Controller Martin of Ndola Airport.

"Are you proceeding Salisbury after landing Ndola?"
"Negative."
"Roger are you night-stopping Ndola?"
"Negative."
"Due parking difficulties would like your intentions."
"Will give them on the ground..."
"Will you require refuelling Ndola?"
"Standby."
"May require a little."
"Roger."
"Your lights in sight overhead Ndola, descending, confirm QNH (AD200 317 degrees)."
"Roger, QNH 1021 mb, report reaching 6000 feet."
"Roger 1021."

Then the plane hit the trees and burst into flame.

The next day, after some delay, the search for the missing plane had gotten underway. Little planes went up from Salisbury, scanning the jungle for signs of disaster, and across the bush the airwaves carried a conversation between Salisbury Information Center and Ndola Tower which sounded to us almost profane with its workaday slang and professional chitchat.

"Can you confirm Jacko 169 departed Thornhill 0830 elapsed time 57 minutes still nil contact?"
"Roger. He'll probably be quite close in before he contacts you, Bud."
"He's descending to I think to about 3000 feet agl to have a look for this queer job..."
"Confirm that victor papa echo has been requested to look out for this bloke on the way over"

"You are fading say again please"
"Roger would you confirm that VPE has been requested to have a look for this missing aircraft en route over."
"He is in the picture but whether he will look out I can't say."
"Roger."
"Call."
"Reply."
"The wreckage has been located will advise later."
"Thank you."

With this "thank you" the tears began to flow in Sweden, in New York, and indeed the world over. From the Royal Medical Board of Sweden doctors came to the scene of the disaster, A. Frykholm and M. Ringertz, and they examined the Rhodesian medical reports and assessed them favorably. They said that the postmortem reports, though brief, were adequate and gave an impression of careful examination and reliability.

> Secretary-General Hammarskjöld's body was the only one of those found dead on the scene of the accident which had completely escaped burning; the position of the body indicates that he was thrown out of the rear part of the aircraft. His traumatic wounds were appreciable and included *inter alia* a severe fracture of the spine between the second and third thoracic vertebrae, several broken ribs and broken breast bone, severe internal haemorrhage in the pleurae (500-700 ml), and a broken thigh bone. Haemorrhages were also found under the skin in the region of the temples and in the meninges, but no brain damage.
> Severe congestion was found in head and neck.
> The results of the post mortem indicate that he lived for a certain period of time after the crash. The congestion gives some support to the assumption that suffocation as a result of breathing difficulties (severely crushed chest, high spinal fracture and crushing of the lungs as a result of haemorrhage

are significant as the ultimate cause of death. It is not possible to estimate with certainty how long he may have lived after the crash. The haemorrhages which took place as a result of the wounds could have developed in a shorter time than a few hours.

We agree with the pathologists in their opinion that Hammarskjöld's wounds would have been fatal in any case. If he had been rescued immediately after the accident and immediately received medical care equipped with the latest devices, it may perhaps be supposed that the survival period could have been somewhat lengthened. . . .

In the time Hammarskjöld lived after the crash, he had clutched in his agony a bunch of grass, and it was found in his fist.

Some people thought it was strange that at the moment of impact the Secretary-General was thrown clear of the aircraft, falling outside the area of fire. Had he the strength to crawl away? The fact that he was the only uncharred victim has been used as an argument that he committed suicide in flight.

But Hammarskjöld had a foible not mentioned in any of the reports though it was known to his security guards: he had an aversion to seat-belts. A passionate speed-demon, he liked to sit in the front seat of his car, next to the driver, zooming at eighty miles per hour, and on these occasions, it was the constant worry of his bodyguards to force a seat-belt around him. On the ground he usually acquiesced, but in the air he put up more of a struggle—and Dag Hammarskjöld could be a very stubborn man.

It is therefore a possibility that while those who wore seat-belts were charred to death, the Secretary-General, having refused it, was catapulted out of the plane and beyond the burning area.

The crash occurred in the Ndola West Forest. The nearest settlement was the Ndola West Charcoal Burners' Compound, and on the night of September 17/18, many of the charcoal burners were at separate places in the bush, attending their kilns within a mile or two of the crash site. Three of them, Messrs. Banda, Daka, and Moyo, were awakened during the night by loud bangs and they saw a fire burning. At dawn they went to look for the source of these phenomena, and they found it; but they did not report the crash. Instead, they carried away from the wreckage a code machine, in the belief that it was a typewriter.

Several other charcoal burners testified before the two Rhodesian, as well as the United Nations Commissions. A Mr. Farie Mazibisa, President of the United African Charcoal Burners' Association, said that on the night of September 17, he had "slept in the bush tending his charcoal kiln . . . He was awakened around midnight by a terrific noise which appeared to come from the north. He saw two airplanes, one a bit ahead and one a bit behind . . . After a few minutes he heard a very big noise. He got up and saw the whole bush lit up and heard many smaller noises like shooting. He was frightened and ran to his house in the charcoal burners' compound . . ."

Mr. Mazibisa said he had not told what he saw to the authorities at first because he had been afraid that he might be accused of having caused the crash.

Mr. Davidson Simango, a charcoal burner, told the Commissions that he was lying down near his work on the fatal night, when hearing the loud noise of airplane engines he looked up and saw "two airplanes flying closer together than they usually fly. . . . The planes were going in a direction away from Ndola. The noise faded . . . and then grew louder . . . He saw one airplane coming back. Then he saw a flash and the plane went down and after that there was a very loud explosion. Later, he heard several small explosions. . . . He lay down and covered his head and stayed there all night. He did not report what he saw immediately because he had been busy . . ."

Mr. Dickson Buleni, a charcoal burner, did not tell what he saw right away because he was afraid the Federal Government would accuse him of having burnt the plane. He had been "sitting outside his home in the charcoal burner's compound with his wife on the night of September 17. He saw an airplane fly over between 10:00 and 11:00 P.M. local time. A long time later he saw a second big plane similar to the one he had seen earlier. . . . A small plane was flying above the big plane. . . . He heard two different engine sounds. . . . He saw a fire coming from the small plane and light on the roof of the big plane and he heard the sound of a fire. Then the big plane fell down and began burning and there was much light."

Mr. Buleni maintained that he had not been drinking and neither had his wife. A number of others in the compound had been drinking, however, and most of them were very frightened, especially when someone suggested that the Katanga war had come to their compound.

The evidence was heard of Mr. A. J. Lemonson Mpinganjira, a charcoal burner, ex-Provincial President of the Malawi African Congress. He said that he had seen a big plane approaching Ndola airport from the north, and that a little while later a big plane which he had taken to be the same one flew back from Ndola towards the north and turned west. Just as it was turning, "he saw two small aircraft, one flying very high and the other low . . . The lower of the small aircraft overtook the big plane . . . It flew just above the bigger plane and a red flash came on the big plane. The big plane dipped down, followed by an explosion. Afterwards there were a series of explosions . . .

"About thirty minutes later, he saw two Land-Rovers with two European occupants each, driving at breakneck speed towards the site of the crash. Ten or fifteen minutes later the flames increased and the Land-Rovers returned with the same speed . . ."

Mr. Mpinganjira was hiding behind an anthill throughout

these happenings, and he had not given evidence before because "he did not trust the Federal Commission. He would have nothing to do with anything Federal." However, he had noted in his diary for September 17, "Dag Hammarskjöld Mystery Flight."

Besides the charcoal burners, some other eyewitnesses were interviewed. Mr. Davison Nkonjera, a storeman, was at the African Ex-Servicemen's Club that night, about a mile from Ndola Airport. He had seen an airplane come from the north and circle the airport three times before flying off towards the west. While it was circling, "the lights at Ndola airport went off both in the tower and on the ground."

After the lights had gone off, Mr. Nkonjera said he heard two jets which sounded to him as if they had taken off from Ndola Airport and he saw them following the big plane. He saw a fire or flash coming from the jet on the right and landing on the big plane.

The watchman of the African Ex-Servicemen's Club saw "two jets take off from Ndola airport and return there and land, both in darkness, as the lights of the airfield were off. He said that he had been afraid to testify earlier, because he thought he would be killed in the same way as the Secretary-General because he had revealed this."

The Commissions could not ignore the fact that although some of the witnesses had given an impression of honesty, they may have been confused about what they saw or have indulged in "imaginative reconstruction." Also, those who displayed strong antifederal feelings might have testified in a way deliberately intended to embarrass the Rhodesian Government.

I asked a member of the United Nations Commission who had helped to prepare the report what he believed had happened to the Secretary-General's plane. He said he believed it was a pure accident: the aircraft was ready to land, the landing wheels were lowered and locked, the flaps were in the proper position, the engines were operating, and there was no sign of excessive speed. Captain Hallonquist, the pilot in command, was accustomed to navigate by night; not only was he considered a cautious and reliable pilot, but he was also a navigation officer and instructor for Transair, the Swedish Airlines Company.

"Some slight error must have occurred," he said. "If you or I had the job to do, we would have sat tight (*serrer les fesses*) and have been so careful we might even have landed that aircraft. But what happened was the error of the perfect."

"Then what about the charcoal burners?"

"They were primitive people who have never seen an airplane at close range," he said. "Besides it was in the night."

To this day the arguments simmer. It is only necessary to mention the name of Hammarskjöld in the Headquarters Building to bring to the surface the old outrage and raise again the riddles and rumors about his death. Was it really an accident? Did he commit suicide, carrying with him fifteen others to their deaths? Was there a stranger in the plane who killed the pilot, thus causing the crash? Was he shot down by Moise Tshombe's single jet fighter piloted by a Rhodesian? Was his plane purposefully given wrong instructions from the Air Traffic Control at Ndola to make certain of the crash in the bush?

"Of course they killed him," said an American who lives close to the heart of UN affairs.

"Who killed him?"

"The British. Not the London British. The Rhodesian British."

"Why would the Rhodesians have killed Hammarskjöld?"

"Because he was a dangerous man."

He was indeed a dangerous man as all pure souls are dangerous, iconoclastic and upsetting. They see before them the empty chair that stands eternally awaiting its brief occupants. And though it is plainly marked *This is the Siege Perilous*, they do not hesitate to sit on it, on pain of death.

2

Agnes Hammarskjöld's Son

CONFERENCE Room 8 at the Headquarters Building is
the "British Room." That is to say, it was furnished and
decorated at the expense of the British government. The walls
have oak panels divided into squares, and in the center of every
square is a bird or a beast carved in bas-relief. The room is a
veritable zoo where you may contemplate a bat, a weasel, a
crab, an inkfish, a kingfisher catching fish or a hawk laying
eggs.

It was among such doubtful diplomatic symbols, in a secret
meeting held by the Security Council on March 31, 1953, that
Dag Hammarskjöld was designated as Secretary-General of the
United Nations.

Outside Conference Room 8, the first basement foyer had
been transformed into an electronics jungle: film and TV
cameras stood vigil like three-legged marabou in strategic positions; floor managers with earphones walked about, pulling on
their wire vines. In the sizzling glare of kleig lights, correspondents of the world press loitered with hands in their
trousers pockets among the cables that undulated like black
cobras across the designs of the Indian carpets from Equador.
I was not present in this melee, but as television director, I
had a monitor's view of it from my control booth. From time

25

to time, the president of the Security Council, Ahmed Bokhari of Pakistan, would emerge from Conference Room 8 to stand before my cameras and say there was no news. Late in the evening he vouchsafed some further information: that the conferring gentlemen were going to adjourn for a snack.

One hour later, fortified, they reconvened, and after a while Mr. Bokhari appeared again to tell us—*habemus papam!* A Swede by the name of Dag Hammarskjöld had been agreed upon. As one man the world press jumped on Mr. Bokhari to ask him the burning question: how do you spell it?

I was one of the few who had heard this name before. In 1923, at the League of Nations in Geneva, I had drawn the portrait of a Hammarskjöld named Åke; and again in 1932, one Hjalmar Hammarskjöld, a baldheaded man with a goatee had been with the Swedish delegation to the Disarmament Conference. As it turned out, Åke was Dag's brother, and Hjalmar his father.

I ought to have recalled Dag Hammarskjöld also, for in 1951, he had been Vice-Chairman of the Swedish delegation to the Paris Assembly; and the following year he had headed the delegation in New York. But although faces are my business I had not noticed him. He was the sort of man one does not notice in a crowd, and that was the very fact that landed him the job of Secretary-General.

Secret meetings are secret to all but the participants, and when enough of them have committed small indiscretions, it is often possible for journalists to piece together a panoramic view of the entire proceedings. In this way, the tortuous diplomacies that had taken place in Conference Room 8 were eventually revealed.

It seems that there were four candidates for the office of Secretary-General: Lester B. Pearson of Canada; Paul-Henri Spaak of Belgium; Carlos P. Romulo of the Philippines; and Mme. Pandit, sister of Prime Minister Nehru, of India.

The Russians, through their delegate, Andrei Vishinsky,

vetoed both Pearson and Spaak, because Canada and Belgium were NATO countries. They vetoed Romulo also because they considered him to be an "American stooge." They refused to countenance Mme Pandit for obscure reasons, possibly out of sheer gallantry. It was after this stalemate had been reached that French delegate Henri Hoppenot suddenly pulled out of a hat the name of Dag Hammarskjöld. Neither Mr. Vishinsky nor Henry Cabot Lodge of the United States had ever heard of him—nor, for that matter, had M. Hoppenot. The name had been carefully pronounced in his ear by British delegate Sir Gladwyn Jebb, who had heard of him from his chief, Foreign Secretary Sir Anthony Eden. Eden had known him in Paris in 1948, where Hammarskjöld had helped to draw up the charter for OEEC—the Organization for European Economic Cooperation. His reputation was that of a brilliant economist, an unobtrusive technician, and a Swedish aristo-bureaucrat.

The British, having already bitten the dust in the matter of their favorite candidate, Lester B. Pearson, could not risk a second defeat by proposing Hammarskjöld; they felt that this Swedish name would fall more gently upon Russian ears if it came from the lips of a Frenchman: certainly it would have to be chewed on before it was vetoed, because most of them had never heard of it.

One thing remains for diplomats to do when they are baffled: adjourn for a snack. This gives them the opportunity to ask for instructions from their home governments. In perfect accord, for once, the Russians and the Americans proposed the adjournment, and within one hour Mr. Vishinsky received a reply from Moscow that the Kremlin found no objection to Dag Hammarskjöld.

In fact, they could have raised objections had they chosen to do so. Only the previous year stiff notes had been exchanged between Stockholm and Moscow on the subject of some Swedish planes that the Russians had shot down over the Baltic Sea, and Hammarskjöld had been the man who signed the notes. Perhaps in spite of this the pedantic earnestness of Hammarskjöld's official prose style had given them the notion that here was the perfect bureaucrat if they had ever seen one.

At the same time, Mr. Lodge telephoned the State Department where the politicians asked the economists if they had ever heard of a man named Hammarskjöld. Upon learning that they had and that they thought favorably of him, instructions were conveyed to Mr. Lodge to support the candidacy of this economist for a political job.

In Stockholm, Hammarskjöld was not altogether unaware that his name was before the high councils of the world. It is said that a message had come to him from the Swedish delegation in New York, informing him that a slightly befuddled old lady was peddling his candidacy about. He had replied, "Amused, but not interested." His friend, Bo Beskow, the artist who was painting Hammarskjöld's portrait at the time, said he thought he was exactly the right man for the job. Hammarskjöld brushed off this compliment: "No one would be mad enough to propose me—nor would I be mad enough to take it."

And so when, on March 31, late at night, the news services called him to have his reaction to the dispatch that he had been chosen to succeed Trygve Lie, Hammarskjöld was not sure that it was not a premature April Fool's joke, and a bad one. But official notification soon followed from Mr. Bokhari. A close friend of his was privileged to hear one of the few colloquialisms that the world was ever going to hear from him: he said that he felt as if he had been "hit by a truck." Later he was heard to say: "You know what has just happened to me . . . is like being lifted by the scruff of the neck, as if I were a little dog . . ."

His father, Hjalmar Hammarskjöld, was seriously ill at that time in the hospital, and Dag went to him there and asked for his advice. He also telephoned his chief, Foreign Minister

Östen Unden, who was having a brief vacation in Capri. Both of these elders advised him to accept the offer.

He cabled Bokhari: "With a strong feeling of personal insufficiency, I hesitate to accept the candidature, but I do not feel that I could refuse the task imposed upon me, should the Assembly follow the recommendation of the Security Council by which I feel deeply honored."

And then, he went to Uppsala. That is where his mother, Agnes Hammarskjöld, lay buried, and he wished to visit her grave.

Once a lady wrote to me from Sweden that she had read an article of mine about Hammarskjöld's father and brother; and she asked me why I neglected Agnes Hammarskjöld. She was right. Mothers of important men often get short shrift in history, unless they happen to resemble Napoleon's mother of whom her son said, "She has a man's head on a woman's body."

Agnes Hammarskjöld was nothing like this. She was a feminine person of plump tendencies; gentle, gracious, and charitable; the outline of her face was softly circular, and she had a mildly rounded brow. But in the center of her face, in the close-set eyes, the thin, longish nose, and gently convex upper lip, one may trace the mold of her son, Dag.

She came from a family of clergymen, but there was a black sheep in their midst, her father's half-brother, Carl Jonas Love Almquist. He was a famed romantic poet, a genius with a touch of the delinquent: upon becoming entangled in a black-mail-and-murder scandal, he had to flee to America where, in those wild and woolly days, neither his genius nor his delinquency attracted attention. Nevertheless, it was to this adventurous individual rather than to her clerical forebears that Agnes Hammarskjöld's son later compared his mother: she shared his "radically democratic view of fellow humans, 'evangelic' if you like, a childlike openness toward life, an anti-rationalism with warm undercurrents of feeling...and personal generosity toward both intimates and strangers..."

Dag was born on July 29, 1905. His father, a conservative politician and civil servant, was in Karlstadt at the time, a member of the delegation negotiating the peaceful separation of Norway from Sweden. This was busy work, for there were those who did not wish this partition to be so very peaceful, and Dag's christening was therefore delayed until late fall when his father could come home. He brought with him as a christening present from his colleagues in Karlstadt a silver chalice on which was inscribed, "For one too long without a name."

Agnes was forty when Dag was born, and since she already had three sons, she naturally hoped that he would be a girl. Some have suggested that his mother's wish, together with her habit of dressing him in lace-rimmed skirts and letting his locks grow long had a bearing on Dag's future sex interests. I am not impressed with this opinion. Oscar Wilde was not the only person who wore skirts and locks when he was young: Franklin Delano Roosevelt did too, and so did Winston Churchill; so did I. In Victorian times and well into *la belle époque*, especially in Europe, many little boys dressed like girls without detriment in their later years to the population explosion. First we wore lacy skirts; next we got pants with a fly in the back and then pants with a fly in the front. Only when our voices changed did we change, with elation, into a pair of long trousers. Thus we advanced from boy to man by stages, as the spawn graduates to the frog.

Dag was a beautiful baby with silky hair twirled like woodshavings around his creamery butter face, and his eyefolds slanted over his pupils in a curtain. He had a baby's soft sucking mouth, and sitting in his three-wheeled perambulator, he fed on his index finger. Once he fell out of the carriage when one of his elder brothers, Sten, climbed on it to kiss him. In due course, he acquired a rake and a toy horse.

When he was eight, a friend asked him what an idyll was. Dag wrote in his friend's notebook, "An idyll is a lamb with a blue ribbon and a bell."

Dag's childhood home was in Uppsala, one of Europe's oldest university towns. In early times it had been the pagan capital where the Vikings built a temple to the god, Frey, and performed human sacrifice in his honor; possibly some of them bore a device of Thor's hammer upon their shields. Today, however, it is the seat of the Archbishop of the Church of Sweden.

Dag's father, Hjalmar Hammarskjöld, was *Landshövding,* provincial governor, and the family occupied an immense red castle that had been built by Gustavus I, the Vasa king who in the sixteenth century detached Sweden from Rome, freed her from the domination of the Danes, welded her into a national state, and then, with an empty treasury, went to work and built a navy exactly as any modern chief of state would do.

The old castle had nothing of the delicacy of a French château. With its massive walls and many small windows, it looked more like a monastery or an Austrian prison. But there were towers, cul-de-sacs, battlements, and they offered a romantic playground to young Dag who used to lead his playmates on explorations of the murky underground passages leading to the prisoners' dungeons, where the echoing walls and squeak of heavy doors sounded in their ears like the moan of bygone days.

The castle was cold, but the family life had old-fashioned warmth. At Christmas, the Hammarskjölds would sit at a long table laden with all the goods of the land, and Hjalmar himself would put the knife into the huge cheese that was always presented to him as president of the dairy farmers' association. Afterwards the personnel of the castle would gather with the family around a giant Christmas tree, and there, amid flickering lights, Agnes Hammarskjöld would read aloud to them from the Apostles.

On New Year's Eve she read a Swedish hymn whose first line was an admonitory: "Night is drawing nigh ..." and this line shows up many times in *Markings,* as the Secretary-General's first entry for the New Year. The elder Hammarskjöld saw to it that all holidays were celebrated in his house exactly as they always had been and always would be. Conservatism is not merely a political credo—it is a way of life.

The Hammarskjöld family traces its history back to 1611. In the family archives, the name is spelt variously, -skjöld, -skiöld, and -sköld, testimony that even Swedes are a little shaky about the spelling of it. Although they are among Sweden's oldest nobility, they wore no titles, for in Sweden all privileges for noblemen have been abolished, except the right to be beheaded with a sword instead of with an axe— an empty honor since the death penalty has been abolished also.

Hjalmar Hammarskjöld was a tall man with long legs, a bald head and an Émile Zola goatee. His pince-nez, which pinched his small piercing eyes close to his nose stem, lent him an air of professional severity. His family tree was jammed with soldiers and civil servants; there was one poet in the family named Lorenzo Hammarskjöld, and Hjalmar himself translated Spanish and Portuguese folk-songs into Swedish.

In 1914, when Dag was nine, his father became Prime Minister of Sweden. Such an event would have caused most boys' hearts to soar high, but it brought the young Dag low. The Secretary-General was fifty-one years old when he began to write haikus, but even then he found reason to express in precise syllables the sad account of the time he was boxed on the ear to teach him the odium of his father's name. According to one of his childhood friends, Sven Stolpe, the poem referred to an incident when some schoolmates of liberal families jumped on him and beat him because of his father's politics.

Perhaps Hjalmar Hammarskjöld's initial crime in liberal eyes was that he had been named by the king above the heads of parliament. Throughout the war he strictly and uncompromisingly maintained Sweden's neutrality; it was he, it seems, who drafted a famous joint Scandinavian note to both belligerents in 1914, with the tart comment that after the war they would be satisfied to find inviolate some of the principles that they themselves had earlier treasured. But from his political opponents, his stand drew on him the accusation of being Germanophile, even of "being sold to the Germans." When the British blockade caused acute scarcity of food in Sweden, he was baptized, Hungerskjöld.

He was disliked even by his supporters, being authoritarian and disciplinarian, a sort of pocket Bismarck who refused to delegate authority and tended to make decisions by himself; furthermore, he was cold and failed to establish warm personal relations with others. In 1917, the animosity directed against him forced him to resign in an atmosphere not precisely of disgrace, but of popular disapproval.

Yet, Hjalmar Hammarskjöld's actions had helped to perpetuate in Sweden a tradition of neutrality; and this has been gradually transmogrified from a political position to a national philosophy devoted to the principles of conciliation, mediation, and outright pacifism. This Scandinavian attitude was already burgeoning in the nineteenth century when Alfred Nobel, overcome with shame for having invented dynamite, established the Peace Prize; and it is reflected today by squadrons of Great Scandinavians who are also great humanitarians and peacemakers: Hjalmar Branting, Fridtjof Nansen, Karl Lindhagen, Folke Bernadotte; and Dag Hammarskjöld.

This is an astounding development in a people who for their size have given history a great deal of trouble. It was, after all, not too long ago that mothers and children found it necessary to pray, "From the fury of the Northman, the good

Lord deliver us"; and yet, today, there are those who pray just as ardently to be delivered from Scandinavian peace-makers.

Dag Hammarskjöld always nurtured a certain residue of resentment on his father's behalf. In 1954, when he was elected to the seat of the Swedish Academy left vacant by his father's death, his inaugural address was a memorial to Hjalmar Hammarskjöld, and also an apologia for him. He spoke of his father's faith in supra-national justice, in a *Civitas Legum* that would replace or rather give modern substance to, the medieval notion of the *Civitas Dei,* the city of God, where "nation states lived under the protection of an internation-alism which gains its strength from the very logic of justice." He emphasized that his father "remained outside the parties all his life," and insisted that "regardless of how close he was to conservatism, there was much in the views of this man . . . to set him apart from the twentieth century views of the Con-servative Party."

In 1960, he communicated to *Kamelposten,* a publication of the Swedish Ministry of Foreign Affairs for the Swedish troops stationed in the Gaza Strip, a dictum of Hjalmar Ham-marskjöld's "Neutrality is not saying yes to both sides, but saying no to both sides . . ."

As Secretary-General of the United Nations, he was able to proclaim his father's underlying idealism from a position of authority, and even to prove it in a sense by the direction of his own life. But as a boy, he could only watch with a son's pain his father's career slide into comparative inactivity when he resumed again his position of provincial governor at Uppsala; and perhaps in this religious Christian family, Hjalmar Ham-marskjöld's ordeal might have called forth thoughts of Calvary.

Dag's brother Bo was fourteen years older than he, and Åke twelve; there was an unbridgeable gap between them in behavior and interests. Sten was five years older. It has been observed that the late-born children of elderly parents out-rank in mental abilities those born when the same parents were young, and perhaps that is why in folk literature the world over, the youngest child is so often starred as destiny's hero. The young Dag was a wonder of diligence and achievement in school, house-high above his fellow students. His final high school marks consisted of eight capital A's, four little a's —corresponding to A minus—and one B in physical exercise. His father viewed the little a's with disapproval, saying that elder brother Åke's marks had been better at Dag's age; indeed, we ourselves shall have some stern comments to make, in due course, about that B in gymnastics.

For a boy like this, congenial friends were hard come by, and one day he would note sadly in a haiku his youthful sense of exclusion. It has been assumed that this splendid isolation contributed to his habitual loneliness in later life, but it could only have developed what was already latent in him. Loneliness is constitutionally motivated, and Dag Hammarskjöld would have been a lonely man even if he had been raised among fellow prodigies. A more pertinent comment upon such gifted children is advanced by the psychologist Jung: "His excellence puts him in an exceptional position and exposes him to a great many risks, the chief of which is an exaggerated self-confidence. Against this, the only protection is humility and obedience, and even these do not always work."

Isolated among brothers, confronted with an even more intimidating figure in his elderly, disciplinarian father, it was natural for Dag to turn to his mother. A child flourishes in "participation mystique" with someone, and Dag's tender disposition inclined him to participate in his mother's feminine occupations. It was he who accompanied her to church on Sundays and he who followed her when she visited, like other great ladies of her time, the homes of the poor on the outskirts of Uppsala. And when she received guests, Dag served the tea.

On a group photo showing both parents and three of the brothers, it was Dag, aged fifteen, whom his mother held by the hand with fingers interlaced.

Friendly relations were maintained between the governor's family and that of the Archbishop, Nathan Söderblom; in fact since Agnes Hammarskjöld had been born on the same day as the archbishop, they were often called "the twins." In this clerical ambience, and with the blood of numerous clergymen running through his veins, Dag thought of studying for the church, and he adopted as his ideal, Albert Schweitzer, the man who had translated "love into action." He confided in Fru Söderblom a rather strange complaint for a teen-age boy: he said that he was disappointed that at school in his French literature class, instead of ideas, he had to learn about the love affairs of the authors. Fru Söderblom then asked him if he had read Blaise Pascal; and it was probably following this suggestion, that he not only read, but adopted the form of the *Pensées* for *Markings,* as well as Pascal's tone of worldly wisdom with a twist of irony.

But in the end it was his father's influence that was decisive in Dag's choice of a career. After dinner, Hjalmar Hammarskjöld liked to hold conversations—to which young Dag listened in—with his elder sons, Bo and Åke, about the politics of the day, the problems that followed in the wake of World War I, and particularly the affairs of the League of Nations. For the career of the elder Hammarskjöld had flared again for a brief while when he was named chairman of the League of Nations committee for the codification of international law; and later he was Swedish delegate to the Disarmament Conference in 1932, before being "placed entirely aside."

The Hammarskjöld boys bore out Jung's observation that "extraordinary kinships exist in the psychological *habitus* of members of the same family that can amount almost to identity." All four of them followed their father into the civil service. Bo became Undersecretary in the Ministry of Welfare, and later, like his father, a provincial governor. Åke was for many years legal adviser to the Swedish delegation to the League of Nations; then he became *greffier*—chancellor—at the International Court of Justice in the Hague. He died of rheumatic fever in 1937. Sten served on Sweden's National Housing Board.

Dag, when he was twenty-five, started his public service career as a secretary to the Royal Commission on Unemployment. Here he drew the attention of Ernest Wigforss, evangelist of the Swedish Welfare State.

His career was nothing short of meteoric. When the Social Democrats came to power, Wigforss became Finance Minister, and he offered Dag Hammarskjöld the post of Undersecretary. He was not yet thirty, and the youngest man ever to hold such a high office in Sweden.

In 1941, he became Chairman of the Governors of the Bank of Sweden, a post that he held simultaneously, for a while, with that of Undersecretary.

But nothing has a more lasting effect upon the personality than the place a child occupies in the family hierarchy. Throughout his life, no matter how high he rose, Hammarskjöld remained something of a baby brother, and his friends and colleagues did not fail to note in him "the playful lad."

His tender attachment to his mother never weakened, and even as Undersecretary he continued to live with his family at their Stockholm house; he never omitted to bring flowers to her when he went home for lunch; nor did Agnes Hammarskjöld ever forget to advise him to dress warmly when he went on a ski-tour, or ever cease to implore his colleagues in the Treasury Department not to let him work so hard.

The Stockholm house was only fifteen minutes' walk away from the Treasury Department, but if Dag was delayed in the evening, he took a taxi rather than keep his mother waiting. And once, the story goes, he was a quarter of an hour late for a rendezvous with a young lady, his only excuse being that he had not liked to interrupt a conversation with his mother.

Many of the Hammarskjöld "mysteries" have their root in this deep rapport with his mother: his celibacy, his ardent desire to be wanted and needed, to "belong"; his willingness to submit to loving care—and also his knack for getting his own way.

After his death, among his snowdrift of papers was found preserved an old piece of cardboard, with a faded violet glued to it amid sticky fingerprints. It bore the inscription, "To mother, because she cannot go out." *

Agnes Hammarskjöld died in 1940. In her Bible was found the following inscription:

> The day you were born, everybody was happy—you
>   cried alone.
> Make your life such that in your last hour, all others
>   weep
> And you alone are without a tear to shed.
> Then shall you calmly face death whenever it comes.

* *Barbara Fraser Archives.*

3

To Say Yes—Without
Looking Back

AGNES HAMMARSKJÖLD had every reason to worry
that her son was going to perish of industry. As Undersecretary of the Treasury, Dag was a demon for hard work.
He arrived at his office every morning at nine-thirty. Usually
he returned to the parental home in the Sturegatan for luncheon; then back to the office until dinner time. After dinner,
about nine o'clock, he would return to his office to work for
a long stretch until five or six in the morning, relieved only
by a visit to the local *keller* for tea or coffee; occasionally he
might linger there with a friend for a talk about literature,
music, modern art, philosophy or religion.

But even when he had worked most of the night, he was
always back in his office by nine-thirty, as crisp and fresh as
a newly minted bank note and with enough energy overflowing to infect others. His fellow-economist, Gunnar Myrdal,
said, "He could enthuse insignificant persons to achieve results
beyond their ability."

This schedule continued day after day, year after year.
Snowed under with self-inflicted work, Dag said, "One feels
like a seal who has difficulty coming up between ice-blocks to
breathe." His colleagues took an even more austere view of

these record-setting habits. "Work is a means of enjoyment," said one of them, "but it should be enjoyed in moderation."

Sometimes for relaxation, Hammarskjöld would disappear into the mountain tops or else lose himself on the plains of Lapland; or he would go for a ski-tour, returning home suntanned and refreshed. In skiing he was said to have been better at going up than coming down, but this did not prevent him from talking eloquently about the art of skiing. He liked also to escape from the office trap in summer by going for bicycle rides with a group of friends, riding thirty or forty miles outside Stockholm. But on returning to the city, Dag would always stop in the suburbs and pull a pair of flannel trousers over his trunks, lest some Member of Parliament should see the Undersecretary of the Treasury going about bare-kneed.

The walls of his office were decorated with paintings. Among them was one by Nils Nilsson showing a green landscape upon which rested a little out-house painted red.

One dawn, after he had worked all night at the office, Hammarskjöld went walking about the city with a colleague, Henrik Klackenberg, and they strolled along the river bank among rats and drunken derelicts. Passing under a railway bridge, they noticed at some distance on it a man throwing a package to a girl. The girl then turned and walked away from him, while the man jumped into the river. By the time Hammarskjöld and Klackenberg got near him he was floating head down, unconscious in the muddy waves. Eventually with the help of a hook, they managed to pull him out.

Laid out under a street lamp, the man regained consciousness. He was very young and had just come out of the army. The bundle he had thrown to the girl were love letters she had written to him, but during his absence she had found someone else, and life was now over for him.

Dag leaned over the young man, comforting him and reasoning with him, while Klackenberg went to look for a taxi. The taxi arrived and the young man got into it, but while Dag was paying his fare—with an extra ten kronen for the mud the driver would have to clean out—he jumped out of the taxi and again ran towards the river. They managed to catch him, and this time Dag succeeded in persuading him to remain alive. The taxi drove off with the young man.

The incident worried Hammarskjöld. "Did we do him a service?" he wondered. "Or is it right to die for a great love? Anyway, we couldn't have acted otherwise."

But the image of the drowning suicide must have continued to haunt him, because twice, in *Markings*, he returned to this theme. In the first case he obliquely related it to himself, and in the second he changed the boy into a woman. In both reflections, he made the suicide a successful one.

Klackenberg's comment on the adventure was, "I am not certain that I could have succeeded in finding my way to the boy, as Dag did." Perhaps it was a case of Hammarskjöld's "quiet diplomacy" at dawn on the river bank.

While he was still Undersecretary of the Treasury, Hammarskjöld's remarkable diplomatic skills had already become apparent. Quite frequently, violent disagreements flared between the various governmental departments, and these involved what for bureaucrats is far more serious than politics: they involved prestige. It was observed in the passage of years that whenever Hammarskjöld was called upon to preside over such stormy debates between men up in arms, the disputing parties were apt to emerge from his office afterwards with happy smiles upon their faces.

There would come a time when "Leave it to Dag" would become a catch phrase in the counsels of nations because of his extraordinary ability to mediate between conflicting interests. Yet he was not a typical "mediator" of the kind frequently seen in history and in life; such men are usually comfortable, plump individuals, as if the talent for mediation dwelled in an opulent belly. Benjamin Franklin was a man of this sort, and so were Mirabeau and Teddy Roosevelt. In my own life I have

observed particularly the magic of Albert Thomas, director
of the International Labor Office in Geneva, and also that of
Paul-Henri Spaak of Belgium. All of these were round, charm-
ing men whose easy humor and friendly manner, not unforti-
fied by considerable common sense, cast oil on troubled waters.

But Hammarskjöld was not this kind of man at all; he was
remote and stiff, his manner showing only in twinkling flashes
the tenderness that was in him. Klackenberg's explanation,
which I believe to be the correct one, was that he brought
about reconciliations by his sheer integrity, by the force of his
rectitude which placed a moral obligation upon parties in dispute to reach an agreement. Hammarskjöld's own credo as a
mediator was characteristic of his strictly formal and abstract
mind: he said that it was necessary to see the parties objec-
tively, while imagining himself in their position. Balanced on
this tightrope of principle, but with human understanding,
solutions could be reached.

In those early Stockholm days, it must have been something
of an agony for conservative Hjalmar Hammarskjöld to watch
his two sons, Bo and Dag, help the Social Democratic Government to establish the Welfare State in Sweden. Bo, as Undersecretary of the Ministry of Social Welfare said, "I am a conservative man; but the best thing a conservative man can do
is to put forward social welfare measures. When people feel
they have a part in the welfare of their nation, that the nation
is something of their own, they will defend and stick by it." *

Dag's chief in the Treasury Department, Ernest Wigforss,
the Social Democratic Minister of Finance, called Dag a "Tory-
Democrat," and in assessing these two qualities in him, he
wrote, "His emotional attitude to people and class differences
did not differ much from my own. The democratic levelling
process appeared natural to him." But in political thinking,
Wigforss found that some of Dag's opinions about the role of

* Joseph P. Lash, *Dag Hammarskjöld*, Doubleday & Co., Garden City, New
York, 1961, p. 33.

the state showed "signs of his old conservatism." Still, he considered Dag to be "more of an advocate of planned economy than economic liberals."

Wigforss also made an observation that "His ability to give clear and concise explanations of the essentials of a matter made it a pleasure to listen to him—provided you were alert and interested enough to follow his argument; but it was in some way analogous to the study of mathematical truths: if you had not understood what came before, you got very little out of what followed." *

One day, the whole world would have reason to sympathize with Mr. Wigforss's occasional lapses of interest in mathematics lessons.

During World War II there sprang up in Stockholm a club, called the "Tuesday Club," pro-Ally and anti-Nazi, whose activities the police of neutral Sweden watched with a vigilant and nervous eye. Dag's friend, Klackenberg, and some other members of the Treasury Department belonged to it, but Dag held aloof. When Klackenberg became engaged, through the club, in smuggling anti-Nazi literature to Norway, Hammarskjöld raised no objection on principle, but he warned of the painful consequences in the Treasury Department, should the undertaking be discovered.

Neutral though the government was, the Swedish press was mostly anti-Nazi, and when too vivid descriptions of Nazi terrorism in Norway were published, the Third Reich protested. Thereupon, the Swedish Minister of Justice, Westman, confiscated seventeen newspapers, and a bitter debate flared up in Parliament on this account. Conservative politicians defended Westman, saying that he had been correct in encroaching upon the rights of the press. This statement aroused the ire of Dag Hammarskjöld who made an angry comment, "Let's not forget, rights are the strongest defense of a small nation." **

* Sten Söderberg, *A Pictorial Biography*, p. 46.
** *Dag Hammarskjöld, En Minnesbok*, p. 58.

Hammarskjöld withstood ten years at the Treasury Department, according to Klackenberg, "with heart and stomach undamaged." From the Treasury, he moved into the Foreign Ministry, at first as Secretary-General. In 1951, he graduated to the post of vice-minister of foreign affairs. Here he surrounded himself with a group of able men. "It wasn't a brain trust," recalled one member of the group. "He was his own brain trust." A definition of intelligence runs: "the ability of storage and utilization of concept." Hammarskjöld's friend, Klackenberg, recalls his fantastic memory, adding that "he knew how to use it." The saying that "those who have good memories do not need wisdom," had no reference to Hammarskjöld, says Klackenberg. "He had almost the wisdom of an old man." But when he told this to Dag, it was not taken as a compliment.

Although he was in the thick of Social Democratic politics, he had not joined the party. All of his life he was to nurture a certain amount of contempt for the "one-sided splendor of party men." When he was offered his first decoration by the king, he showed little enthusiasm for accepting this royalist insignia. A Social Democratic friend had to talk him into it. "If you do not accept it," he said, "people will think that you have joined the party. In your circle, it is natural to wear decorations. If you do not, you will appear to be navigating under false political colors."

Hammarskjöld accepted the decoration, and perhaps wore it, without, however, mollifying conservatives who raised their eyebrows at his intimacy with the Social Democrats and labelled him a "fellow traveler," and even a "Wigforss stooge." It is curious that life is so often shaped like a cork-screw, and that one man must face the same problem again and again, as if it had been given him alone to solve. Characteristically, and rather oddly for a man whose habitual attitude was cool and self-contained, he took this criticism rather sensitively, and he wrote an article in *Tiden* magazine, to explain himself, which he called "some marginal reflections on a personal problem." They were in fact a formulation of his notion of the ideal civil servant, from which he was not to deviate a jot, even when he had translated it into terms of an international Secretariat. "The basic and obvious commandment in the code of the civil servant," he wrote, "is that he serves the community and not any group, party or particular interests. This does not by any means mean that he ought to be—or that it is proper that he should be—politically indifferent, but it does mean that, however deeply engaged politically he may be, *as an executive civil servant* he must not work for his political ideals . . ."

This radical division between the public and the private man, raising visions as it does of an automaton-bureaucracy, in which individuals are devoid of will, drew outcries from both sides of the political field. One cannot help wondering if one who is party-homeless can ever speak on the same wavelength as those who are politically anchored; his words may have mathematical logic, but some vital theorem has been omitted from the argument, preventing the two kinds of men from understanding each other.

Hammarskjöld enumerated four types of civil servant: (1) the one with no opinion, who lets himself be influenced by various interests; (2) the political independent who has a definite personal scale of values, but who thinks that one is free to try what one thinks right; (3) the man who is, so to speak, his own party, in that he has translated his own value judgments into a series of practical standpoints that do not entirely coincide with those of any party; and (4) the party man.*

Of these, the only automaton surely is number four. Hammarskjöld falls into categories two and three.

He pointed out how the technician, through his knowledge, anonymously and unseen, may influence the politics of the day. For if he has a "strong political ethic," he might change

* Söderberg, *Pictorial Biogr.*, p. 49.

the administrative attitude without transgressing the obligation of the civil servant to be objective. Simply by having strong convictions, such an unobtrusive being might quietly and decidedly influence developments by "open criticism or by his presence at private discussions with those in political power."

Since he must have been drawing on his own experience, this sounds very much as if Hammarskjöld's "compelling integrity" had been making itself felt, of all places, in a foreign ministry. Since his own "strong political ethic" was founded on Schweitzer's "reverence for life" it becomes obvious that Hammarskjöld's automated civil servants were not at all the sort of hypothetical bogeys the party politicians were grumbling about. They are in fact, the members of the ideal International Secretariat which, in 1961, he was to describe in his speech before Congregation at Oxford; and the sooner I become civilly served by automatons who have "reverence for life" the better I shall like it.

This, then, is the Secretary-General Sweden sent to us, gift-wrapped and ready made, even though few had ever heard of him: he was a work demon of "alarmingly swift perceptions," whose moral rectitude exerted a quiet pressure on others simply because it existed; a person whose diplomatic skills were so subtle that they cancelled even the disadvantage of honesty; a man his friend Klackenberg characterized as "courageous and good"; and who was politically a "conservative-liberal-social-radical-internationalist." In what pigeonhole shall we place such a man, asks his biographer Sten Söderberg. Hammarskjöld had no real doubts about himself. He suspected that he was the ideal Secretary-General of the United Nations.

He accepted his massive task as an exhilarating challenge, and wrote in *Markings:* "To be free, to be able to stand up and leave everything behind—without looking back. To say yes . . ."

On April 9, 1953, he descended from his plane at New York International Airport, a slightly built, sandy-haired man without hat or overcoat. Statistically-minded journalists immediately ascertained that he was five feet ten inches in height and weighed one hundred and sixty pounds. He was greeted with the hearty handshake of his burly predecessor, Trygve Lie, and by his dampening words: "Dag Hammarskjöld, you are going to take over the most impossible job in the world."

Hammarskjöld then made a statement to the press in which we learned that he was a mountain climber: "That much I know of this sport, that the qualities it requires are just those which I feel we all need today: perseverance and patience, a firm grip on realities, careful but imaginative planning, a clear awareness of dangers, but also of the fact that fate is what we make it and that the safest climber is he who never questions his ability to overcome the difficulties."

The press could not have been too well impressed with his words, "I want to do a job, not to talk about it—not even afterwards..." The great powers who elected him, though, could not possibly have taken exception to the innocent thoughts he drew forth from his Swedish civil service experience about the role of a Secretary-General. "I... have my views and ideas on the great international issues facing us... But those views are mine as a private man. In my new official capacity, the private man should disappear and the international public servant take his place. The public servant is there in order to assist, so to say from the inside, those who take the decisions which frame history."

And then, in the midst of these seemingly innocuous and rather conventional remarks, the real Dag Hammarskjöld emitted a dire threat—although it was not recognized as such at the time. He said, "Don't think that he (the Secretary-General) takes but a passive part. It is a most active one. But he is active as an instrument, a catalyst, perhaps an inspirer."

4

The New Secretary-General

HAMMARSKJÖLD began his appointment with a gesture of shy friendliness toward the Secretariat. Almost immediately upon his arrival, he arranged a tour of the vast Headquarters Building in order to shake hands with every individual—close to four thousand of them—employed there. I don't think anybody was greatly impressed at first by his stature or beauty; he lacked the stony face that is the internationally respected passport of the executive type. There was something jumpy about his gait, and his handshake was far from hearty.

In the course of this journey, which took several days, he arrived at my office. No word was exchanged, not even "How do you do?" There was simply the stiff handshake, the swift, self-conscious smile, and that was all. Nevertheless, knowing that I should one day have to draw a caricature of him, I looked at him with malice aforethought. His eyes were a cold blue; his enemies would call them steely, and we were to learn that he could look awesomely severe. Yet, the Nordic eyefolds that slanted steeply downwards, even obscuring part of the iris, gave him a kind expression, and they turned into a twinkle at the corners of his eyes. But neither twinkle nor his nervous smile emanated jollity: they were rather twin signs, to me, of an

49

extrasensitive man on the defensive because he was vulnerable.

Most striking was the steep and high forehead, quite out of kilter with the rest of his face, which was fragile. I have seen a similar towering forehead on portraits of Kant, and also on Mme. Curie. I noted too the extraordinary puffy jowls that made him look as if he had hidden a couple of chestnuts in his cheeks.

In photographs where the light is favorably placed to emphasize the aristocratically narrow bones, the well-moulded brow and elegantly pinched temples, Dag Hammarskjöld had intellectual beauty. But light is not always a flatterer, and at our first swift meeting I had time to grasp the peculiar possum-like quality of his midface with its small eyes, elongated nose and cheekpockets, and to realize that I should have a struggle, in drawing him, to capture the elusive shrewdness of his countenance.

He terminated his tour of the offices, but he was not yet done: there were the guards to be greeted. Since they were disposed all over the building, Mr. John F. Cosgrove, Chief Security Officer, ordered them lined up close to their stations, and the Secretary-General's Odyssey began again as he went from group to group, shaking hands silently. At last four thousand hands had been taken, and hardly a word spoken. The visit ended in front of the building, and Hammarskjöld turned for a final handshake with his guide. Mr. Cosgrove, a religious man, threw protocol to the winds and said the proper words for all of us: "God help you, Mr. Secretary-General!"

Some sort of transcendental help is certainly necessary for a Secretary-General of the United Nations. Not only is the magnitude of his task intimidating, but every historical precedent with which he might guide his actions is one of failure. It is his lot to deal with, even to give direction to, men of power without having any other power but that which they agree he should have. Sooner or later in the exercise of his duties, he must have the temerity to stand on Article 99 of the Charter, which reads: "The Secretary-General may bring to the attention of the Security Council any matter which in his opinion may threaten the maintenance of international peace and security."

The false bottom here is "in his opinion." For opinions can be questioned, especially by the troublemakers themselves. The Secretary-General, therefore, is charged with an obligation, even granted a power by the Charter—but Heaven help him if he uses it.

Trygve Lie had been a magnificent organizer. He had the huge task of setting up the World Organization, and he did it out of nothing. But when in turning his attention to matters of international peace and security he supported the Soviet position, Capitol Hill labelled him a Communist; when his stand gave comfort to American causes, in the Kremlin he was stamped as a lackey of the American monopolies. The French and the British flinched at every move of his that touched upon their African and Asian interests.

When, in the summer of 1950, Lie, acting on the ominous Article 99, was instrumental in organizing resistance to the Communist invasion of South Korea, his head was already in the noose. The Russians snarled that he was "an abettor of American aggression who, having finally discarded his mask, has given up all pretense of respecting the Charter." * When his reelection came up, the Russians vetoed him in the Security Council. But it is the General Assembly, where there is no veto, that elects the Secretary-General and the members voted 46 to 5 to extend Lie's term of office.

This did not, of course, leave the Russians at a loss. They simply declared Trygve Lie nonexistent, and refused to have anything to do with him.

The situation made Lie's functions awkward, if not impossible, and in 1953 he made it known that if a suitable successor

* Andrew Boyd, *United Nations Piety, Myth, and Truth,* Penguin Books, p. 95.

could be found, he would willingly resign. But when, on March 31, United States Ambassador Henry Cabot Lodge told him that his "suitable successor" had been chosen and that it was his fellow-Scandinavian, Dag Hammarskjöld, it seemed that Lie, for one, had heard of him and his remarks were uncharitable.

It was indeed bitter luck for Mr. Lie that the die had been cast. For in the spring of 1953, Stalin died; and on the very day that Vishinsky had accepted Hammarskjöld's appointment, the Communist Chinese Foreign Minister, Chou En-lai, had given the green light for a Korean armistice. With these events, milder winds could be expected to circulate from the Communist world, and Trygve Lie's chances of stabilizing his position would have brightened. "The change in Moscow's policy may explain why Trygve Lie took Hammarskjöld's selection with such ill grace, emerging in fact as the bitterest behind-the-scenes opponent of the decision," as Joseph P. Lash has put it.*

The great powers had learned a lesson by their experience with the energetic Mr. Lie: never again did they want a political Secretary-General heading a world organization. No doubt some of the old timers let their minds hark back nostalgically to the days when Sir Eric Drummond had been appointed first Secretary-General of the League of Nations. He got his job, so the story goes, when Clemenceau saw him sitting behind Lord Balfour at the Versailles Peace Conference, incessantly laughing, and thought he was the ideal fellow to head Wilson's utopistic League. Sir Eric was the ideal bureaucrat. He organized the first international civil service. But so far as I recall, between 1919 and 1933, he never opened his mouth in the Council or the Assembly of the League, except for laughing. After he retired from office, his government rewarded him with an appointment as ambassador to Fascist Italy.

Now they had found again a silent, industrious, unobtrusive

* Lash, *op. cit.*, p. 10.

bureaucrat, and that was the opinion we all had of him in the first weeks after his appointment. We could not avoid comparing him with our paunchy, tubby, departed Trygve Lie, and some of us did so unfavorably, for Lie had been a Norwegian Labor politician who never lost his vote-getting handshake. He used to stop people just to talk to them. He knew the age and sex of the children of every guard in the building, and he was never tired of inquiring after their health, conduct, and progress at school.

The new Secretary-General had taken the trouble to shake all of our hands in one gruelling operation; but when that was over, he shook less hands in years than Trygve Lie had in one week. The first to suffer from his aristocratic aloofness was Jimmy, the shoeshine boy, accredited to the United Nations, who shines shoes in twenty-seven languages and knows the capitals of every country in the world. His place of business is halfway between the bank and the cafeteria. "Hammarskjöld won't let me shine his shoes," he lamented. "Trygve Lie used to call me into his office once or twice a week, and sometimes we'd watch the world series together on TV. Five times, I've been to the 38th Floor to offer my services to Hammarskjöld, and five times he refused it.

"I guess," said Jimmy in a resigned, lackluster voice, "his valet shines his shoes." But then he gathered his spirits together and added proudly, "Now, if the Secretary-General wants to have his shoes shined, he'll have to come to me!"

We were all to learn that Hammarskjöld was not an unfriendly man, but he measured out friendliness with precision in the right place, at the right time, and with the right dose. Some said that even this was only the well-calculated public relations of a naturally remote man. Still, simplicities were apparent in him and they, too, appeared to be natural. When waiting for an elevator, he would, in a simple manner, invite others who waited to ride with him, a thing Trygve Lie never did. When he was in New York for Christmas, he took his

Christmas dinner with the maintenance men in the third basement, and with apparent genuine pleasure, although he could
not often have engaged them in long chats about Vivaldi and
Proust.

He dressed neatly, and elegantly; and yet so modestly that
he was not sartorially intimidating. He alternated bow ties
with long ties. He hardly ever topped his ensemble with a hat,
and preferred to shiver than to wear an overcoat.

When he addressed the staff, he assured us that he "cared,"
that he was happy "to belong," that we were important to him.
He always referred to the vast edifice of steel and glass in which
we labored as "this house" as if it really were a roof over our
heads. The threshold of his office was always open, he said.
One takes such statements with a grain of salt, but the Staff
Council, whose function it was to approach the Secretary-General with our problems, soon found that it was true. And so
did individuals. He had hardly warmed his chair on the 38th
Floor than Grace Barbey of UNICEF asked for an appointment to meet him. She was going to Stockholm, she told him,
to an international conference of Nongovernmental Organiza-
tions, and "people there will ask me, do you know Dag Hammarskjöld? And I would like to tell them that I do."

"But Miss Barbey," said the Secretary-General, "I am glad
that you came to see me. Because after you have come back
and I return to Stockholm, people will ask me, 'Do you know
Grace Barbey?' And I would like to tell them that I do."

A beautiful Georgian princess named Nina sits at the information desk in the Public Lobby, and since she cannot remember the names of all four thousand employees who enter "this
house" in the morning, she has developed the pleasant and safe
habit of greeting everyone, "Good morning, sweetie."

One day, as she heedlessly uttered this stereotyped greeting,
the corner of her eye registered the shape of the Secretary-
General. She looked up hastily and corrected herself, "Good

morning, Mr. Secretary-General." Hammarskjöld said with a smile, "I prefer the first greeting."

Another day, a middle-aged couple approached Nina and respectfully asked if they might see Hammarskjöld. It quite often happens that people want to talk to the Secretary-General and give him good advice, and Nina tries to maneuver them into another direction.

"Why don't you take the guided tour first?" she suggested.

The visitors remained adamant. "We have just taken it," they said. "Now we would like to speak to the Secretary-General."

She stretched out her hand to pick up the telephone, and the gentleman said, "But please don't disturb him if he's busy."

"And who shall I say wishes to talk to the Secretary-General?" asked Nina.

"His brother."

An excited telephone call to the 38th Floor brought an excited secretary plunging down to the public lobby to escort the visitors in state upwards. "Imagine," said Nina, "taking the one dollar guided tour, when your brother is Secretary-General."

Of this direct and unpretentious simplicity, which appears to run in the Hammarskjöld family, I myself saw an example in 1955 on the occasion of the tenth anniversary of the founding of the Organization when the General Assembly held a commemorative meeting at the San Francisco Opera House. I was sent there to televise the festivities. On the day of my arrival I discovered to my despair that the flags of nations had been arranged in such a way that they covered up the delegates' faces, and also that of the speaker on the rostrum. I expressed my objections in thunderous fashion.

Some one thumped me and pointed to the Secretary-General on the floor. It was he who had arranged the room and he had approved it. I walked up to him and voiced my reservations in a whisper.

"Which flags are in your way?" he asked me.

I told him. Before I could make a move to help him he had skipped nimbly forward and whipped the offending flags out of their sockets. He stood back, loaded with flagstaffs and peeked at me from between the flamboyant billows. "Satisfied?" he asked.

But all this simplicity did not add up to bonhomie by any means; in fact, had we known it, it was the very badge of a complex man. His abstruseness was beginning to make itself felt in certain perplexing objects of abstract art that were invading the lobbies; and others were rumored to inhabit his office and his New York apartment.

His apartment on Park Avenue had been chosen for him before he came to New York, and Audrey Langston, the United Nations Photo Liaison Officer went there with a photographer to have a look at it. Afterwards, Hammarskjöld, who had not yet seen the place, asked her, "How do you like it?"

"It is a boudoir," replied Miss Langston.

Hammarskjöld appeared disturbed by this opinion. Audrey explained, "Some old dowager must have lived there. The place is full of lace and family photos in silver frames from the turn of the century."

"Well, come up and see it when I have furnished it."

Some months later, Audrey again visited the apartment, only to find it almost completely unfurnished. She tackled the Secretary-General on the subject, and he explained to her soberly, "You see, I enjoy the solitude of bare walls."

In due course, with the assistance of Hank Roskam, an artistic Dutchman in the United Nations Maintenance Section in whose judgment Hammarskjöld had full confidence, the apartment was furnished.

The Secretary-General had brought a few props with him from Sweden. One of them was the painting by Nils Nilsson with the red outhouse, that had hung in his office at the Treasury Department. Another was an old-fashioned bird's-eye maple bureau that had belonged to his mother. This object was completely incongruous with the rest of the furniture which was severely and geometrically modern.

Nilsson's outhouse also seemed uneasy in the company of an abstract painting by Bo Beskow. A menorah from Israel was on the mantelpiece, and the fireplace was filled with chaste logs of white birch, a wood characteristic of Småland, the province of his ancestral origin. A hollow wood-carving with a hole in it stood on a pedestal, the work of Barbara Hepworth— the same artist who put a hole in the Hammarskjöld Memorial which stands today in front of the Headquarters Building.

The bookcases were loaded from top to bottom. Against the wall hung a mountaineer's ice pick, the gift of Sherpa Tenzing Norkay, who, with the New Zealander, Sir Edmund Hillary, had put the United Nations flag along with their national flags on Mount Everest. It bore the inscription, "So that you may climb to greater heights."

Also on the wall hung a magnificent fan from Africa, made of peacocks' feathers. In the land of my birth, they say that peacock feathers in the house bring bad luck.

When all this was completed, and Audrey Langston again visited the apartment to take pictures, the Secretary-General said to her, "Now then, is it monastic enough for you?"

Hammarskjöld made himself known to us by degrees; to the outside world he remained a silhouette. He loathed personal publicity, and it was with reluctance that he agreed to an interview with Alistair Cooke in 1955. He sat and fidgeted, while with some difficulty Mr. Cooke elicited from him a few brief remarks about his personal relaxations and pleasures: that he liked hiking; in fact, cross-country hiking; and that it was all right if you put a few mountains in it. It turned out that the Secretary-General did not read Mickey Spillane, and that he had little patience with novels, in general, because "they use too many words to say very little." Not even to please the Americans would he confess to an admiration of Hemingway.

"I do feel that the American novel is running a risk at present, and that is that by accumulating realistic details they seem to believe that they create an impression of reality. I don't think so. They just put too many things on the stage." His favorite American novel was *The Red Badge of Courage,* and he thought the first part of *Huckleberry Finn* was "just perfection."

No, there was no losing himself in imaginary realities for the Secretary-General; but in the craftsmanship of words that gives shape to the nebulous spirit, he could immerse himself: "If I manage to get off the high wire, I would rather switch over to poetry than anything else."

"You would?"

"Yes."

"As a relaxation?"

"Yes."

". . . What do you read, I won't dare say favorites?"

"Well, it's a very wide range indeed . . . Speaking to the American or British world, well I know, for instance, the newspapers are always talking about my liking for Eliot; well, it's quite true that I do like Eliot, but not in any exclusive sense of the word. And here in America you have a man like Robert Lowell. He is an extremely remarkable poet. That is a very good example."

"Do you go for Karl Shapiro?"

"Oh yes . . ."

"Greenberg, all the new men?"

"Well, Robert Lowell I would mention first of all. He impressed me most . . . Of course, you take to poets slowly, and you take to painters slowly. It would be rather rash to say that this is *the* one."

"As for the post-Eliot poets in England, do you have many people that you are particularly fond of?"

"Well, I do admire Dylan Thomas quite a lot. But I must

say that he is rather difficult for someone who has not grown up with the English language."

"Well now, some people find that they relax, let's say, with poetry, but then they have to have an absolutely non-intellectual relaxation too. Are you a man who reads mystery stories?"

No, the Secretary-General was not a man who read mystery stories like Mr. Dulles and other great statesmen. A man's relaxations condition the mind as does anything else. Hammarskjöld's dealings with nations were always conditioned by exposure to the cold white light of abstract thought, instead of being pickled in Whodunnits and He-dunnits.

But we did not know this at first. We accepted the Secretary-General on his face value as a quiet man with the tastes of a cultivated gentleman, something of a *Schoengeist*. We were grateful for his introduction of such events as the United Nations Day Concert where artists of the first magnitude shared their aura of culture and dignity with "this house." None of us could have dreamed that he was extraordinarily subtle and that he would one day be described as "cunning in the service of God"; that he thoroughly intended to use his diplomatic skills to change the habits of diplomacy; and that in the privacy of his diary he had already beseeched fate to give him something to die for.

We did not even know that at the very outset of his tenure of office, he had achieved a very nice stroke of diplomacy on our behalf, so quiet that it was invisible; and of course, never spoken of until years later.

His arrival in New York had coincided with the heyday of the Senator McCarthy troubles when the Headquarters Building suffered an invasion of FBI agents carrying black pads with which they fingerprinted every American in sight. Investigations were being made of all United States citizens employed by the Secretariat, and as a professional refugee since 1919, I was naturally one of the more suspicious characters. In fact,

I am an innocent sort of refugee; nevertheless, I could not help recalling the Paris prefect of police who, when he was asked, "What would you do if someone accused you of having stolen the Eiffel Tower?" replied, "I'd take the first plane to London."

When Trygve Lie had recruited in a hurry close to four thousand employees for the World Organization, it was inevitable that some persons should have entered who, having had some kind of Communist tinge, were later disapproved by the United States government, which then requested their dismissal. However, this indication that Uncle Sam had his eye on us was peculiarly embarrassing to American employees. An international civil servant is not expected to be under the instructions, still less under pressure, from any national government, including his own. He is there, in whatever capacity, great or humble, to serve the World Organization, and his obligation is very often reinforced by devotion to its ideals. It was therefore with considerable irritation that American members of the Secretariat lined up in a conference room to let the FBI smudge up their fingertips. Thereafter, morale was at a low ebb, and there was an effervescence of discontent and feelings of insecurity, especially as our daily work brought us into contact with Communists whom we were now afraid to wish "Good morning." This was the mood of the staff when Hammarskjöld arrived on the scene.

After a while the mood subsided and the pressure appeared to have been lifted; at any rate the FBI was no longer present in visible form. Not for years did we learn the firm position he had taken with the United States government. In 1961, he expressed it in his usual expensive language to Congregation at Oxford University:

"... the Secretary-General ... affirmed the necessity of independent action by the United Nations in regard to selection and recruitment of staff ...

"It was recognized that there should be a relationship of mutual confidence and trust between international officials and the governments of Member States. At the same time, the Secretary-General took a strong position that the dismissal of a staff member on the basis of the mere suspicion of a government of a Member State or a bare conclusion arrived at by the government on evidence which is denied the Secretary-General would amount to receiving instructions in violation of his obligation under ... the Charter, 'not to receive in the performance of his duties instructions from any government.' "

That Hammarskjöld had been able to make the United States government listen to his point of view and agree to abide by it at a time of national scare certainly demonstrates diplomatic talents of no mean quality. This was the period of his honeymoon with all the delegations. They were absolutely charmed by his quiet and unassertive ways. Cautiously, he never embarked upon any measure without talking it over with the chiefs of delegations. Once, when a suggestion of his was turned down by Andrei Vishinsky, the Soviet delegate added with a flourish, "But for you, Mr. Hammarskjöld, we would jump out of the window."

But when Hammarskjöld told this story, he added wryly, "That, of course, might change."

I have sometimes thought that in addition to financial, legal and military experts, governments ought to employ psychologists. Had a psychologist been privy to the counsels of the gentlemen in Conference Room 8, he might have looked less at Dag Hammarskjöld's unobtrusive manners and bureaucratic speech, and more at his taste for modern poetry and abstract painting; and he might have viewed with especial suspicion his passion for mountaineering.

So far as I can see, mountain climbing is a sport that is best left to Abominable Snowmen. But, some time after Dag Hammarskjöld came among us, I wrote an article about him for a Swedish newspaper in which I reflected upon the significance of having a Secretary-General who is a mountaineer. My conclusions were:

1. That a mountaineer is prudent and thinks twice before putting his feet anywhere.
2. That even so he must accept the challenge of the peak, advance, and never retreat.
3. That he has a taste for solitude and the courage to risk his neck.

As it turned out, these observations were not too far from the mark. But this was not apparent for some time. We did not particularly notice the sudden intrusion of God upon the international scene. The new Secretary-General made several speeches upon his arrival in which he spoke of "humility," "loyalty," and "devotion and integrity." He also told the representatives of nations that his work would be guided by the "strict observance of the rules and principles laid down in the Charter of this Organization." He reminded the Assembly of the festival of Easter that had just been celebrated by the Christian world and indicated the "redeeming power of true dedication to peace and good will towards men"; he also quoted a Swedish poet who said, "The greatest prayer of man does not ask for victory, but for peace."

The skeptics among us—and non-skeptics are short-lived in the diplomatic thicket—smiled at all this. We had heard such diamond-studded words before falling from the lips of mendacious men. This was, after all, the way the perfect Secretary-General ought to express himself; and so we found them no more remarkable than his promise to be "an instrument, a catalyst, perhaps an inspirer."

It was not realized at all that the new Secretary-General meant every word he said.

菜　單

大拼盤：

醬鴨　　　　紅椒　油鹽　腰鯽　片魚

鹽水鷄

西紅柿　芹菜

黃瓜

清湯燕菜

蟹肉魚翅

鷄油扁豆拼乾燒冬筍

口蘑燒鮑魚果

蠔油油菜果

鍋燒鴨

火腿蒸菜花

桂花賛丸加櫻桃

點心四樣

一九五五年一月十日

HAMMARSKJÖLD : 68

birthday, he received a cable that eleven of the flyers would be released. Some deduced from this coincidence that the Chinese had actually saved the flyers up in order to give the Secretary-General a birthday present; but whether this was so or not, it was Hammarskjöld's first major personal triumph.

In a letter to Bo Beskow, his artist friend, Hammarskjöld wrote, "The journey to China was a fantastic experience. In a sense, after it I was more grown up than before. It is grandiose and devastating, intensely distant and yet intensely true. This is so for the countryside, for the atmosphere in Peking (a splendid camp for the nomad princes who came from the desert across the low mountain ranges—a camp with an endless number of heavy tent-tops) and this is true for Chou En-lai (with a heart of steel, bloody hands, stern self-control, and a very warm smile)."

Chinese are one thing, Jews and Arabs are another.

On November 29, 1947, the United Nations General Assembly voted the partition of Palestine into Jewish and Arab states. The United States, the Soviet Union and France voted for the resolution. Thereafter, as soon as the British departed from Palestine, the Jews declared their half of the partition to be the sovereign state of Israel. Harry S. Truman and Joseph V. Stalin promptly recognized it, and the Arab League promptly declared war on it. Assam Pasha, Secretary-General of the Arab League promised that "This will be a war of extermination and a momentous massacre." To which the Grand Mufti of Jerusalem added, "When the sword speaks, everything else must be silent." They were both right: it was a momentous massacre of both Jews and Arabs, but it was the Israeli sword that had the last word.

The United Nations set up a Truce Commission, appointing the president of the Swedish Red Cross, Count Folke Bernadotte, as mediator. Bernadotte went to the Holy Land, and there on September 17, 1948, he was murdered by Israeli terrorists. His aide, Ralph Bunche, succeeded him, and by July, 1949, he had procured from four nations four separate armistice agreements which were published with a preamble stating that their purpose was "to facilitate the transition from present truce to permanent peace." Permanent peace in the Near East is like the magician's egg: now you see it and now you don't.

With the advent of "Nasserism," the Soviets switched their support from the Israelis to the Arabs. Czechoslovakia, which had been selling weapons to the Israelis to fight Arabs, now sold them to the Arabs to fight Israelis. France stepped into the breach and sold weapons to Israel. Things were moving along nicely towards a major war when Hammarskjöld moved onto the 38th Floor of the United Nations Building.

Complicating the military heroism was, as always, the human tragedy of refugees, close to half a million Arabs who had fled Israel during the war. The Arabs blamed the plight of the refugees on the United Nations for having created Israel; Israel blamed it on the Arabs for having started a war. The refugees, therefore, remained in a United Nations camp as a permanent obstacle to Israeli-Arab reconciliation, and by this time they have increased their numbers to over a million, testimony that while man bears with suffering, he still breeds.

By 1955, Nasser, with the help of Czechoslovakia and the Soviet Union and in military alliance with Saudi Arabia and Syria, was piling up huge armaments in the Gaza Strip. On April 4th, Israel complained to the Security Council of repeated attacks by Egyptian guerrilla fighters—*fedayeen*—based in Gaza. On August 30, the complaint was repeated.

One week later, Egypt complained to the Security Council that Israelis had killed thirty-six soldiers and refugees in the Gaza area. In January, fifty Syrians were killed in the Lake Tiberias region.

By this time the United Nations Truce Supervision Commission's cup was running over with border incidents.

On March 20, 1956, the Security Council met, and acting upon the proposal of the United States requested the Secretary-General to go to the Near East and "reestablish compliance" with Bunche's 1949 armistice agreements. In other words, his mission was to put an end to pointless murder.

The following day, Hammarskjöld made a note in his diary, in which he seemed to liken himself to a triumphant Biblical figure, Phinehas, who by a decisive act averted the wrath of God from his people. He may have done this in hope, determination, or prophecy; or even in self-mockery, for this ingredient was by no means lacking in the complex Secretary-General.

Hammarskjöld established his headquarters in Beirut, Lebanon, and spent the next four weeks visiting the various capitals to negotiate with the men in power. He must have felt like Gulliver in the land of the horses. He could have had no sympathy for wild-eyed Arab nationalism, yet he had ears for Nasser's legitimate complaints as well as for Ben Gurion's grievances and the Jewish plight. His dealings with Nasser were smoothed by a man with whom he had something in common: Mahmoud Fawzi, Egyptian Foreign Minister, a career diplomat, cautious, tight-lipped, high-strung, pedantic, and like Hammarskjöld, an island by himself. He was the last survivor of the royal Farouk regime, and it was with him rather than with Nasser that Hammarskjöld dealt.

He went to see the King of Jordan, Hussein the Short. This little king is one whose life is considered a poor risk by insurance companies. His cousin, King Faisal of Iraq was murdered, and so was his grandfather, Abdullah (one of Lawrence of Arabia's companions-at-arms) on the steps of the Jerusalem Mosque. King Hussein's own father, Talal, had previously tried a shot at Abdullah who later spoke of the incident: "Talal is a good son; he missed me."

Although such goings-on had become uncommon in the Hammarskjöld family since Viking days, Dag took a fancy to the King of Jordan whose simplicity and courage he admired, and he appreciated his difficult position between the giants, Nasser and Ben Gurion.

Prime Minister Ben Gurion was a thornier problem. This hard-knit, stocky man whose domed head was garnished with the light plumage of a snowy egret, had originally been called David Green, but he had chosen for himself the name of Ben Gurion, Son of the Lion, and it was more than a name: it was a program. He frowned upon Hammarskjöld because he considered him hostile to Israel. This suspicion had nestled in Ben Gurion's heart ever since Hammarskjöld had addressed to Dr. Nahum Goldmann, leader of the World Jewish Congress, remarks that gave Ben Gurion to believe that Hammarskjöld questioned the wisdom of the partition of Palestine. Furthermore, Ben Gurion had a low opinion of Hammarskjöld's famed diplomatic technique. "In the Israeli view, Hammarskjöld thinks that situations can be solved merely by formulating them," as *Time* Magazine put it (November 26, 1956).

Paula Ben Gurion, the prime minister's stately wife, on the other hand, had enormous diplomatic talents, and she displayed them to Dag. "Why don't you get married?" she asked him. "Then you would have to worry about your wife and you would leave us alone." *

Still, staying at Sdeh Boker, Dag and David had friendly discussions about art, literature, and religious philosophy, and when Paula asked him to help peel the potatoes, the Secretary-General helped. "Ben Gurion is nobody's friend," an Israeli commented skeptically upon the visit, "His religio-philosophical conversation was only an effort to bridge their insoluble differences."

But on May 9, when, back in New York, Hammarskjöld re-

* Lash, *op. cit.*, p. 73.

ported to the Security Council, he told them to their considerable admiration that he had received from all the kings of the East, friendly and unfriendly, from Israel, Egypt, Syria, Lebanon, and Jordan, written assurances that the cease-fire provided for in the 1949 armistice agreements would be observed.

At some time in this triumphant year of 1956, Hammarskjöld reflected upon the heady responsibilities of joining battle with principalities and powers; his diary shows his feeling of having guidance from an even higher source than the Security Council. And so, while he permitted himself to rejoice at his successes, he abjured the credit for them. He seemed to share the scruples of the surgeon, Paré, who said, "I treated, God cured."

As it happened, he was taking a wise precaution, because six months later more trouble broke loose in the Near East and zigzagged across the earth. Nasser had married himself into the Communist family, and in retaliation the United States and the United Kingdom withdrew their offers of aid in the financing of the Aswan High Dam. With epileptic suddenness, Nasser then nationalized the Suez Canal. Next, Britain blocked Egyptian funds in the United Kingdom, and the United States followed suit, freezing all assets of Egypt and of the Suez Canal Company in the United States.

Nikita Krushchev watched and warned that if war broke out over the Suez Canal, the Arabs would not stand alone.

On September 29, 1956, Israel invaded the Sinai Peninsula, explaining to the Security Council that this was done "... to eliminate the Egyptian *fedayeen* bases, from which Egyptian armed units ... invade Israel's territory for the purpose of murder, sabotage, and the creation of permanent insecurity to peaceful life."

Washington wanted to call an emergency meeting of the Security Council if only they could find Henry Cabot Lodge. They finally dug him out of the Metropolitan Opera House where he was attending the opening in the company of British ambassador Sir Pierson Dixon. The same night, resplendent in his gala outfit, Lodge visited the office of Dag Hammarskjöld to tell him that his government wished to call a meeting of the Council.

The next day the Council met and Lodge asked for "immediate cessation of military activities of Israel against Egypt"—only to be balked by the veto of his opera-companion, Sir Pierson Dixon. The French doubled the veto, although one would have been plenty.

France and Britain, both vitally interested in the Suez Canal, had their own ultimatum to Israel and Egypt, but it was a mock one. It asked for a cease-fire within twelve hours and the withdrawal of both armies to a point ten miles from the Canal—and if this was not done, "British and French troops will intervene."

Of course, they were only too eager to intervene, as the Israelis very well knew; in all likelihood, the Israelis had agreed not to budge in response to the ultimatum. Thus, on October 31, 1956, the French and the British attacked Egyptian airfields.

Nasser had been properly framed.

On that dramatic day, with war—and probably a contrived war—in full blast, Dag Hammarskjöld read what was for him the riot act to the Security Council:

"This afternoon I wish to make the following declaration: The principles of the Charter are, by far, greater than the Organization in which they are embodied, and the aims which they are to safeguard are holier than the policies of any single nation or people.

"The Secretary-General has the duty to maintain his usefulness by avoiding public stands on conflicts between Member nations unless and until such an action might help to resolve the conflict. However, the discretion and impartiality thus imposed on the Secretary-General ... may not degenerate into a policy of expediency. He must also be a servant of the principles of the Charter, and its aims must ultimately determine what for him is right and wrong. For that he must stand.

"A Secretary-General cannot serve on any other assumption than that—within the necessary limits of human frailty and honest differences of opinion—all Member nations honor their pledge to observe all articles of the Charter . . .

"The bearing of what I have just said must be obvious to all without elaboration from my side. Were the Members to consider that another view of the duties of the Secretary-General than the one here stated would better serve the interests of the Organization, it is their obvious right to act accordingly."

This sounded something like an offer to abdicate, and spontaneously, the great powers chimed their eloquence to express confidence in the Secretary-General, including France and Britain. Sir Pierson Dixon said, "We have the highest regard for the integrity and the impartiality of Mr. Hammarskjöld." He could well afford to take this position with British troops safely en route to cut the throat of Nasser.

All action in the Council was paralyzed by the Anglo-French double veto. The gravity of the situation brought four foreign ministers rushing to New York: Selwyn Lloyd of Britain, Dmitri Shepilov of the USSR, Christian Pineau of France, and Secretary Dulles from Washington. On the night of November 1/2, a special emergency meeting of the General Assembly took up the matter and called for a cease-fire. Two nights later, the Soviet Union threatened the United Kingdom and France with "volunteers," and also rocket warfare, if the cease-fire did not immediately go into effect.

When this cease-fire resolution was adopted on November 2nd, there was a notable abstention: that of Lester Pearson of Canada. His explanation was that no cease-fire could possibly prevail because the Arabs and the Israelis would obviously continue to be at each other's throats—unless they were kept apart by a truly international peace and police force.

When one has spent four decades, as I have, watching diplomacy in action, amid the outrage and the duplicities one sometimes witnesses historic moments. At least that is what one thinks. But who can tell when a moment is historic? The diplomat cannot, or the journalist, or the onlooker. Only history can tell.

But I do believe that the day Lester B. Pearson of Canada stood on the rostrum and submitted to the Assembly a resolution requesting Dag Hammarskjöld to submit "within forty-eight hours a plan for the setting up, with the consent of the nations concerned, of an emergency International United Nations Force to secure and supervise the cessation of hostilities . . ." was historic. For the first time a world organization was going to get teeth in it. Lack of teeth had been the main trouble with the League of Nations; indeed, probably it was that of the Holy Alliance. A world organization is one gift horse you have got to look in the mouth.

Whose idea was it to set up an Emergency Force? Some druids say that it was Pearson's. Others that it was Hammarskjöld's, but that the Secretary-General had judged that it would be more acceptable if proposed by a delegate. I turned to Andrew Cordier, now Dean at Columbia University, who in 1956 had been Hammarskjöld's executive assistant. He told me, "We had dinner at the Drake Hotel, Pearson, Hammarskjöld and I. Pearson suggested a peace force made up of the British and French. Hammarskjöld was set against this.

"The next day we had lunch on the 38th Floor, and the same night Pearson presented the resolution. There was no mention of the British and French in it.

"No doubt Pearson had his merit in the idea."

The resolution adopted on the night of November 4/5, 1956, specifying that the troops of the great powers were not to participate in the United Nations Emergency Force, certainly seems to show the fine Swedish hand of Hammarskjöld. In setting up UNEF, the Military Staff Committee, which is made up of the five powers, was not consulted at all, although its liaison officer, Lt. Col. Victor de Guinzbourg, was asked occasionally for advice on logistics. UNEF troops were composed of Indians, Danes, Norwegians, Swedes, Colombians, Finns, far-flung peoples whom nobody of consequence greatly hated.

It was by no means an easy thing to put over: there were days of noisy quiet diplomacy on the 38th Floor. Finally, on November 7, Israel, Egypt, France, and the United Kingdom accepted the cease-fire order from the Assembly, and Egypt accepted the notion of UNEF landing on her territory. Small details had to be ironed out. Europe and North America were raked for berets that could be dyed United Nations blue, in vain; instead, blue-sprayed United States helmets were used, and they were provided by the U.S. Army Base in Leghorn, Italy. At Hammarskjöld's request, the Italian government agreed to permit use of Capodichino Airport near Naples as a staging point for the flight to Egypt, and the United States agreed to move the troops from their homelands to that point. Since Egyptians do not greatly hate the Swiss, Hammarskjöld spared their feelings by asking Swissair to lift the UN troops from Italy to Egypt.*

Such was the Secretary-General's faith in the common sense of his fellow man that he supposed his troops would stay on the Sinai Peninsula for two or three months, but after eight years, they are still there. However, the cease-fire is still there also.

In his Introduction to the Annual Report to the General Assembly for 1956-57, the Secretary-General wrote, "There is need for careful analysis and study of the UNEF experience in all its aspects, in order to give the United Nations a sound foundation, should the Organization wish to build an agreed stand-by plan for a United Nations peace force that could be activated on short notice in future emergencies to serve similar

* *Time*, November 26, 1956.

ways. Steps have been taken for such a study to be undertaken in the Secretariat."

The steps to which the Secretary-General referred were these: with the Suez crisis happily weathered, he asked each department that had participated in the great adventure to prepare papers describing their role in the setting up of UNEF. He thought to submit the lessons learned to the General Assembly. The department chiefs obediently submitted great mountains of reports, each extolling the importance of his own department in the operation. These the Secretary-General ordered digested, and when the digest was reduced to hundreds of pages, he ordered the digest to be digested. Satisfied at last, he added his own thoughts, which were as long as the digest itself.

But this report did not reach the Assembly floor. The Russians warned Hammarskjöld that if he presented it, they would tear it apart. The analysis of the UNEF experience hides to this day, for fear of the Russians, in the archives of the United Nations, and all that was made public of it was that Hammarskjöld noted its existence before the First Committee, and said that he had not wished to insist upon presenting it because "the time is not ripe."

And yet, Hammarskjöld did not advocate a standing international army. His idea was only that a master-plan should be available upon which a police force could be quickly made up whenever it was needed, in such a fashion that would conform to the political realities. When Czechoslovakia and Rumania offered troops to UNEF (for the Gaza Strip) he politely declined them. In the Congo he preferred to compose the force mostly from Afro-Asian countries.

With "Ach und Krach" peace established in the Near East, there remained the clearance of the Suez Canal which was obstructed by scuttled ships, toppled bridges, and fallen airplanes. The French and the British offered to do the job, but Nasser preferred that the UN should do it. Hammarskjöld engaged the services of Lt. Gen. Raymond "Jack" Wheeler, former chief of the United States Army Corps of Engineers. "Typical of the United Nations," snorted Viscount Hailsham, "to send an old Middle Western grocer to do a difficult technical job." However, Jack Wheeler cleared the canal in four months, faster than anyone had expected. Full of success, he procured a photo of Hammarskjöld upon which he wished to have the Secretary-General's autograph. His secretary thought this was a doubtful enterprise: she had heard that Hammarskjöld, as a matter of principle, never autographed photos. But Wheeler went to see Hammarskjöld and handed him the photo with these words, "Mr. Secretary-General, I'm told you never autograph your photos, so I'm giving you a chance to say no." Face to face with fate, Hammarskjöld was a man who said yes, and so he signed it.

More difficult was the clearing away of diplomatic debris. Egyptian interference with Israeli shipping through the canal remains a cumbrous affair to this day, and it was a long time before Ben Gurion, Son of the Lion, consented to talk to the man who had saved the skin of his prey, Nasser. Israeli Foreign Minister Golda Meir talked to him though: a former schoolteacher from Milwaukee, she upbraided Hammarskjöld as if he had been a schoolboy. And upon his next visit to Israel, he was greeted by demonstrators carrying posters calling him "Nassershield"; a hurtful reminder, perhaps, to the Secretary-General, of the days when his father had been called "Hungerskjöld" in Sweden. Eden in his memoirs wrote bitterly that after the cease-fire on November 6, "it should have been possible to shape a lasting settlement of the Arab-Israeli conflict and get some secure guarantees about the freedom of passage through the Suez Canal." He said that "he never would have anticipated that the cards that were in the hands of the United Nations and the United States would have been thrown away as they were in that situation."

Queried about the latter statement at a press conference,

Hammarskjöld replied: "What were the cards that the UN had? The presence of French and British and Israeli troops in or close to the Canal Zone, regarded as enemies by the country through which the canal runs—regarded as enemies by the whole Arab world? Is that a card which is a useful one for a negotiation about peace, if it is not an imposed peace, and do you believe that any peace imposed on the Near East would have been a lasting one?" He was standing on the conviction (unfortunately a sound one) that the day is long past when the mere appearance of a British gunboat in choppy waters can impose discipline on swarthy populations for decades to come.

To the present day it is a mooted question whether the world would be a better place to live in had Nasser been destroyed in 1956. But this is not the point at issue regarding Hammarskjöld. His business was not to destroy Nasser or the state of Israel; he was there to preserve them both until such time as they might be willing to talk about their conflicts instead of fighting about them. Whatever the political expediency may have been, the fact remained that an awesomely explosive situation had been handled with moral rectitude.

Just as the Suez crisis was reaching the boiling point, revolution flared in Hungary. Double urgency was on the agenda as every move of the Security Council was blocked by veto, and this was inevitably followed by an emergency meeting of the General Assembly. Now, we in the Secretariat got our first spectacular display of the Secretary-General's formidable staying powers. Day after day the meetings lasted until four or five in the morning, and they started again at three in the afternoon. Regiments of people grew faint and weary, but Hammarskjöld throve. He sat in his chair for hours, alert as a bird. About six o'clock in the morning, after the meetings had adjourned, he would drag his staff to his office where, sipping a little champagne he would hold a postmortem, at the same time planning for the future, organizing UNEF, and keeping an eye on Budapest. At seven, he would go home to his Park Avenue apartment.

"Tomorrow I'm going to let you sleep," threatened Bill Ranallo after this had been going on for some time.

"No," said Hammarskjöld. "Wake me as usual: eight-thirty."

He telephoned Leif Belfrage in the Swedish Foreign Office to ask for Swedish troops for UNEF. "Aren't you very tired?" asked Belfrage.

"Oh, no," replied Hammarskjöld. "I don't think I've slept more than two or three hours this week, but I'm doing fine." *

Once he called a delegate at noon, and the delegate said with some peevishness that it was Sunday and he needed sleep. Hammarskjöld could not stop repeating in amazement, "That sissy needs a sleep! That sissy needs a sleep!"

During these hectic days, my television crew had to pass their own "United for Peace" resolution, for every time a veto blocked the Security Council followed by a General Assembly meeting "without delay," their scene of activities shifted; they had to pick up the heavy TV cameras and heft them from the Security Council Chamber to the Assembly Hall. And then, when at dawn something new arose, as it usually did, that needed to be vetoed in the Council, they would pick them up again and carry them back. It was to our intense relief when the Assembly switched from the Suez debate to the Hungarian question without interruption so that we were saved a moving. My own work as director was exceptionally exacting, for at any moment, cameras roving over the faces of delegates might catch one asleep in his chair. Since it is against UN policy to show snoozing delegates on the air, extra wakefulness was demanded of me. Once, when a camera accidentally came to rest on the sleeping Liberian, I bellowed, "Pan over to Lebanon!" The cameraman panned, but Lebanon was asleep too.

About this time, Hammarskjöld enriched the diplomatic

* Lash, *op. cit.,* p. 89.

vocabulary with the term "UN Presence." Asked to define it, he replied, "There is a UN Presence whenever the UN is present," which is as nice a definition as I have ever heard of a diplomatic phrase.

UNEF is, of course, an extreme form of UN presence. But there are cases where UNEF cannot be used without raising the hobgoblin of UN intervention in the internal affairs of nations. Such a case was the Lebanese crisis of 1958, which had strong elements of civil war. It was feared that the presence of an armed UN police force might change the balance of the sides in dispute, thus making it impossible for the Lebanese to have a peaceful fracas. Following Lebanon's complaint that the United Arab Republics were interfering in her domestic affairs, therefore, a UN Observation Group consisting of several hundred unarmed civilians and soldiers was sent to keep a watch on the Lebanese border and make sure that there was no armed infiltration into the country and that weapons were not being smuggled across the Lebanese border. It was, the Secretary-General said, "a very good example of what UN Presence can mean in a very hot situation without any resort even to military units..."

Jordan too complained of the Arab Republics' interference —in fact, someone had twice tried to shoot down her little king's airplane. Nevertheless, the last thing she wanted was a UNEF police force trampling about under her blue heaven. At the request of the General Assembly, Hammarskjöld negotiated with the Jordan government a new sort of UN Presence, still further removed from the concept of a force: this was a kind of United Nations ambassador whose function it was to live in Jordan as long as need be, keep an impartial eye on the mischief there and make his report to the Secretary-General. It was a one-man civilian operation, dear to Hammarskjöld's heart: it meant to him his own ears and eyes on the spot. Besides acting as a deterrent to malefactors, the ambassador also was to help, through negotiation, the reestablishment of neighborly relations between Jordan and the rest of the Arab world.

Said Hammarskjöld: "... We have learned that UN physical presence is a new and decisive element in the solution of conflicts ... through reconciliation. It may take varying forms. The forms must be chosen after careful analysis of the situation. We may, on the one hand, need to have military units, but without fighting tasks. We may, on the other hand, follow the range (and) arrive at the opposite conclusion: one man, civilian, on the spot."

There is still another aspect to UN Presence which Hammarskjöld was too quiet a diplomat to give voice to—for a while: it can be used to keep the great powers out of trouble spots where they have face to lose and nothing much to gain. It was precisely this sort of situation that was the genesis of the famous "vacuum" that the Secretary-General was expected to fill. The powers, by sheer reluctance to incriminate themselves by calling a spade a spade, might bring forth an ambiguous resolution, that is, one with a large hole in it, or vacuum, where presumably they feared to tread. In this case, they "left it to Dag" to interpret the resolution as seemed good to him and then to act accordingly. This was dizzying work, especially as the powers, in a succession of resolutions have a habit of filling one vacuum with another. For the Secretary-General it entailed grave political risk.

But Hammarskjöld was nothing if not courageous, and he was a perfect glutton for vacuums, sometimes getting to them before they even existed officially. Such a case was the dispute that arose between Cambodia and Thailand concerning an ancient Buddhist temple that stood upon their borders. Without submitting the case to the Security Council—though not without holding private talks with its members—Hammarskjöld sent a venerable Swedish diplomat to the scene as his personal factotum to straighten the matter out. Questioned about it at a press conference, the Secretary-General made light of the affair. It was a simple case, he said. However it could have become complicated, because at the bottom of it was the hand of Red China. "You can see," he told the journalists, "how much more effective and smoothworking such a technique is than the regular one which involves all the meetings and debates and so on."

He went even further than this. With his alarmingly swift perceptions, he noted where vacuums were likely to be about to exist, and he made certain that they were precisely where he wanted them to be. Many of the ambiguous resolutions passed by the Security Council were written by Dag Hammarskjöld in his own convoluted and delphic style. In the case of a delicate issue, it is this sort of document alone that has a chance to pass or at least have the benefit of abstentions, for anything short of ambiloquence is promptly beheaded by the veto.

Once he had gotten such a resolution passed, its vague language left him a wide margin for interpretation, and he was able to perform diplomatic magic. Someone has suggested that Hammarskjöld's motto ought to have been *Per Ambigua ad Astra*.

The Secretary-General's ways were cunning, but they were not sly. The fact is that the Charter, as it was framed in San Francisco, no longer embraces the troubles of our modern world. The great power unity that was supposed to prevail and keep our peace never really existed. The veto, which the great powers granted to one another was never more than a *ceinture de chasteté*, a sorry symptom of distrust. Not great power harmony, but great power discord became the pedestal of peace around which Hammarskjöld hopped, skipped, and as a matter of fact, dodged.

As cold as death were the vacuums that yawned when cold war issues were at stake. Hammarskjöld handled the cold war as a physician handles a pernicious disease. As Dean Cordier put it, when a crisis arose, his policy was "to elbow the cold war out of the situation, lower the tension, isolate the cold war element in it—then to the solving of the problem."

In due course, this technique acquired a twist which may be paraphrased thus: "Elbow the great powers out of the way and solve the situation with the assistance of small powers." It went very well indeed until, in the Congo, the great powers had something to gain. Then they elbowed Hammarskjöld out of the way.

But there were years when through loopholes of quibbles and minefields of contradictions and vacuums of equivocal decisions, the Secretary-General led the World Organization into pastures undreamed of by those who framed the Charter. And when we in the glass house saw the Secretary-General going to the Gaza Strip as one goes to the cafeteria, and visiting the Kremlin to talk about Berlin, and discussing disarmament problems with Khrushchev in a rowboat on the Black Sea, and walking unscathed through the hornets' nest in Laos, it was difficult to avoid being contaminated with hope.

He had made of himself an instrument. As a catalyst, he had put honesty to work in politics. And as an inspirer—well, some people think that moral rectitude is a great untapped source of power in practical politics, and Hammarskjöld was inspiring them.

6

Something to Lose

THE SECRETARY-GENERAL plotted his wonders in his offices on the 38th Floor, a sort of Mount Olympus where deities—or at least the Deity—never slept, and where a quarter of a mile above the fracas of public debate, quiet agreements were reached. Once, during the Suez crisis, with acrimony building up in the Security Council, Hammarskjöld scribbled a little note and passed it along unobtrusively to Mahmoud Fawzi of Egypt, Christian Pineau of France, and Selwyn Lloyd of Britain. It said, "Meet me in my office."

He had a coterie of advisers and assistants, some of whom were inherited from Trygve Lie. His chief executive assistant was Andrew Cordier, a stocky, compact Hoosier with two feet planted solidly in the world of reality; it was he who guided him at first through the intricacies of procedure, and he seemed to have almost a paternal attitude towards his chief. "It was easy to work with him," recalls Cordier. "He knew where the Organization had to go and where it stood, and he laid his groundwork accordingly." He had not found his collaboration with Mr. Lie so easy. Lie would agree on a certain program in the morning, then change his mind over luncheon, without informing his executive assistant. "But Hammarskjöld kept me informed totally," reflected Mr. Cordier.

It is a surprise to learn that the secretive Hammarskjöld kept less administrative secrets than the expansive Mr. Lie.

He showed a preference for sensitive, subtle, quick-minded men. When the new African countries bowed onto the world scene Hammarskjöld adopted as his adviser, Heinz Wieschhoff, a lean and stringy man whose face reflected the same quizzical unrest as that of the Secretary-General. Conor Cruise O'Brien, UN representative in Katanga wrote of him, "Wieschhoff had a hard, lucid mind and a strong, even formidable personality . . . there were several other people in that room who were far from being nonentities, but Heinz Wieschhoff was the only one who when Mr. Hammarskjöld was there seemed to continue to radiate on a wave length of his own." This is no mean compliment from a man who habitually oils his typewriter with vinegar.

By profession, Wieschhoff was an ethnographer who had been for eleven years a professor at the University of Pennsylvania, where among his students was Kwame Nkrumah, later President of Ghana. He had himself been a pupil of the great German explorer and authority on African art, Leo Frobenius, whom he had accompanied on several expeditions to South East Africa to study the culture and archaeology of the region. Frobenius propounded the theory that civilization undergoes an organic development similar to that of plants, animals, and man, and it is interesting to find this monistic notion occasionally flickering in the background of Hammarskjöld's thought, perhaps through the influence of Wieschhoff:

"However primitive a basic institutional pattern may be, it carries within it seeds for the growth of higher social organisms, . . . I believe it is useful, in the discussion of the development of human society, be it national or international, to keep in mind this sociological perspective, taken over from theories of biological evolution . . ."

One day, shortly before Christmas, Mrs. Wieschhoff, an American of Quaker stock said to her husband, "You ought to give Mr. Hammarskjöld a Christmas present." Wieschhoff was taken aback. Raised in a strict Westphalian family, he retained a European's respect for rank, and it seemed to him a presumption to intrude upon Hammarskjöld with a Christmas present. Then, a few days before Christmas, he came round. "I'll give him a present," he said, "but what?"

"Give him one of those clay pipes you brought home from Africa."

And so, Mrs. Wieschhoff neatly boxed and wrapped a clay pipe whose bowl was shaped like a human head, and Wieschhoff took it to the office with him, where with great discretion, he entered Hammarskjöld's sanctum when he was not there, and placed it on his desk. A little later in the day, he saw Hammarskjöld, who asked him, "Did you get my present?"

"No," said Wieschhoff, puzzled.

"Oh. Well, I left it on your desk."

Neither of these constrained and reserved men would conceive of exchanging gifts casually, face to face.

Hammarskjöld's present was a cream and sugar set of geometric design, handmade in Sweden.

One Christmas morning Hammarskjöld visited the Wieschhoffs in Bronxville. He sat under the tree amid the pile of sparkling papers and spoke eloquently to the Wieschhoff children on the art of skiing. But although he was taken into the kitchen and introduced to the goose, he refused to participate in the family dinner. Before leaving the Wieschhoff home, he accepted one for the road: a medium-sized medicine bottle containing a brown liquid was placed before him which bore a handwritten label reading, "Benjamin Franklin's Orange Shrub—after a recipe written in Paris, 1778-1784. *Fecit* W.J.R." The initials were those of Dr. Robbins, President of the American Philosophical Society.

Hammarskjöld and Wieschhoff died together in Ndola the following year. The orange shrub was not opened again until Mrs. Wieschhoff offered a glass to me.

Frequently the Secretary-General spent Christmas with the UNEF soldiers in the Gaza Strip. A Christmas tree was usually flown in from Canada or Norway and decorated with bits and pieces of color, more as a symbol than for beauty's sake. Before leaving New York, the Secretary-General always placed in his buttonhole the UN insignia to please the soldiers.

In 1958, he dined with the soldiers and afterwards, a reception was held in his honor. Noting the presence of the young girl secretaries in their Christmas best, Hammarskjöld felt embarrassed that he had brought no presents to offer them. On an inspiration, he pulled a case of cigars out of his pocket and handed them around to the girls. When this story was related to me, I was skeptical. "He must have meant it as a joke," I said.

"Not at all," I was told. "Those cigars were handed around in dead earnest."

The worst of it was that the waiters immediately moved in with lights for the girls, so that every one of them in line of duty was obliged to smoke a cigar. "I never was so sick in my life," lamented Frances McAuley, who had never smoked before.

Again and again the anecdotes and episodes of Hammarskjöld's life fall into place like shards to show the vessel that he was—a man who for all his diplomatic skills was maladroit in commonplace human situations and furthermore infected others with his own constraint. His qualities of mind were winning him admiration, and his quality of spirit was altogether elevating to the atmosphere of "this house." But he was not popular in the usual sense. There are many who remember resentfully that he was personally inaccessible, even though his "threshold was always open." Such criticisms persist mostly in the middle strata of the Secretariat, among people too highly placed to draw his tenderness and too low to merit his confidence. Maintenance men, security guards and typists found him informal and lovable. His cabinet on the 38th Floor found him an inspiration of whom to this day they cannot speak without emotion. But it cannot be denied that some have been deeply wounded by his frosty selectiveness and his abrupt intoleration.

A particularly vicious attack on him widely published throughout the world after his death called him "ruthless," "arrogant," a man who demanded "blind submission in subordinates," and was unable to "delegate authority"; and it accused him of deliberately creating a "Hammarskjöld myth."

The article drew forth an indignant response from Dr. Ralph Bunche: "I am simply appalled . . . it grossly misrepresents and distorts the character of one of the truly remarkable men of our times . . . There was nothing formidable about him; he not only tolerated but seemed to relish views at odds with his own; and if he had a messianic complex he concealed it well from his working associates . . .

"Dag was admired and respected by his associates, but he was not idolized by any of us and never gave the impression that he expected to be; quite the contrary in fact. He demanded quality and high standard in work, of himself as well as others; he was contemptuous of mediocrity; he was impatient with dissimulation; but he was not arrogant or overbearing . . .

"He could be ecstatic about a literary gem, a fine painting, or a superior musical performance. I have seen him dance a jig of elation when late at night some good news would come by cable from some critical spot. He could tell jokes, sometimes on himself."

These sincere and certainly truthful observations about Dag the ideal chief and jolly good fellow do not obviate the fact that there is and was such a thing as a "Hammarskjöld myth." But Hammarskjöld did not make the myth; it was generated automatically out of the conflagration of his many conflicting temperament traits which were in turn reflected in the manifold faces he turned to various people. He himself was only too conscious of his "robust" sense of superiority, and he realized that he could never conceal this from others. The humility and warmth proper to his ideal self did not come easily to him. And yet he had learned the lesson of St. Paul: without these golden ingredients of the soul, he would be condemned to live in an abstract hell in which his desire to help the many would be mocked by his inability to win the love of his few intimates. He stared with sore eyes upon his faults, his selfishness, his ambition, his death-wish. What virtue could ever balance them? What virtue but love, the "outflowing of power released by self-surrender."

Here we have all at once the Hammarskjöld who was self-absorbed and coldly ambitious, and the Hammarskjöld capable of such direct self-surrender that each one of his closest collaborators, in conversation and in writing, tend to the conviction that the light of the Secretary-General's countenance shone most strongly upon himself.

Hammarskjöld wound up his brilliant self-analysis with the observation that far from being contradictory, these two aspects of himself mutually supported one another.

It is not too often that executive types are found to harness their cold ambition to their better selves, and while I believe this came naturally and inevitably to Hammarskjöld, it obviously did not come easily.

Equally myth-provoking were the Secretary-General's contacts in his official capacity with the world at large. He had the utterly astonishing habit, for a bureaucrat, of replying to every communication personally and at once. During the Suez crisis a schoolteacher in Göteborg, Sweden, asked his pupils to write essays on the event and Dag Hammarskjöld's role in it, and one small boy was inspired to suggest that all the papers be sent to the Secretary-General in New York. Their reply came by return mail, and it showed that he had read the papers and found that all the young pupils were growing up to be good, earnest pacificatory Swedes.

A British lady journalist, Mrs. Campbell Cooke, sent him an article reprinted from the magazine, *Women Speaking,* and received a telegram of gratitude the next day at three o'clock in the morning. A clergyman sent him a sermon to read asking him whether he agreed with the sentiments expressed therein and by return mail received his answer: "No."

Authors sent him their books, groups sent him their prospectuses, and old ladies to whom he might conceivably have offered a cigar had he met them face to face snowed him under with literature of one sort or another. All received prompt, informed, personal response. Was it bureaucratic tidiness, or sense of duty, or noblesse oblige? Perhaps it was all of these in mutual support with an "outflowing of a power" which alone was an antidote for his loneliness.

If so, one could wish there were more lonely bureaucrats in this world.

Hammarskjöld took mischievous joy in the intricacies of the political game, and he adored being a success at it. But he reminded himself that now he had "something to lose." He reflected in his diary about the orders he obeyed: they had to be obeyed at once, staking everything.

When the UN General Assembly, after ascertaining the will of the majority by vote, makes a decision, this does not have the force of law. It is only a recommendation. Some critics of the World Organization might ponder how long order could be kept in their home towns if the judge on the bench were empowered merely to hand a rope to a guilty person and recommend him to hang himself.

When such an Organization acquires a Secretary-General who regards the principles of the Charter as a sort of Bible and feels that it is his responsibility to carry out recommendations of the Assembly even though this interferes with the purposes of a great power, that Secretary-General is sitting on a Siege Perilous.

Hammarskjöld's first rebuff came with the Hungarian revolution—or counterrevolution, depending upon the language in which you are reading this book. The affair was especially prickly because it involved the old diplomatic argument about "internal" and "external" affairs. We have yet to invent a Charter which will contain the notion that all affairs are ambivalent; that internal affairs are external, and external affairs are internal.

Compounding the diplomatic delicacy of the situation was the fact that whenever revolution breaks out anywhere, two governments are temporarily in force, that of the revolution and that of the status quo, and it is difficult to tell, especially from a distance, which is which.

It started in October, 1956, with a bloody battle between Hungarians and a combination of Soviet troops and Hungarian police. The next day at dawn, Soviet tanks rumbled down the streets of Budapest meeting with fierce resistance. They withdrew.

On October 27, France, the United Kingdom and the United States requested an urgent meeting of the Security Council. The revolutionary prime minister, Imre Nagy, then protested United Nations interference in an "internal affair." But when the Soviet forces returned, that same Imre Nagy cabled Hammarskjöld, asking for UN help in upholding the neutrality of Hungary—that is, her right to hold aloof from the Warsaw Pact, the counter-NATO.

Prime Minister Janos Kadar, leading the forces of the status quo, cabled the same day that the request of Nagy was illegal, and he objected categorically to any discussion of the Hungarian question by the United Nations.

On November 4, the very day when the Assembly took the momentous decision to set up UNEF, Soviet tanks returned to Budapest and were met by fierce resistance. The uprising spread throughout the land; 23,000 people in all were killed. Houses crumbled, the prison gates were opened, and refugees fled in all directions across the borders. Meanwhile in New York, Security Council action was blocked by Soviet veto.

An emergency session of the General Assembly called upon the Soviet Union to stop the armed attack on Hungary; but by this time Imre Nagy was overthrown. Janos Kadar was in power, and he notified Hammarskjöld and the world that "Soviet troops are in Hungary at the request of the Hungarian government."

Hammarskjöld then appointed an Investigating Committee and the Assembly called upon Hungary and the USSR to permit it to enter Hungary; but Kadar replied that "the presence of UN observers in Hungary is not warranted."

Now Hammarskjöld offered to go to Budapest himself. Back came the reply that he was welcome as a tourist but not as Secretary-General; but, said Kadar, government representatives would be glad to meet him as Secretary-General in Rome. Hammarskjöld saw no point in observing the Hungarian uprising from Rome; but on November 21, he reiterated his offer to go to Budapest as Secretary-General. The Hungarian government waited twelve days before declaring its willingness to welcome Mr. Hammarskjöld in Budapest "at a later date appropriate for both sides."

But Hammarskjöld, by quiet diplomacy, continued his negotiations, and finally was able to inform the General Assembly that he planned to go to Budapest on December 16 and stay there for three days. But on December 12, the Hungarian delegate informed him that December 16, after all, was not deemed "appropriate" by his government. In fact, not for five months, long after the relics of uprising had been cleared away did the Hungarians find it in their hearts to offer the Secretary-General a chicken *paprikás* on their home hearth "at any time convenient to him."

Hammarskjöld never went to Budapest.

The position of the Hungarian government was that no revolution had taken place, but a counterrevolution, fomented and supported from abroad. Vasily Kuznetsov, Soviet Deputy Foreign Minister told the General Assembly: "People who are loyal to the high ideals of the United Nations ... will, I am sure, draw the necessary conclusions from Hungarian events— so that never in the future will counterrevolutionary forces basing themselves upon assistance from international reaction be able to unleash ... sanguinary orgies." *

The Hungarian refugees, 200,000 of them who in the days of the uprising had fled into adjacent countries, as well as their sympathizers, blamed Hammarskjöld for their plight. They said that during the Nagy regime there were twenty-four hours when he might have gone to Budapest, and history would have taken another turn. Three years later, before the Student's Association in Copenhagen, Hammarskjöld explained, "In the Hungarian crisis, the United Nations confined itself to an 'expression of principle' ... with the exception of one or two of the smaller countries, no one in the United Nations urged measures going further than those which were taken."

Hammarskjöld in fact had taken on his own "fairly new-fangled" initiative what steps were within his powers. Since his first Investigating Commission had been denied the opportunity to visit Budapest, he had urged the Assembly to appoint another five-member Special Committee whose mandate was to maintain direct observation on Hungary by collecting evidence and taking down the testimony of eyewitnesses. One hundred and eleven of these eyewitnesses were interviewed in New York, Geneva, London, Rome, Vienna, everywhere except in Hungary. The Russians were angered by these activities. Kuznetsov reproached Hammarskjöld for having overstepped his functions in creating the Special Committee, and Janos Kadar protested its establishment as a violation of Hungary's sovereignty.

On June 20, 1957, the Special Committee published its find-

* *Time*, Nov. 26, 1956.

ings, and they were grave. They said that the Soviet Union had oppressed by force of arms a spontaneous uprising of the Hungarian people, had removed the legitimate government and replaced it by one not supported by the people. The UN released the report to all member nations. This is normal procedure, but pandemonium broke loose. Arkady Sobolev, permanent delegate of the Soviet Union accused Hammarskjöld that in permitting the Secretariat to distribute the report, he had tacitly disseminated western propaganda.

But in diplomacy, there are *protests of procedure,* and *protests of substance;* a country making a protest of procedure does not really have its heart in it. Mr. Khrushchev understood very well that Hammarskjöld, as an agent of the United Nations had duties to execute. Perhaps he felt that Hammarskjöld had panted heavier than need be over the Hungarian affair, but Nikita Khrushchev was not really cross with Dag—not yet.

As for the Hungarians, though they had not permitted Hammarskjöld to come to Budapest, they remained friendly to him—indeed, they admitted his four-man Committee sent to establish the Hungarian people's need for food, medicines, and clothing. Hungarian enmity toward Hammarskjöld was to begin with the Congo affair.

In 1957, when Hammarskjöld's reelection came up, the Soviet Union cast its vote for him. On September 26, in a speech before the General Assembly, he called his task, "as deeply rewarding as it is exacting, as perennially inspiring as, sometimes, it may be discouraging."

His sense of the immensity of his task or his response to its challenge had not been impaired by success or failure. "Service of the United Nations," he said, "... is profoundly meaningful—whether it bears immediate fruit or not. If it paves one more inch of the road ahead, one is more than rewarded by what is achieved. This is true, whatever setbacks may follow: if a mountain wall is once climbed, later failures do not undo the fact that it has been shown that it can be climbed . . ."

In 1956, at a press conference, he had been asked whether he saw any prospect of agreement, or even any progress in disarmament talks then being held in London.

"Well, I do," he answered. "You may feel that I am a blue-eyed fool, believing in all sorts of things . . . but I do believe in possibilities . . . I am an optimist."

Belief in possibilities where disarmament is concerned takes optimism of the rarest sort, and this issue landed the Secretary-General in more trouble, this time with the United States.

In the spring of 1958, the Soviet Union announced the unilateral suspension of nuclear testing and invited the United States and the United Kingdom to suspend their tests also. Washington dismissed this as a clever propaganda trick, being convinced that the moment the Soviets needed to make an atom test, they would find no difficulty in suspending the suspension. But, when Dag Hammarskjöld, at a press conference welcomed the Russian decision, thus turning the propaganda trick into a major propaganda victory, teeth gnashed on Capitol Hill and eyes bulged as they tend to do when they see Red.

A few weeks later, the Russians came up with a complaint to the Security Council. They said that the operations of the United States Strategic Air Command over the Arctic Zone were tending too far in the direction of the Soviet Union and that this constituted a danger to peace. They asked the Council to condemn the flights and call for their cessation. President Eisenhower then made a counterproposal: he suggested setting up a zone of international inspection in the Arctic. His idea was that this would be to the advantage of both countries, since it would guard them from surprise attack—at least from a northerly direction.

After these matters had been before the Security Council for a while, Hammarskjöld intervened in the debate. He expressed himself in favor of the United States proposal. He particularly liked the "inspection" angle because he thought that such a "limited system of inspection" might break up the stalemate that existed (and still exists) in this aspect of disarmament problems. Now it was the Russians' turn to pounce on him. *Pravda* roared that he had forgotten "that he holds the post of Secretary-General of the United Nations and not Secretary-General of NATO." Arkady Sobolev accused Hammarskjöld of "praising an American propaganda maneuver." By this time, it should be clear that the term, propaganda, when used in diplomacy, is not a simple gerund: it means any proposal of your opponent which you do not like.

The Russian protest was now not one of procedure, but of substance, for the American proposal had evoked what is to the Soviets the horrid spectre of "international inspection." Hammarskjöld explained himself to the Council:

"The stalemate in the field of disarmament has been permitted to last for far too long. Attempts to break it through negotiations have so far proved of no avail.

"I think there are reasons of different kinds behind this deeply worrying failure. One is that in a sense the governments have been too ambitious, not being satisfied with just making a dent in this intricate and vital problem from which a rift could develop, opening up the possibilities of a true exchange of views. Another reason has been the tendency for each government to wait for others to take the first step. Still another reason, and of course the basic one, is the crisis of trust . . ."

He pointed out to the gentlemen of the Council that having faith in one's fellow man is not the same thing as letting down one's guard, and he continued, "Each government is in close contact with the opinion of the man in the street in its own country ... I am sure that all governments are in a position to confirm my statement that the peoples are eagerly and anxiously expecting leadership bringing them out of the present nightmare. The government taking a fruitful initiative will be hailed as a benefactor by the peoples. The governments responding in a positive spirit ... will share the merit ...

"I hope that each one of the governments represented around this table will wish to try out the line of trust ..."

This revelation of the Secretary-General's blue-eyed foolishness caused an uproar among the press-men who collected in a buzzing hive at his press conference on May 1, 1958. Hammarskjöld expressed himself further on the subject:

"Disarmament is of course an extremely complicated problem ... But there is a point in the development of disarmament where every time an initiative is taken in good faith and its possible consequences, its possible values, are not fully explored, I have the feeling that we have missed the bus. And we should not be too sure that the road will remain open for buses in all the future ..."

He told the journalists that it was his sense of urgency that had prompted him to make a public statement on the issue.

"It is all right to continue disarmament talks if it is just a high political game of some kind of refined chess ... But if, in the meantime, the armaments race continues up to a point where it does represent a risk of ... collisions which are unintentional, then, of course, an element of urgency is introduced which makes it impossible to look with equanimity on the diplomatic game.

"I do not believe that any of the governments concerned have less of a sense of urgency than I have. But it may be that the way in which discussion has been pursued has tended to mislead public opinion, so that they have felt: 'Well, this is in the hands of the governments, and they talk and write letters and discuss matters and meet, and we can go on in the shadow of that somewhat costly but not harmful operation . . .' "

The *vox populi* is often praised as *vox Dei,* the voice of God. I have rarely heard a statesman point out its dreadful, indolent fatality.

Hammarskjöld then apologized to the newsmen for having used in his speech to the Council strong language:

"The use of the word 'nightmare' may shock you as it in a certain sense shocked me, because it is the kind of language I rarely use. However, it was completely adequate for me as a description of what I had in mind . . ."

Yes, and for what most of us have in mind.

Hammarskjöld was no demagogue. He avoided the use of emotion-charged words, and he never addressed his public statements to a hypothetical world citizen, aged eleven. His syntax was involved, and his style so interlarded with qualifying phrases that it is sometimes possible, in reading his speeches, to wish that the Charter required the Secretary-General to compose his thoughts with the verbal brevity of haikus. For this reason, while he lived, many of the most astounding actions and statements of Hammarskjöld's career did not strike the general public so spectacularly as those, for example, of President Kennedy, and only persons who observed closely the workings of his diplomatic world gasped at their novelty. It was not until his haikus were published that people at large understood what sort of man had for a while interfered in their affairs.

A colleague once wrote of him in *Kamelposten:* "He reminds me of a jet plane. When the sound reaches our ears, the plane is already far away."

The outcome of the Council's debate was so classic as to be tedious: the majority voted against the Soviet complaint, and the Soviet Union vetoed the American proposal. While the affair must be counted as one of Hammarskjöld's failures, still, in August 1963, two years after his death, "one more inch in the road ahead" was paved when the Nuclear Test Ban Treaty became reality.

It was inevitable that with his ceaseless agitation on behalf of the colonial peoples of Africa, Hammarskjöld should eventually come to a clash with the redoubtable General de Gaulle.

De Gaulle's sovereign disdain for the World Organization predated the Hammarskjöld era. It was rooted in events at the end of World War II when he failed to capture the confidence of Franklin Delano Roosevelt and Winston Churchill. Roosevelt once said of him, "He thinks he is Joan of Arc." And Churchill said, "Of all the crosses I have borne since 1940, none is so heavy as the Cross of Lorraine." He was referring to the insignia of De Gaulle's Free French forces. The pair of them ignored De Gaulle as far as possible. France was therefore not invited to participate in the Dumbarton Oaks Conference where the United Nations was planned and at which it was decided that France should be recognized as a "great power" only "in due course." Nor was De Gaulle invited to Yalta where the San Francisco Conference was fixed upon. For these reasons Big Charles has held aloof from the world organization, calling it, among other things, the "disorganization," or *"le machin"* which is French for "thingummy."

Now France was watching Hammarskjöld with misgivings and with resentment as year after year the Algerian question was kept on the agenda; nor had his role in the Suez affair won him the heart of France. It was with the French-Tunisian dispute in 1958, however, that the Secretary-General really got himself *dans le petrain.*

In a nutshell, if there exists a nutshell to contain such a many-splendored mess, the situation was as follows: France, which by treaty occupied the Tunisian base of Bizerta, was becoming uneasy because Tunisian President Bourguiba was sympathetic to the Algerian liberation movement.

On February 8, 1958, French planes bombed the Tunisian

village of Sakiet Sidi Youssef, charging that it was an Algerian rebel base. President Bourguiba, furious, asked for the immediate withdrawal of all French troops from Tunisia, including the naval base of Bizerta. He requested the Security Council to take up the Sakiet bombing incident. France, turning the tables, said that the Council might more profitably consider the "situation resulting from aid furnished by Tunisia to rebels, enabling them to conduct operations from Tunisian soil."

This dispute was particularly alarming, because of the resounding words uttered, such as "national dignity," "duty," "honor," "sovereignty," and "legitimate claims," all of which I have observed in my experience to be lethal to civilian populations. As if these expressions were not sufficiently foreboding, there was oil: it had been discovered at Edjele in the Sahara, and to that territory, besides France and Tunisia, Algeria, Morocco, Mauritania, Libya, Senegal, and Mali also laid claim. A good two years of diplomatic catch as catch can ensued. In 1960, France exploded her first atom bomb.

Next, four retired French generals in a *coup d'état* got control of Algiers and tried to prevent De Gaulle from conferring with Algerian rebels. Bourguiba, who had given considerable respite to the French during the revolt, now lost patience and on July 17, 1961, he declared, "The hour has struck for the evacuation of Bizerta."

Tunisian troops blockaded the Bizerta base. Tunisian "volunteers" moved towards the Sahara oilfields. The French broke the blockade at Bizerta. You may be sure that everyone was acting in self-defense. Tunisian dead, 150.

For several days thereafter, the French navy and airforce bombed the town of Bizerta and 800 paratroopers were dropped over the city. French armored units which had been inside the Bizerta base took up positions outside it. Aircraft strafed the area and machine-gunned the roads. killing more civilians.

On July 21, President Bourguiba wrote to the Secretary-General, "I am obliged to my great regret to ask you to arrange for the immediate repatriation of the three battalions of the Tunisian Army stationed in the Congo (Leopoldville)."

The same day the Security Council met to discuss the crisis. Their words were no longer resounding; in fact they could not have been more delicate and evasive. It seems that the Tunisian crisis was so involved that all sorts of matters had to be ironed out before a resolution could be arrived at. The sad fact (for Tunisian civilians) was that France was a NATO ally, and Bizerta a handy base for the United Kingdom and the United States. Nobody really wanted it to be evacuated. Of course, Bourguiba picked up a sudden ally in the Soviet Union which, having chastised him in the past for his western sympathies, now gave him wholehearted support, brandishing the old crowbar of French colonialism, and above all, crusading against military bases on foreign soil as a threat to peace. Another helping hand came unexpectedly from Nasser who, after feuding with Bourguiba for his western leanings, now discovered in him an Arab brother.

By and by the Tunisian dead totaled 1300.

On July 22, Hammarskjöld spoke to the Council: "News reaching us from Tunisia indicates that a serious and threatening development ... continues, with risk of irreparable damage to international peace and security. In view of the obligation of the Secretary-General under Article 99 of the Charter, I consider it my duty to make an urgent appeal to this Council ... to get a complete and definitive resolution."

He told them that action could not wait for "the more time-consuming considerations," and in doing so he invoked the ominous Article 99 that gives political power to the Secretary-General—provided he does not use it.

Hammarskjöld used it. He demanded a cease-fire and a return of both sides to their original positions. Liberia sponsored the resolution on his behalf.

France now ordered its forces to halt their offensive and Tunisia ordered cease-fire. However, somebody must have used the wrong codes. The shooting continued and French troops maintained their positions in the city of Bizerta. On July 23, President Bourguiba wrote to Hammarskjöld, "The gravity of the situation in Tunisia . . . make a direct and personal exchange of views necessary and urgent. I should therefore be happy to receive you in Tunis at your earliest possible convenience."

Hammarskjöld answered immediately, ". . . such a request on your part imposes upon me the clear duty to place myself at your disposal for such personal exchange of views which I hope might help to lead towards peace." The same day he flew to Tunisia.

Hammarskjöld conferred with President Bourguiba and with senior members of his cabinet, and having done so, on July 25, he wrote a letter to Couve de Murville, French Minister of Foreign Affairs:

> The present situation at Bizerta causes me the most serious concern in view of the fact that, more than two days after the Security Council's decision, no progress has been reported regarding the withdrawal of armed forces requested by the Council as an essential sequel to the cease-fire itself.
>
> In view of the responsibilities incumbent upon the Secretary-General for the execution of this resolution . . . I consider it my duty to explore the possibilities of improving this disturbing situation by making an effort, at least, to establish immediately the necessary contact between the two parties, the basis for which must obviously be strict compliance with the terms of the resolution and respect for Tunisian sovereignty.
>
> Having heard the Tunisian authorities' account of the situation, I should now like to have corresponding information on the French attitude. . . .

Couve de Murville replied in terms that expressed, in the diplomatic dialect nothing short of contempt, as well as a subtle accusation of partiality.

> I have the honor to acknowledge the receipt of the letter dated July 25, 1961 which you sent to me from Tunis where you now are at the invitation of the President of the Tunisian Republic. This letter, which appears to me to set out the views of the Tunisian government...

Instead of the expected invitation to Paris, the letter ended:

> The French government has decided to issue a statement clarifying the facts with which you are concerned. For your information I am enclosing a text of this document, which is to be published.

To this repulse Hammarskjöld quickly replied in the same stately language:

> I think it hardly necessary to embark on an exchange of views by correspondence... I have noted with some surprise that what I said in my letter appears to you to set out the views of the Tunisian Government. This remark of yours might be interpreted as meaning that I have acted as the spokesman of one of the parties to the present conflict. I am sure, however, that such is not your intention...

With the door to France shut in his face, Hammarskjöld went to Bizerta to seek talks with French Admiral Maurice Amman, commander of the base. Upon entering the base, French paratroopers stopped his car, though it flew the United Nations flag, and asked for his identification. They obliged him to get out of his car while they searched it. Eyewitnesses state that the Secretary-General submitted to this grave insult with a smile and allowed his car to be searched without protest, but it is a safe assumption that a man so sensitive and proud as he, and sincere in his purpose, was deeply hurt. Furthermore, Admiral Amman refused to receive him.

UN officials had the opinion that holding up the Secretary-General's car was a violation of the Charter which provides, "the Organization shall enjoy in the territory of each of its members such privileges and immunities as are necessary for the fulfillment of its purpose." The French explanation was that the Secretary-General's attempt to make contact with a military commander was out of order. Hammarskjöld himself did not mention the incident again, or express any resentment, but he made an oblique reference to it in a speech before the Security Council. In informing the members that the troops at the Bizerta base were mostly French paratroopers, he added, "By personal experience, I can also confirm that these troops, at the time of my visit, exercized functions for the maintenance of law and order that normally belong to organs of the sovereign governments."

France did not participate in this rather awkward meeting because "the French delegation has no new facts to communicate."

In the end it was not Hammarskjöld whom De Gaulle consented to receive in Paris, but United States ambassador to the United Nations, Adlai Stevenson, who went there at the request of President Bourguiba. As a result of these talks, the French were persuaded to recognize the principle that Bizerta ought to be evacuated. As for the Sahara oil, under French guidance, it is now exploited in the common interest of the nations laying claim to it.

De Gaulle further displayed his animosity to the United Nations by his refusal, when he visited New York, to follow the custom of other heads of state of addressing the Assembly in session, or holding a press conference at Headquarters, or paying a courtesy visit upon Hammarskjöld. Instead, it was Hammarskjöld who paid De Gaulle a visit in his New York hotel. Apart from politics, these two gentlemen did not get along badly. Once, when they met for luncheon in Paris, at the Élysée Palace in 1959, the atmosphere was described as

"cordial" as one might expect between two literary gentlemen, goldsmiths of words, "civilized Europeans."

It has always amused (and instructed) me, as a caricaturist,
to observe the similarities and differences between statesmen.
These two, at the very foundation of their being, had something in common as one may grasp by studying their photographs as teen-agers: both were the "string-bean" type with
small face, close-set eyes, long neck, sloping shoulders, the
image of weedy, studious, soul-searching, sensitive youngsters.
But in maturity their differences became overwhelming:
De Gaulle, heavy-boned and sluggish with broad gestures,
Hammarskjöld light and lively with gestures tight and
subdued.

Both had family backgrounds which were religious and
military, both had mystic courage, and both carried crosses.
Big Charles carried the flamboyant cross of soldiers, while
Hammarskjöld's was the invisible one of contemplative men;
and in spite of everything I have been taught, I am not convinced that one cross has much to do with the other.

7

A Room of Quiet

"THE UNITED NATIONS stands outside—necessarily outside—all confessions, but it is, nevertheless, an instrument of faith," said Dag Hammarskjöld before the World Council of Churches.

This is precisely what distinguishes our modern World Organization from the League of the Iroquois, but although a comparison is often made, the distinction is seldom drawn.

In his diary, it appears that the Secretary-General had studied the Sufi philosophers of Islam who, like most mystics, hold that the perfect communion with divine love is quite enough religion for anyone. It looks very much as if he, too, stood outside all faiths, although he arrived at that position by the road of a boy who had followed his Christian mother to church. The religious basis that underpinned his mundane thoughts were quite evident when he was alive. But if anyone ever thought of likening him to Christ, it would have been only in the sense that Goethe said of Schiller: "He was like Christ, and so ought every man to be."

I was astonished therefore when shortly after Hammarskjöld's death *Markings* was published in Sweden I heard from Sven Åhman, the UN correspondent of *Dagens Nyheter,* about the outcry that was being raised in Scandinavia about Hammarskjöld's religious contemplations. The critique in Åhman's own paper, by Olof Lagerkrantz, had said, "He identified himself increasingly with Jesus ... and by 1957, Jesus turned in Hammarskjöld's diary into a politician."

Ambassador Bartels of Denmark had written a lengthy critique, using the word blasphemy. It seemed offensive to him and to others that Hammarskjöld had identified his actions with God's, and by logical extension had worried that his own failures were really God failing mankind.

Widespread fears were being expressed in the Scandinavian languages for Hammarskjöld's sanity.

It seems to me the question is, what did he mean by God?

"There are innumerable definitions of God," wrote Gandhi, "because His manifestations are innumerable. They overwhelm me with wonder and awe and for a moment stun me. But I worship God as Truth only ... Absolute Truth."

Hammarskjöld defined God in the indirect fashion of the doubting intellectual. God was a "non-God, a non-Spirit, a non-Person, a non-substance." He was simply the One, pure and absolute, and as such he must be loved.

He came close to Spinoza who thought God was everything: "All is God; all lives and moves in God."

If Hammarskjöld believed, and I think he did believe, that God is all-inclusive and His will is the sum of all causes and laws, and, with Santayana, that "the mind of God is all the mentality that is scattered over space and time, the diffused consciousness that animates the world"; if he believed that the myriads of external forms, living or dead, in substance and in essence are an expression of God, that God is in fact Unity, then Hammarskjöld's incriminating boomerang phrases, such as "What is in me God gives of Himself to Himself," and "The gift is God's—to God," should not worry anybody very much. They are but word-patterns, similar to palindromes, symbolic of dynamic unity.

I asked one of Hammarskjöld's closest friends if the Secretary-General had been a church-goer. The answer was "No." The Secretary-General's former colleague, Klackenberg, has the same opinion. He writes, "After his death, Hammarskjöld was designated in some quarters as a great man of the church. In some respects this surprised me . . . It is always a touchy affair to talk of the convictions of others, and also there are different periods in a man's life. But the many years I worked with him, to my knowledge he never went to church—except occasionally to keep his mother company. Nor did he indicate any need to attend a religious service."

While he was not a church-goer, it was well known in the Secretariat that Hammarskjöld was a dedicated church-visitor and that wherever he went on official business, he would try to squeeze time to visit local churches, temples and mosques. In New York he frequently dropped in on Catholic, Protestant, Jewish, and Greek Orthodox places of worship. He even attended services at the Wall Street Church, until the minister, unwitting of the exclusive ground on which he trod, announced from the pulpit, "Today, we have among us . . ." Hammarskjöld never went back again.

In 1958, in Rome, he visited the Basilica of St. Peter. "I travel so much," he said. "Why shouldn't I see what I really want to see?" He remained under the Dome, deep in thought, for several hours.

That same morning he had seen the Pope, Pius XII, with whom he had a talk about disarmament, and he had been greatly impressed by the fact that the Pope knew every detail of this knotty problem. "Isn't it odd that I had to come to Rome to learn about disarmament?" he said to his companion, Gibson Parker, head of the Information Office in Geneva. The Vatican was in fact a major supporter of the World Organization because of Pius' interest in Technical Assistance; and later, Pope John's forthright favor brought thousands of Roman Catholic pulpits to the support of the UN.

On this visit to Pius XII, the conglomerate faiths of the

United Nations had resulted in a worrisome question of protocol. The Pope had received the Secretary-General alone in
his study, but afterwards he accompanied him to the ante-
chamber where Hammarskjöld presented to him Gibson
Parker, and also to his bodyguard, Bill Ranallo. Ranallo, a
Catholic, knelt and kissed the apostolic ring. Gibson Parker,
an Anglican, kissed the ring without kneeling. The Secretary-
General, a Lutheran, clicked his heels and bowed his head, but
remained erect.

Flying back to Geneva, Hammarskjöld began to bother himself about this undisciplined scene, especially his own behavior.
Although he had given Gibson Parker some papers to study,
he kept interrupting him to return to the subject as if he
wanted to be reassured that he had been right in remaining
erect. "I treated him as I would the head of a state," he ex-
cused himself. "Isn't he the head of the biggest state?"

At the interview, Pope Pius had told him, *"Vous êtes mon
homologue laïque"*—You are my lay counterpart. W. H. Auden
wrote that once Hammarskjöld had explained to him jokingly
that to be Secretary-General of the United Nations was very
much like being a secular pope—but that the papal throne was
a lonely eminence.

This could not have been altogether a jest. In the very core
of his being, Hammarskjöld felt himself to be the custodian
of the world's political conscience, and the Charter was his
Holy Writ. His chapel was the Meditation Room at Headquarters Building. This room was his creation, and it is today
his best memorial. But that he was able to establish such a
room at all is a latterday miracle.

Before 1951, it was not possible to meditate anywhere in
or around the United Nations. That year the General Assembly was held in Paris. One day, there turned up at the Palais
de Chaillot, a museum which had been quickly transformed
into a crowded warren of busy offices, a gentleman named
Weyman C. Huckabee, a member of the Laymen's Movement,

whose slogan is "Let's Try Christianity." He wanted to know
why no room had been set aside for the purpose of prayer.
A colleague of mine in the Secretariat told him, "It will take
an archangel to find space for a prayer room in this building." * I suppose it did not occur to him that an archangel
could possibly be named Huckabee.

Mr. Huckabee evidently managed to make his complaint
felt in the right quarters, because a room was established in
the Palais de Chaillot for prayer. It was not a big room. The
space might perhaps otherwise have served to store a stack of
flags. It was hung with curtains of a neutral color and a UN
flag was in the corner. About half a dozen small chairs with
backs were lined up; it was a place where a modest soul might
relax. I visited it with my wife just as a café-au-lait colored
gentleman was removing himself. Although many people
signed the visitors' book, I cannot recall ever seeing anyone
actually meditating there except a few invincible meditators
who looked as if they came from the sub-continent of India.

Nevertheless, when in March, 1952, the Assembly folded its
tents in Paris, we carried the contents of the Meditation Room
back with us to the Sperry Gyroscope Factory at Lake Success
where the United Nations was then housed, and a room was
found to set them up. What was more, a junior architect went
out to the Bronx and for $150 bought a three-hundred-year-
old African mahogany stump which was placed in the center
of the room as a sort of nondenominational altar, but I must
confess that it looked to me more like a chopping block upon
which one might sacrifice a Thanksgiving turkey.

Those who undertake the task of planning an immense
bureaucratic headquarters probably have too much to pray
for to worry about a room for prayer. When the new UN glass
house was on the drawing board, no space was provided for
a Meditation Room, and when Trygve Lie was beleaguered
on this account by devout persons, he gave them the answer

* *The Christian Science Monitor,* Dec. 3, 1956.

that a good secular Secretary-General should: "We have no money."

Once more an archangel jumped into the breach and money began to pour in: nickels and dimes from children's piggy banks came rolling into the United Nations and dollars from adult pockets, to the amount of $8000. This made it possible to edge out a part of the ground floor in the new building as a modest prayer-room. In the corner stood, as usual, the UN flag which kept having to be replaced, since it was frequently filched by visitors. And there was the line-up of little chairs.

By this time, the Laymen's Movement had formed a subgroup called "Friends of the United Nations Meditation Room." It consisted of Christians, Jews, and Moslems who were combined in an interfaith effort to keep an eye on this prayer-room lest anyone should get the notion of turning it back into mundane use. They must have been stunned when the stranger from Sweden, Dag Hammarskjöld, arrived upon the scene to find that he not only gave ear to their purpose, but was actually willing to plot with them to get the Meditation Room past the "experimental stage." If only they could get him the money—he estimated the amount he would need at $25,000—he promised to establish something of a Meditation Room. The Laymen were confident that money would be forthcoming, and work on the room began, with Hammarskjöld supervising every detail of its enlargement and remodelling.

It is altogether possible that the scheme for the Meditation Room was already full-blown in his mind before the Laymen got to him. In Löderup, Sweden, where he had a country house, he had once planned the erection of an interfaith chapel. His devotion to and his knowledge of the manifold religions and mystical philosophies of the world were by no means a planned conception of his duties as Secretary-General of the United Nations. There had developed in him long before he came to New York, a realization of the unlimited God, and it must have been for the economist, Dag Hammarskjöld, a magnificent reward of his sudden elevation to a position of enormous responsibility, that with the help of the Laymen he was able to give expression to it.

The Laymen's drive for funds brought in an immediate check for $10,000 from an anonymous donor. Piggy banks and pocketbooks again poured forth their riches, so that they were soon able to hand over to Hammarskjöld an additional check for $12,600, which was in fact only the beginning of the large sum of money they were to collect for him. At a luncheon held in the delegates' dining room where the check was presented, Hammarskjöld made a speech in which it became clear what singular thought he had devoted to the project, and how he had personally conceived it in detail. The Meditation Room as it exists today at the Headquarters Building was the "project" of many, but it remains one man's work of art.

"This house must have one room," said Hammarskjöld to the Laymen, "one place which is dedicated to silence in the outward sense and stillness in the inner sense. We must do everything possible in creating such a room to create an atmosphere where people could really withdraw into themselves and feel the void."

The first thing Hammarskjöld had done was to banish all the little chairs and replace them by benches, saying, "The men who come here will have enough force to support their own backs." These were lined up in several rows along the north wall, which he made somewhat wider than the south wall so that anyone sitting on them feels that he is gazing through the gloaming along a perspective. He replaced the mahogany stump with a six-and-a-half ton rectangular block of iron ore which, polished on the top sufficiently to bring forth a sheet of minute lights and illuminated from above by a single spotlight, shimmers like the moon on water. The block was a gift of the King of Sweden, and a Swedish mining company had to wrest from the earth about sixty chunks of iron before the right one was found.

"We wanted a room of stillness," Hammarskjöld said, "with perhaps one or two very simple symbols, light, and light striking on stone. It is for that reason that in the center of the Room there is this block of iron ore, glimmering like ice in a shaft of light from above. That is the only symbol in the Room—a meeting of the light of the sky and the earth...

"The original idea was one which I think you will all recognize; you will find it in many great religions; it is the empty altar, empty not because there is no God, but empty because God is worshiped in so many forms. The stone in the center is the altar to the God of all... In this house with its dynamic modern architecture, there are very few things that give you the feeling of weight, solidity, and permanence; in this case we want this massive altar to give the impression of something more than temporary..."

Certainly, no one can accuse Hammarskjöld's piece of iron ore of lacking permanence. The floor of the old Meditation Room had not been strong enough to bear its weight, and so a special support had to be built that goes down from the main floor of the public lobby to the garage in the Third Basement, which presumably rests on good Manhattan rock. Hammarskjöld had much more to say about its significance:

"In this house, we are trying to turn swords into ploughshares, and we thought we could bless by our thoughts the very material out of which arms are made. For that reason we felt that it was appropriate that the material to represent the earth on which we stand, as seen by the light of the sky, should be iron ore, the material out of which swords have been made and the material out of which homes are built. It is a material which represents the very paradox of human life; the basic materials offered by God to us may be used either for construction or destruction.

"This leads our thoughts to the necessity of choice between two alternatives."

At home in Sweden, he ordered from his friend, Bo Beskow, an abstract mural for the room. The story is told that this ordering was accomplished by "a few questions and a quick nod," * which, since Beskow also has a house in Löderup, seems to suggest that the two men might have discussed such a room even before Hammarskjöld came to New York. When Beskow visited the United Nations, I met him, and he looked to me to be a somewhat more robust and more richly bearded Hammarskjöld-type, a sensitive man with a warm, vibrating core. It is his chief business to make church windows, for which he bakes his own glass. His father, too, had been an artist, but reversing the natural order of things, he had escaped from that profession to become a clergyman.

Beskow's mural on the narrow south wall of the Meditation Room is a composition of geometric patterns which is supposed to present to the senses a feeling of the essential one-ness of God. "We had one difficulty," Hammarskjöld told his angels, the Laymen, "that in a room of this kind in a house of this character we could not use any of the symbols with which man has been used to link his religious feelings; we had to work on the basis of symbols common to all."

Geometry is certainly common to all. However, the various religious symbols of mankind are also geometric. It is therefore possible in studying Beskow's shapes to discern in the mural almost any religious symbol one wishes to see. There is a cross, a crescent, a sun, and triangles, the foundation of the Star of David; but all are intersected by one another, and they are broken up in color and shade. They appear to fold intricately and to lose themselves in transparencies. If one stares long enough at this painting, it is easy to imagine oneself standing under the scaffolding of some unfinished man-

* Elvira K. Fradkin, "Revisiting the United Nations Meditation Room," in *The Laymen's Movement Review*, Vol. VIII, no. 1, p. 15.

made structure on an asteroid, gazing beyond into the unlimited realm of space. I am not an admirer of abstract art in
its great chaotic spate, but this painting of Beskow's seems to
me to be complete in its purpose, and exact.

Nothing short of perfection suited Hammarskjöld for his
Room. In enlarging the old room, he had added a foreroom
and ordered it panelled in light rose-wood with its delicately
ordered grain. When upon viewing the finished job, he noted
that care had not been taken to match the grain of the panels
so that the rippled progress of the design was disturbed like
a quiet pool in which a herd of horses had been bathing, he
commanded them to be torn down and refitted. This was done
at great expense.

On the north wall of this foreroom is an abstract sculpture
by the American artist, Cronbach, and it is baptized *Ship*.
It is a shape of skimming verve and spirit, but I should not
like to cross the Atlantic in it.

Hammarskjöld's Room was not yet completed when he
received the check from the Laymen, but already—as any artist
might have warned him in advance—he was beginning to find
fault with his work of art. He explained to the Laymen this
"very curious problem indeed": the Room was an astounding
success. Although it was not on the route of the guided tours
and was not—and he said "should not be"—one of the sights
of the house, four or five thousand visitors were daily invading
the building and a very large number of them were curious
about the Meditation Room. It was not that they wanted to
meditate. They just wanted to have a look at it. They were
"very welcome, of course," but . . .

"We want to bring back the stillness which we have lost in
our streets and in our conference rooms, and to bring it back
in a setting in which no noise would impinge upon our imagination. In that setting we want to bring back our thoughts to
elementary facts, the facts we are always facing, life struck by
light while resting on the ground. We want to bring back the

idea of worship, devotion to something which is greater and higher than we are ourselves. . . ."

Hammarskjöld had built a room dedicated to stillness and solitude, which, if it is the deepest, the most submerged, is also the most necessary need of mankind; now he was wondering how on earth a little peace and quiet could be achieved. He besought the Laymen to turn their minds to the problem, and no doubt they did: some good soul gave a thick carpet, which, laid all around the area outside the room muffles somewhat the footsteps of visitors.

And yet, who can finally solve the problem of the mystic? He spends his life in a solitary cave forging his spirit in solitude into a shape resembling—so far as its possibilities exist—perfection; but then he looks out of his cave to find multitudes of people waiting to touch him, to gaze on him, and thus to gain a share in his perfection. Hammarskjöld's room, as he said, was only a shell, like any other room. But within it he had managed to place the simulacrum of his own questing soul. While avoiding all ordinary symbols, he had the art to place there the deep magnetic core of all creation, and put it in a perspective leading to the unimaginable future. The Meditation Room is a smashing room, and a beautiful place to be.

By the time the Room was finished, he had by his own actions reminded the world that among the sovereign nations which at present live outside the law as much as any assassin or pirate of the past, only a moral law holds true, and thus, in the Meditation Room, he gave to the glass house its soul. Not many government buildings have souls, but they need one, and with sure instinct, people will always buzz around their need.

And so the visitors came, and they still come in their millions to see Hammarskjöld's room of quiet, and those who wish to meditate there must choose a quiet hour or else they must have the force to support their own thoughts as they support their backs. In the foreroom on a little table stands a book where visitors may register their names, addresses, countries, and religions. I don't know why, but one I saw registered his telephone number.

In the column for religion, one discovers all existing faiths, and also such entries as "none," or "Catholic (tolerant)"; "none of your business" is there of course, and so is "atheist," upon which (the one I saw) someone had scribbled "Terrible!" and underlined it twice. In the column for countries, one reads the names of all the lands of the earth, and also, "internationalist" and "the world." Another person wrote, "USA, the Greatest Catholic Country in the World."

Sheldon Green, born in Kansas City, but now residing in Brooklyn, started to write his name, but becoming entangled, finished with the help of his mother who added an explanation that Sheldon was only five and a half. Paul Zloba of the United States Marine Corps, offering a grim reminder of events of the sort that were discussed in the enormous chambers nearby, registered his address as "somewhere."

What can comfort the ghost of an ancient artist who, having lovingly articulated the bones of the feet of the dead Jesus, sees his work obliterated by perpetual kissing? Nothing, except acceptance of the loss. As long as Hammarskjöld lived, these visitors' books, once filled, were delivered to his office on the 38th Floor, though not before the vigilant guards (sacrilegiously I think) had erased the smut that godless teen-agers wrote on them.

Hammarskjöld visited his chapel regularly, two or three times a week, and he never went anywhere without visiting it. For him that crude iron block, drawn with difficulty from the earth's centers, was the symbol of earth's veritable spirit in which all mankind shares and which mankind seeks; a common source and goal, the complete purpose of creation. It was his Sermon on the Mount which explained the glory of simple being, without effort or calculation.

Other statesmen also visited the Meditation Room. Dwight D. Eisenhower spent a few minutes in it accompanied by Secretary of State Dulles, Hammarskjöld, and UN ambassador, Henry Cabot Lodge. Pope Paul VI went there in 1965.

I visited it with evangelist Billy Graham who, leaving his followers outside, sat on a bench, forwards bent, his head resting on his folded hands in deep devotion for some time.

"We were trying to create a Meditation Room where men of all kinds and from all regions of the world would have a place where each could find his own God..." said Hammarskjöld.

On the south wall of the foreroom which is made of green Vermont marble there hangs a bronze plaque commemorating Count Bernadotte who on September 17, 1948, was assassinated in the Holy Land. Hammarskjöld himself unveiled this plaque before Countess Bernadotte.

The day before Hammarskjöld left for his last journey to the Congo he visited, as usual, the Meditation Room. About that time, he ordered another tablet for the west wall of the foreroom, close to the entrance. It was to be made of black marble with some words of his own inscribed on it. Then he went to Ndola and died on the night of September 17/18, exactly thirteen years after Bernadotte.

The ordering of this plaque was one of his last official acts. It now hangs, thinly carved in black on black, hardly visible, a whisper in stone:

"THIS IS A ROOM DEVOTED TO PEACE AND THOSE WHO ARE GIVING THEIR LIVES FOR PEACE. IT IS A ROOM OF QUIET WHERE ONLY THOUGHTS SHOULD SPEAK."

He had written his epitaph.

8

I and Thou

WE HAVE with us today a very famous traveler. He has kindly consented to answer any question you may have on travel. He is also a member of the Swedish Academy, and if any of you have any questions on literature, he will be happy to answer them. In addition to that, he is a distinguished mountain climber, and he is perfectly willing to answer any question on mountain climbing if anyone wants to put any questions. Then, he has been talking recently to a number of delegates about some world problems, and some of you may want to talk about those. But in any event, he is very agreeable to answering questions today...

"I am very happy to welcome here today, the Secretary-General of the United Nations, Mr. Dag Hammarskjöld."

These words were uttered in Danny's Hideaway by Bruce Munn of United Press International, President of the United Nations Correspondents' Association, at a correspondents' luncheon. Convivial as they seemed there was a bite in them, contained in the words, "He is very agreeable to answering questions today..."

Hammarskjöld's relationship with the press was not always cordial. He never developed the taste of Franklin D. Roosevelt for the ping-pong game of speech and counterspeech, nor

John F. Kennedy's impish joy in repartee. Never did the newsmen see an expression of transcendent delight creep over
Hammarskjöld's countenance as he delivered himself of the
mot juste, after the manner of Adlai Stevenson.

He recoiled from the crowd of journalists, those front men
of the profane masses which he kept at a distance, and yet
loved. Shortly after his arrival in New York, he told Bruce
Munn: "You Americans have a way of abbreviating the names
of your leaders. You talk of FDR and Ike. I'm afraid you will
call me Ham."

"Like Connie Mack!" laughed Munn.

"McGillicuddy," rejoined Hammarskjöld. He dreaded the
popular nickname, but he had already learned the real name
of the popular baseball manager.

The newsmen happily settled upon calling him Dag, but
perhaps they wished he had been more of a Ham-type Secretary-General. "What's this 'quiet diplomacy'?" one of them
once loudly complained. "All it means is that the New York
Times gets the news. That's where it leaks to."

This was unjust. The Secretary-General was quite impar-
tially secretive when it suited him. In 1958, a major correspondent, returning from Lebanon where he had been stationed
during months of crisis, blanched to learn that Hammarskjöld
had smuggled 250 more United Nations observers into that
country than he or anyone else knew about. The Secretary-
General's purpose was to build up a private stockpile of
observers, so that when they were all officially asked to leave,
they should be able to take as long as possible to go about it.

He was one of the most photographed of men, but it was
an ordeal for him to have his photo taken, and by far the best
photos of Hammarskjöld were taken when he wasn't looking.
One of the most delicate diplomatic jobs in the Secretariat
was held by Miss Audrey Langston, an Englishwoman whose
duty it was to see that the Secretary-General obediently made
his physiognomy available to the multitude. Noting that Ham-

marskjöld was impatient, and even contemptuous of persons who were intimidated by him, she slipped into the no-nonsense attitude for which Englishwomen are famous in a pinch. Every time a new ambassador presented his credentials, a photograph had to be taken. One week it happened that five new ambassadors arrived. After the third, Hammarskjöld declared, "I'm not going to do it again."

"You have to," replied Audrey Langston. "These ambassadors send their pictures shaking hands with you back to their home countries."

"The Queen of England doesn't have to," hazarded Hammarskjöld.

"Well, you do," said Miss Langston. "You are just part of the furniture in your office."

Once when a great news magazine wished to take Hammarskjöld's picture, Audrey Langston sent a memo to his secretary asking her to put the matter before the Secretary-General "at an opportune moment." By mistake the secretary passed on the memo to Hammarskjöld who wrote on it, "No, no, no, a thousand times no!—unless she insists."

The photographer, Philip Halsman, who had induced a number of celebrated people to let him take pictures of them jumping into the air and wanted Hammarskjöld in his series, really had a forlorn hope.

American television can be dismaying to foreigners of earnest disposition. I once had a small skirmish with Mrs. Alva Myrdal, a distinguished Swedish diplomat, who found herself appearing on a program on which puppy-dogs were sold. It took considerable suavity on my part to explain this fruitcake atmosphere to her and to persuade her that it was a means of carrying her significant remarks to a much wider audience than if puppy-dogs, or other popular favorites, were absent.

One may imagine, therefore, the commotion on the 38th Floor of the Headquarters Building when the Secretary-General brought himself to appear on Ed Murrow's popular

Person to Person show which consisted of a live, impromptu dialogue between Ed in the CBS building, and Dag at the UN. The Secretary-General was to occupy the latter half of the time-period, and he settled down to view the first half of it: the interview was with a French actress, very loose of brassiere and tongue. Hammarskjöld was scandalized. He absolutely refused to appear on the same program with the lady in question. With cameras, kleig-lights, and engineers standing at the ready all around him, and half of an expensive national program yet to run, it was a painful affair, and it was due to the quiet diplomacy of Gibson Parker, at that time Deputy Director of the Radio Division, that Murrow's interview with Hammarskjöld went on the air at all. It was a fiasco in any case, and this was not altogether due to the Secretary-General's rebellious frame of mind. An abrupt and reticent man like Ed Murrow was an excellent interviewer of French actresses and politicians whose conversation is free-flowing, but when he found himself face to face with a man even more reticent than he, the interview repeatedly jammed or fell into an abyss of silence.

We of United Nations television encountered no insuperable difficulties with the Secretary-General, perhaps because of the deference shown him, or else because his own shyness was less on his home ground and he was able to be patient and even affable. Once when Joe Nichols was directing a world-wide radio hook-up which broadcast the Human Rights concert along with a previously taped message by the Secretary-General, he shouted, "Kill the music, cue in the Secretary-General." He heard a quiet voice from behind him where Hammarskjöld was standing: "I'm glad you didn't call for the contrary."

On March 8, 1956, I directed a show for the Canadian Broadcasting Corporation in which the Secretary-General and four journalists engaged in a round table discussion about the relation of the United Nations to the proposed Atomic Energy

Agency. Before he arrived we got a call from the 38th Floor
to say that he was on his way. "And clean up those cigarette
butts from the ashtrays," said the Voice from Above.

The Secretary-General arrived and waited patiently until
the cameras were made ready. In the meantime, I explained
some procedure to him and advised him that when he wished
to address the camera, he should look at the one that had the
red light on, indicating the picture then on the air. This information, which is usually received with gratitude by politicians,
was completely ignored by the Secretary-General. Not once
did he bother to look for the red light or turn his face towards
the proper camera. No ounce of Ham was in him. He was un-
theatrical, economical in his gestures, an island bare of light-
house.

He usually appeared in the studio smoking a cigar or cigarillo, which he continued to smoke during the broadcast. This
was a nuisance, as the smoke interfered with the picture. The
film people had an even greater struggle with the Secretary-
General's smoking habit, for in a five-minute film, shot over
a much longer period of time, the cigar would shrink as he
smoked and stretch as he lit a new one. This Alice in Wonder-
land cigar disturbed the continuity of the film. Yussuf Karsh,
the photographer, faced with the problem of Winston Churchill's cigar, had simply walked up and taken it out of his model's
mouth; but Karsh was not an employee of Churchill's.

Once he came to the film studio to record a United Nations
Day message—an important event which was filmed on 16 and
35 millimeter film and distributed all over the world to be
shown on thousands of television stations and cinemas. He was
smoking a Webster cigar. He sat down, and no sooner did
producer Tom Baird call out, "Ready? Roll it!" than the
Secretary-General gave a great puff on his cigar and blew out
such a cloud of smoke that it covered his entire face.

"Cut!" called Baird, and he said, "Mr. Secretary-General,
this was the greatest commercial ever filmed for the Daniel

Webster Cigar Company." Thereafter he laid the entire cigar situation before the Secretary-General for his consideration.

The next time Hammarskjöld turned up in the film studio, he brought with him a large supply of cigars which he lit one after the other, but he never smoked them very far, so that in each take he appeared with a cigar of nearly full length. The studio was left to contemplate a hecatomb of half-smoked first quality cigars.

During the years that I stared at Hammarskjöld's face sometimes for hours on end, I never grew tired of looking at it, particularly at the narrow midface with the fleshy lips and curled-up Mona Lisa smile. The furrows of his forehead won my admiration, because I have examined enough furrows to know what stories they tell. Confused men have confused furrows. Hammarskjöld's furrows ran in even, parallel lines across his brow; they showed a habitual attitude of attention, reflection, and questioning, but no sign of hostility. Had Hammarskjöld been a caricaturist and furrow-fancier, he would not have worried about the state of his soul as much as he did.

It was not in him to woo the press, and he held sparse press conferences. Bruce Munn took the occasion of a press luncheon to chide him for imposing this starvation diet, paraphrasing Lady Macbeth, "We have him not and yet we see him still." Without hesitation, Dag retorted, "If I may quote from the same play: had I held a press conference, it would simply have been full of sound and fury, signifying nothing."

"He knocked me cold," said Bruce, "with his erudition and quick mind."

There is no better way to watch how the mind of a statesman works than at a press conference: he sits helpless as a man in the stocks, while embarrassing questions are hurled at him, which he must duck or catch, as best he may. In his face, his gestures, the twitch of his nose as the answer germinates, one may follow the labyrinths of his thought processes.

Hammarskjöld used to sit before the newsmen, seemingly

well-entrenched behind his own "robust superiority," trying to look noncommittal; but in fact he was wary and intent.

He listened to questions, eyes cast down, playing with his pencil, shooting up his eyebrows intermittently towards the even corrugations of his forehead. The gentle sidewards bent of his head indicated that while he listened, he was already formulating an answer, that his mind worked like that of the policeman who stands at the Place de l'Étoile in Paris, and seeing the traffic arrive from all directions, knows in advance exactly where he is going to direct it. But in spite of his shrewdness and his subtlety of mind, he carried with him an aura of vulnerability, and there was something virginal about him as he sat there, unprotected, manufacturing thesis into synthesis.

His replies were prudent, sometimes even evasive. He drew out his remarks with clichés such as "and so forth and so on" —a habit of people who would prefer not to speak at all. Once A. G. Mezerik made up a question which he interlarded with Hammarskjöld's clichés, and this was greeted with great laughter by the correspondents. The Secretary-General said, "I see that your colleagues are as amused by your question as I am myself."

But he was not amused at all.

He could smile, but laughter was not in his repertory. He was intellectually impatient, though never overbearing. It was possible to irritate him, but impossible to shatter his composure. When irritated his Swedish accent became stronger, and he clipped his words or dipped them in irony.

He particularly disliked journalists to fight their national battles in the forum of the press conference. In 1957 when he returned from Egypt to say that he had concluded a "gentleman's agreement with Nasser," an Israeli reporter wanted to know, "How is it possible to make a gentleman's agreement with a person who is not a gentleman?"

"I don't think much of the question," replied Hammar-skjöld frostily and indicated the next questioner.

When a Pakistani journalist told him, "Do you know Israel has been condemned so many times, and yet this condemnation has had no effect on that state?" Hammarskjöld said in clipped syllables: "I think we should not pursue that point any further."

The Secretary-General had little patience with the exaggerated antagonisms the cold war engendered among the UN correspondents: it was as if he thought they, at least, ought to know better. One of the correspondents is David Horowitz of the World Union Press, a Swedish, Jewish, American citizen married to an Irish girl. This human platypus initiated a UN Correspondents' Circle which, meeting once a month in a private house, was to bring journalists of all ideological persuasions together for a few drinks and a friendly chat. The Secretary-General was delighted by this development, and he wrote to Horowitz a benedictory letter in which he provided a directive for the conversations: "There are so many basic human aspects of life which are held in common . . . fundamental and constructive in character . . . The need for devoting so much time and energy to the political crises and problems that so often separate nations and regions should not be so time-consuming as to cause us to neglect those large areas of life in which common ground of appreciation and understanding can be found."

During the Hungarian Revolution in 1956, in addition to my television duties, I received from the United Nations another task: that of reporting UN events by radio to Hungary. This broadcast lasted for years. Like other broadcasters to foreign parts, I made up my report on the basis of summaries given to me by the radio newsdesk, and they were very carefully compiled indeed with relentless objectivity as between the "western" and the "eastern" points of view, measuring out balm for every stomach ulcer in perfectly equal doses. Even the number of sentences devoted to Russian and American pronouncements had to be carefully counted. Of course a balanced diet can be very dull.

But one relief was granted from these monotonous and repetitious statements. That was when somewhere in the world, the Secretary-General made a speech, or held a press conference. His words could then be reported as they stood. He was by no means parsimonious with press conferences when traveling to far-flung regions and sometimes he would put a girdle around the earth with them, setting himself a breathtaking schedule. In 1956, in the course of twenty days, he spoke to the press in Teheran, Beirut, Bombay, Karachi, Bangalore, New Delhi, Rangoon, Djakarta, and Canberra.

As the transcripts came in, the melancholy conclusion was unavoidable that people everywhere look at world affairs through their narrow local binoculars caring little for the world at large, and knowing little about the United Nations, its limitations and capabilities. Quite often when Hammarskjöld was asked a particularly naive question, he would turn the conference into a seminar; and here he was in his element.

It was in translating these galloping seminars of the Secretary-General's that my own admiration of him became fixed. I have been intimately involved with the fortunes of the World Organization, ever since it was nothing but Wilson's babe, abandoned on a quay in Geneva, and like many other members of the Secretariat I am utterly devoted to the ideals it represents. I have heard in the course of almost a half-century much vote-getting and career-advancing bombast spoken in the name of these ideals which in misuse have obfuscated them.

Secretary-General Hammarskjöld spoke to populations Wilson perhaps never dreamed would ever be in a position to ask questions. His words were as modest as they were gentle; they were honest, unevasive and exact. Whatever he said was realistic, undramatic, and it badly needed saying. I believe that realism is an even better servant of an ideal than poetic eloquence, and it was to Hammarskjöld the teacher that I first said "Yes."

Once in Pakistan, the question was posed him: "How can the United Nations be turned into an effective organ, since it has so far been unable to solve most of the major problems of the world? I mean Kashmir, Israel, and the Arab question."

Hammarskjöld replied: "The question is not whether the United Nations has solved the problems. The question is whether it has been helpful in getting the situation under control so that the governments concerned are helped in the direction of a solution.

"The UN is not a sort of super-state organization. It can only use its influence among the member governments for the solution of problems ... Due to its existence, there is a very great possibility of implementing decisions reached amongst these governments ... The UN is a diplomatic instrument which is added to the technique of diplomacy for the solution of problems. It is no panacea ... it is a kind of intermediary ..."

In Jakarta, Indonesia, he was asked, "In your opinion, how long will it be before the United Nations works out its program as effectively as was meant?"

"A very long time indeed," replied Hammarskjöld "because we are all human beings and we were meant to make the United Nations a thing of perfection. We are not ripe for that kind of perfection yet, but I must say what I have said before: if the elephant walks and walks in the right direction, we should not be impatient. It does not move too quickly, but we shall certainly arrive at a goal."

A friend of mine on the radio newsdesk had the task of preparing résumés of Hammarskjöld's press conferences. He told me, "The day I found out that Hammarskjöld was a teacher, my job became easy. All I had to do was quote him: the Secretary-General said . . ."

Hammarskjöld came to terms with the press eventually, simply because it was there, like a mountain to be climbed, a fact to which he had to say "Yes." He learned to use it as a tool: in the spring of 1956, when he traveled to the Near East to obtain armistice agreements, he thought that an understanding with Nasser had been reached. But just as he was ready to depart at Cairo airport, a press agency report was handed to him that seemed to indicate that Nasser had no intention of holding to the understanding. He drove back to Cairo at once, demanded an immediate meeting with Nasser, and told him that he was completely mistaken if he thought that the Secretary-General would be satisfied with the mere appearance of an understanding.*

From that time on, he used to send to the headquarters detailed communiqués to be released to the press, which then served to nail down conferees to agreements reached.

But the relationship that he would have preferred and which he attempted to establish with the press was very much that of teacher and pupils. In Jerusalem, he had become fast friends with the Jewish philosopher, Martin Buber, at whose modest Arab stone house he was a frequent visitor. The melancholy Viennese Jew would sit at his desk behind his stacks of manuscripts, wearing slippers, a robe, and a scarf around his neck; while Hammarskjöld, the grave, impeccably groomed Lutheran from Sweden occupied a chair. Together they soared into the patterned infinities of abstract thought, smiling at each other like David and Jonathan. Hammarskjöld proposed to translate Buber's book, *I and Thou*, into Swedish, and indeed, twelve pages of this translation were found in the wreckage of the plane.

It is by no means astonishing that the Secretary-General,

* Lash, p. 73.

tormented by a sense of isolation and exceptionality, should have been drawn towards the philosophy of Buber which attempts to solve the dilemma of communication between man and man, and man and God.

Buber's phrase, *"I and Thou"* is an anagram of various communicatory relationships. "I and Thou" exists between man and wife, between doctor and patient, teacher and pupil, and the pastor and his flock. Furthermore, writes Buber, "The relation with man is the real simile of the relation with God . . .

"The love of God is unreal unless it is crowned with love for one's fellow men."

The communication or "dialogue" that takes place between such relations was intricately examined by Buber, and his ideas engrossed the lonely Hammarskjöld. The Secretary-General was no more capable of "chumming" with the more refractory UN correspondents than he supposed that Jesus was of consorting with publicans and sinners for the purpose of converting them. But he did seek contact with them on the level of his touchstone, the uncarved block in the Meditation Room, on that which is common to all, indestructible, eternal, and upon which the future, not the present headline, must be founded. He coerced the idealism of the newspapermen. Thus, they found themselves treated to indirectly corrective lectures, occasionally along the lines of Buber's thoughts. One of them was in defense of "quiet diplomacy," a subject that lay permanently between Hammarskjöld and the journalists like a dagger drawn:

"I do believe, to use what has become a famous term, thanks to Camus and Buber and others—I do believe that development in human terms of what they call dialogue is badly needed. But dialogues require a few things: objectivity, a willingness to listen, and considerable restraint. Those are human qualities. No one of them is very remarkable, but they are all called for, and if they lead to a 'dialogue,' I think it is very reasonable to let that dialogue develop within the more or less traditional framework, that is to say, a little bit out of the glare of publicity, which robs you of a few headlines, but helps us all."

Yes, but there is a snag in the development of correct dialogue. The enemy is what Buber calls *inclusion*. It is evident that the *special educative relation* cannot persist between teacher and pupil, if the pupil for his part were to usurp the position of the teacher; any more than a *healing* relation can exist between doctor and patient, if the patient tries to cure the doctor.

The trouble with the United Nations journalists is that many of them are extremely knowledgeable. Hearing them talk and reading their words, one would imagine that they are all the Secretary-General. They practiced inclusion. They badgered and baited him, they objected and knew better. They complained that his private diplomacy and stingy press conferences kept United Nations affairs out of the flow of international news. Gravely Hammarskjöld would persist in his educative role: "... private diplomacy is a means to an end. The avoidance of publicity is in the interest of the success of the operation ... that is to say we sacrifice points ... I would accept the sacrifice because I think it is more essential in the long run for the sound development of international cooperation to achieve the *de facto* successes, even if they are unknown to the public, than to endanger a *de facto* success because of too great a willingness to 'sell' the United Nations."

No, Dag Hammarskjöld was not much of a plum for the newshungry or for any who wished that the United Nations were more of a circus where they could daily watch Communists and/or capitalists being daily fed to the lions; or a baseball game of which the daily score of spurious "diplomatic triumphs" could be posted in a headline.

And yet, when the tragic news came from Ndola, the *I and Thou* relationship with the journalists was miraculously there. It had developed imperceptibly in the meeting of words. The dialogue had offered them something more spectacular and rare than circuses: a prolonged confrontation with a statesman of sincere spirit and purest ideals whose life's work had extended into their own and had endowed it with his own significance and impelling sense of mission. "I would like to enlist you," he had said to them, "as a part of the United Nations which works with very much the same aims in mind ... as in the Secretariat. I have been struck ... how deeply you feel yourselves engaged in that venture in your activities as individuals. To use the word 'heartening' would be sentimental."

And so the newsmen mourned for him, as they still do—at least those do who are not totally bound up in some ideology. Shortly after his death, they set up for him a memorial, and it is significant that they chose one that would have best pleased a teacher. The notice on the bulletin board in the "bull pen" where correspondents congregate read:

"We the journalists at the United Nations, who saw Dag Hammarskjöld at his task, and who mourn his death, have sought a fitting means by which we may perpetuate his memory. To this end, we have established a Memorial Scholarship Fund. It will promote in our profession a wider knowledge of the United Nations; and it will knit closer ties with the countries whose independence and advancement were the object of his unceasing labors during the last years of his life. The Memorial Fund is establishing annual

DAG HAMMARSKJÖLD SCHOLARSHIPS

for young journalists or students of journalism, and the first, from Africa, will take up his scholarship this year."

I and Thou!

9

Surface and Depth

ANY mention of the name of Hammarskjöld at the Headquarters Building plunges one knee deep into specula-
tion, not only about the mystery of his death, but the many
mysteries of his life. That the Secretary-General left a map of
his soul in *Markings* for the guidance of such cafeteria philosophers is not the least of his oddly prophetic actions.

Once I sat with Theodore Fagan, one of the United Nations'
remarkable simultaneous interpreters. I observed that in order
to understand Hammarskjöld, one ought to read *Markings*
together with his speeches on political subjects.

"Yes," said Fagan, "and listen to his voice, too."

Fagan is right. One who engrosses himself in the living
words of statesmen is bound to have discovered the conjunc-
tion between a man's voice and his personality. As an artist,
when I look at a man, I have learned to extend my points of
diagnosis to everything I see, hear, or feel—the setting of the
bones of his face and the expression on it, the quality of his
skin, his posture and gait, what he says and how he says it—and
by this means to try to grasp the miracle of his individuality.

This is not so "unscientific" as it sounds. A psychiatrist may
have laboratory tests at his disposal, but he does not fail to
look well at his patient, observe his manner, and listen to him.

A substantial literature is available to him, besides, dealing with the physical basis of personality.

An artist has not laboratory tests or calipers, and he contents himself with the evidence of his eyes. But in compiling my observations, I am indebted to the work of constitutional psychologists who have provided for me a structural pattern with which to pin them into place.

Most constitutional psychologists of the present day work on the basis of three main physical types which they have described in considerable detail, both in body build and temperament. By temperament is meant those personality traits that lie at the very foundation of the personality, the nature, as Horace said, "that you may drive out with a pitchfork, and yet it will return." Each researcher seems to take delight in devising his own tongue-twisting terminology, but I think of them as they look: the Round Man, the Muscleman, and the Thin Man. In a nutshell, the round, portly man is natural, humorous, practical; his eye is on the ball and he has a sharp nose for opportunity. The Muscleman is tough, tenacious, courageous, efficient, insensitive, and humorless. The Thin Man is sensitive, shy, inward-looking, abstract-minded and systematic.

Of course we are all a wild mixture of these three types, and in addition certain exotic seasonings are thrown in such as femininity (or masculinity in women) infantilism, gigantism, dwarfism, and idiocy. Whatever we are, our inherited temperament traits are modified, qualified, and otherwise acted upon by our environment, family influences, education, social class, religion—in short our whole life history.

When we have a complex, aloof, man like Hammarskjöld, an individual not "easy to know" even by those who knew him best, and the circumstantial evidence of whose person is incomplete and contradictory, it is all the more fascinating to put him to the test of a long hard look; to try to discern, so far as we can, his innate dispositions, impulses and feelings—the raw material, which, when exposed to the pressure of an austerely formalistic Swedish civil service environment, produced the Hammarskjöld we knew.

I worked under Hammarskjöld from the day of his arrival in New York to the day of his departure for Ndola. He was the star of my most dramatic television programs. Whenever he appeared in the assembly or conference rooms, my close-up lens was on him, and far more acute than the lens of my camera was that of my eye. I saw a delicately built man, slender and graceful, but veiled: his gestures were truncated, kept close to the body; his words were abstruse, and even his voice was glazed. His friend, Stolpe, said that he spoke as if through a sheet of glass.

In appearance and manner he signalled the over-sensitive shy man who by nature flees the honky-tonk of daily life to find shelter in the still of nature, in books and poetry, and who withdraws cautiously into a tender inner world in order to—as Strindberg puts it—"spin themselves into the silk of their own souls."

In knottier words, he was what European constitutional psychologists usually call a "leptosome," Americans an "ecto-morph," and I—preferring what I see to Greek exactitudes—the Thin Man. Here rocks the cradle of the Hammarskjöld who was averse to publicity, the bad mixer, the lonely, touch-me-not diplomat with a preference for "quiet diplomacy," whose most spectacular achievements were carried out with less fanfare than Khrushchev's—or even Churchill's—most trivial ones.

Here also is the author of *Markings*, whose only really intimate friend was his diary to whom he could confide his nervous self-analysis and ask in honed phrases rude questions; which if impolitely expressed would read, "What do I have to forgive myself today?" "Whom have I offended?" "Why am I better than other people?" "Am I overbearing?"

A British journalist once summed up Hammarskjöld: "If

he were to find an abandoned child on a street corner, he would take him home, care for him, give him everything—except love."

Not "oversensitive or cold," but "both oversensitive *and* cold" is part of the clinical description of this sort of delicately built man, and we cannot doubt that Hammarskjöld was aware of his own coldness, since his diary is full of exhortations and reminders to himself of the necessity of being a simpler, a quieter, and a warmer man. But in fact, he was a thinking man, and thinking is a cold process. He was abstract-minded and systematic, a mathematician; and "Mathematics," wrote Bertrand Russell, "possesses not only truth but supreme beauty—a beauty cold and austere."

I sensed this coldness in him the first time I saw him, perhaps gaining this impression most forcibly from his eyes. As an artist, I have observed that the color of the iris is an indication of warmth or coolness in the temperament. Eyes of what artists call "warm colors," those with a mixture of red, such as brown, hazel, violet or golden eyes, indicate that warmth is to be looked for in the personality make-up. Cold colors that have the color of ice, such as light blue or green, indicate coolness of temperament. Hammarskjöld had blue eyes of arctic cold.

But coldness does not prevent a man from being consumed by fiery passion, like that of the inflammatory Lord Russell himself; or like the brittle poet, Uhland, who was depicted as: "fiery wine in a bowl of ice"; or as the Swedish playwright, Strindberg, said of himself, "I am hard as ice and yet so full of feeling that I am almost sentimental."

Falling obediently into step with such brothers-in-temperament, Hammarskjöld's self-portrait was, "a touch of frost and fiery skies."

Yet there are some who absolve him of his frigidity. When I asked Mr. Leif Belfrage, one of his close friends, if Dag

Hammarskjöld was a warm-hearted man, he replied, "He became one."

It is true that in some individuals a personality shift occurs at middle age, usually with the putting on of weight. A dramatic case of this kind is that of Florence Nightingale who from a stringy and fearsome crusader turned into a harmless plump old lady who spent her time making useless gift objects. The Germans have a word for this change: *Legierungswechsel.* But I am not sure that it applied to Hammarskjöld. I think that warmth was lacking but that tenderness was certainly present, and perhaps as he curbed and canalized the worst in him, it became more visible to the naked eye.

Eclectic as he was in his friends, preferring artists, writers, musicians, and others of his own psychic atmosphere, he could switch with apparent will to the company of UNEF soldiers, maintenance men, African politicians; with the same graciousness Tolstoy shifted between imperial palaces and peasant huts. It may be argued that it mattered little to such self-absorbed men what company they kept, since among intellectuals or workers, they remained islands by themselves. But the shift would not have taken place at all without the will born of tenderness, the simple desire to behave in imitation of Christ, and if this was not warmly felt, it was strongly felt.

But while Hammarskjöld held his intellectual and social unequals with tenderness, he was apt to talk to them in a language that went over their heads. He had a special fondness for children, but he did not know what to say to them. When he undertook his gruelling Odyssey of Headquarters Building in which he shook four thousand hands—and he shook almost as many again in Geneva—he performed his duty with a modest smile and without condescension, but wordlessly. In his country home in Brewster, New York, he offered a barbecue to thirty maintenance men and their wives and the cleaning-women, and he received them unpretentiously in sport-shirt, slacks, and sandals on his naked feet. It did not occur to him that for most of them it was a state occasion for which they dressed up to the nines.

At this barbecue and at the Christmas party he shared with the UNEF troops, he insisted that the photographers—whom he otherwise feared—take pictures. This was an odd publicity stunt for a man who habitually eschewed personal publicity and was nauseated by the most thoroughly deserved praise and honors. Hammarskjöld wanted those pictures taken for the same reason that Emperor Francis Joseph of Austria wanted people to watch him washing the feet of the poor: he did not care much for the ceremony, but he wanted to be right. To be seen was not important to Hammarskjöld, but to be seen doing what was right.

If there was no warmth in it, and if he seemed to become a warmhearted man, I think it was his native tenderness incarnadined by those passionate fires in which he was forging his ideal self—which was full of warmth and love. But it was a lonely glow at the bottom of his being and to be seen only in flashes, perhaps in the sudden radiance of his smile. A bottleneck impaired the smooth flow of his emotion, and this was the origin of his seeming aloofness and haughtiness. On the same account, the timid, tender Blaise Pascal was called by Voltaire "the sublime misanthrope."

His impersonal formality, his inability to show facile sentiment gained him the resentment of some which remains to this day. Alex Gabriel of the Transradio News Agency does not forget a certain infuriating encounter with the Secretary-General. Gabriel annually went to some trouble to arrange in Bangor, Maine, a forum of discussion of United Nations affairs. One year, at the last minute, after much effort and money had been spent on the necessary publicity, three ambassadors who were supposed to have appeared on the forum sent their regrets: their engagements prevented them from going all the way up to Maine. In this extremity Gabriel suddenly spied in the corridors of Headquarters Building, Hammarskjöld making for the elevator, and passing his own impulsive "Leave It to Dag" resolution, he ran up to the Secretary-General to ask for help. But before he could explain himself, Hammarskjöld threw up his hands defensively, hunched his shoulders, and said in a high voice, "No, no! I don't want to listen..."

"But Mr. Secretary-General, I am in the most terrible pinch," implored Gabriel.

"No, I'm not going to listen," repeated Hammarskjöld and shot like a rabbit into the safe shelter of the elevator.

"He wouldn't even listen," says Gabriel bitterly. "He defended himself like a woman."

There is no doubt that annoyance at this public assault upon his cool and measured elegance lay at the bottom of Hammarskjöld's attitude; his sense of form was outraged and, taken off guard, he abruptly and quite unjustly shut off communication.

He was a bad mixer and detested chitchat. For him the poised personality of the cocktail party whose life-saving chatter is welcome to most of us was nothing but an odious individual with no reserve or respect, empty-headed, light-brained, a blown egg, an empty shell.

It is hard to tell with a man like Hammarskjöld where inhibition ends and self-control begins, or whether indeed they are not two aspects of one and the same thing. Whatever the case, any man who stores emotion must sooner or later let off steam. Dr. Bunche informs us that Hammarskjöld was "not above anger, even fury, or other emotions. He could at times and did erupt."

But he erupted in private. His public demeanor was of a correctness that bordered on stoney imperturbability. Once at a press luncheon at Danny's Hideaway his friend and Undersecretary for Public Information, Mr. Bokhari, sitting between Max Harrelson of Associated Press and Bruce Munn of the

United Press International, fainted. There was commotion at the table, correspondents jumped to help, Miss Kay Gray rushed to the telephone to call a doctor. In the midst of the brouhaha, Hammarskjöld sat quietly at his seat smoking a cigarillo, seeming to adopt the position that it was no more than Bokhari's duty to have fainted while seated between the Associated Press and the United Press International. He honored the occasion with only one move: when Bokhari's wallet fell out of his pocket, he snapped it up with lightning speed, and slipped it into his own pocket for safekeeping. After Bokhari had been taken to the 42nd Street Hospital, the Secretary-General walked quietly out of the hall and held his press conference standing in the bar.

To be sure, he knew that there was no cause for alarm: Mr. Bokhari had an affliction for which he was taking a medicine which sometimes caused him to faint. But another kind of statesman than Hammarskjöld would have seized the opportunity, with all the world's press staring at him, to lose his head a little, and thus gain a great reputation for being a warmhearted man.

Very rarely did he publicly lose his composure. One occasion was on December 20, 1960, when the Assembly was voting the final appropriation for the Congo operation. The Latin Americans upset the applecart, so that the proposal did not get the necessary two-thirds majority. The Indian Ambassador, Mr. Jha, then proposed a recess with the idea of working out a compromise behind the scenes. Late that night when the meeting reconvened, Hammarskjöld was in good spirits, confident that the appropriation would pass. But as the voting proceeded, it again fell short of the two-thirds majority.

Pale of face, the Secretary-General jumped from his seat, ran down the steps of the podium, and sat huddled on a side-seat in the section reserved for distinguished visitors, his body seemingly atremble. No one could have known precisely what he was feeling about this defeat. Hardly three weeks before, he had written a moving poem about his men beleagured in the Congo.

He sat in the darkness until his nerves calmed. Later in the night, the Argentine delegate came forward with a compromise proposal and the appropriation was voted.

Another occasion when Hammarskjöld lost his temper was in late 1961 when he came back from Geneva to offer a state dinner to Ayub Khan. Before dinner, the Secretary-General was supposed to have had an hour's conversation with the Pakistani president, but Ayub did not show up. He was holding a reception at the Waldorf, and had found it impossible to get away. Hammarskjöld began to simmer and rage. He walked nervously around the table, rearranging the seating and objecting to the position of the photographers; it was the only occasion in all his years on which he was heard to direct unflattering epithets towards underlings.

Most strikingly symptomatic of his Thin Man's mind was his taste for abstract art. In his 38th Floor offices hung Picasso's "Still Life With Cake," and it is a cake you may have and eat too, so far as I am concerned. In Fernand Léger's "Woman Combing Her Hair," you may *chercher la femme,* but you will never find her. Fritz Glarner's "Rational Look" a geometric abstract, is at least what it purports to be. Hammarskjöld must have shared Kierkegaard's thought that "all wisdom of life is abstraction," or Plato's that "God always geometrizes." For him abstract art reduced the chaos of the world to purity and order, transformed the temporal into the eternal, and he did not need to "understand" it; he was elated if he could sense eternal order.

Once he rushed out of a meeting, gazed for a while at an abstract painting in his office and sighed, "Now I am refreshed." Then he returned to the meeting.

Form-addicted and system-loving as he was, he must have derived deep satisfaction from counting the syllables of his haikus, making certain that their total number in three lines should be no less and no more than seventeen. I once saw a box that had contained his Christmas present to Heinz Wieschhoff on which he had written his season's greetings. He had composed his words and pedantically placed them, even splitting words in the middle to make them fit into a small rectangular pattern at one corner of the box.

His doodles were geometric; he scribbled them unwittingly while he planned his Congo plan.

An abstract is the essence of things and is the fruit of cogitation that obviously cannot proceed except inwards. The abstract-minded man is "schizoid"; he is split in the sense that he is aware of the processes at the bottom of his subconscious as well as of his conscious mind. The psychologist Kretschmer tells us that many schizoids are religious and that their religious feelings tend towards the mystical and the transcendental.

Deep into his soul plunged Hammarskjöld. By turning inward he found not only God but the company of humankind. The soul is the perfect rebus of being, the abstraction of all that is; it is the truth. And so, "Let the inner take precedence over the outer, the soul over the world wherever this may lead you." *

How tragic for one who looks for guidance to this deep and perfect plan to find it obfuscated by the flaws of the individuality, with its pettiness and crudities, its envies, lusts, shabby vanities, and appalling lack of humility!

The inexcusable Hammarskjöld was occasionally on public display. Once a young woman member of the Secretariat found herself seated next to him at a private dinner party and on her other side was a Brazilian guest who besides his native language spoke only French. Ostentatiously she spoke French to both gentlemen in an effort to impress this situation on the Secretary-General, but Hammarskjöld obtusely insisted upon responding in English. Finally, she told him the fact outright. Hammarskjöld snapped, "Too bad!"

* *Markings*, p. 81.

Then the young woman said to him, *"Comme l'a dit Talley-rand, quel dommage qu'un si grand homme soit aussi mal élevé."*—What a pity such a great man is so ill-bred.

Hammarskjöld remained unmoved by this remark; as a matter of fact he stopped talking altogether. "He was much too well read," she commented, "not to know that these words of Talleyrand were said in reply to Napoleon who had told him, *'Vous n'êtes que de la merde dans un bas de soie.'* "—You are nothing but dregs in silk stockings.

"It took some courage to say such a thing to the Secretary-General," I remarked, "after all, you're employed by the Secretariat."

"I wasn't invited to dinner as a member of the Secretariat, but as a private person," she replied. But the incident must have cut deep into the Secretary-General, for he never spoke to this young woman again, or even looked at her.

On the 38th Floor, the Secretary-General is remembered with affection and piety, although even from those close collaborators he tended to hold himself aloof. It was said by some that he was very swift to eliminate any man who threatened to encroach upon his position or authority, but one close to him positively denied this: "That's ridiculous. There was no such man."

A magazine article was written that accused Hammarskjöld of hardness to little people. Dr. Ralph Bunche denies this: ". . . he was reserved to the point of shyness. The truth is that although Hammarskjöld had been rated highly as an administrator at the United Nations, his greatest weakness in administration was found precisely in the fact that he usually could not be hard when personnel situations demanded it, because of an underlying soft-heartedness."

This was true; Hammarskjöld did not raise a finger against the lady of the dinner party, and I know several cases of officials who spoke bluntly to Hammarskjöld, risking their jobs, but they were not dismissed.

Doctor Bunche's summary of the Secretary-General puts the finger on a subterranean Hammarskjöld in which I see his mixed parental inheritance; and this is plainly written on his physique.

Take a photo of the Secretary-General and cover the upper half of his face; you will see a Hammarskjöld you have not seen before. His lips are full, his chin eminence is small and round as a lady-apple and dimpled. These features, with the puffy cheek pockets and delicate feminine grace of his body, are the legacy of his roundish mother, and in the same package he got her kindness, simplicity, common sense and a woman's indestructible allegiance to external orderliness. Here lay his "weakness," his childish appeal and also his vulnerability.

Now cover the lower part of his face and see the fierce and contemptuous Hammarskjöld: the marked browridge, the steep pinched temples, the heavy skin of the brow ploughed by deep furrows. With them went his erect posture, narrow but big hands, and light but conquering gait, all the muscular heirloom of Hjalmar Hammarskjöld who bequeathed to Dag his self-confidence, pedantic earnestness, firmness of purpose, and the inflexibility which is a precondition of the honest.

Kretschmer has made the curious observation that gifted men inherit intellect from the mother and character from the father. Hammarskjöld's paternal inheritance earned him the admiration of his followers and the hatred of his enemies. Even his admirers did not overlook that "UN Presence," was correlated with "Hammarskjöld omnipresence"; and they spoke of the "one-man brain trust," and "acting as if he owned the United Nations." These hard, uncompromising, and self-assertive traits were of course in constant conflict with the soft tenderness bequeathed him by his mother, as well as with the mystical abstract-minded idealism of the slightly-built man. This "germinal hostility," I feel, is the origin of the many contradictory opinions of him: some say he was considerate, others that he was ruthless; some that he was steely cold, while others speak of his softheartedness; his narcissism is as evident in *Markings* as his quest for humility.

But one does injustice if one tries to reconcile these seemingly contradictory traits, or to excuse one with the other. They were parts of the same picture, sometimes inseparably so. It is a paradox of the mystic, for example, that in order to set his highest goal in life as simple humility, he must be *a priori,* both superior and complex.

The conflict of inhibition and drive in him, made Hammarskjöld a tense man, and tension was written in the tightness of his lips and the alert eyes. This was what made his gestures swift and abrupt, and it sent him walking with such speed through the corridors of the United Nations that Bill Ranallo, his guard, found it difficult to keep in step with him. Once a lady said to Bill, "How nice for you to have all those long walks with the Secretary-General!" and Bill replied, "Nice! I hate those forced marches!"

But this tension was the *force motrice* that drove him to "greater heights"; as water and fire produce steam his conflicts were the driving power that led to his demonic unrest, and also to his greatness.

Another characteristic, very prominent in him, was that he was born a "baby brother." Some women were very quick to sense this fundamental desire of his to be taken care of, sheltered, even "bossed around." Miss Audrey Langston, of the photographic section, who was particularly successful in getting along with him, says, "I bullied him. I had to. My job was to get those photographs. But there was an invisible line drawn between us. Once my job was done, the next day I showed him the utmost courtesy. And that comforted him."

And then she added with insight. "I was his nanny. He saw his mother in me."

He submitted without resistance, and I suspect with covert satisfaction, to the "bossings" of his husky bodyguards whose duty it was to force seat-belts around him and see that he did not begin to drink whisky in the small hours of the morning when it was time to go to bed. Once, off for a weekend in the country, he went to the 51st Street bookshop and picked up nine books to read. The guards took a dim view of these, for they intended that he should catch up on his sleep. They confiscated three of the heaviest books.

In his country house at Brewster, N. Y., he lived like playmates with his guards, insisting on taking his turn at cooking which he did indifferently and at dish washing (at which he was bad). But on Monday morning in his office the guards snapped to attention when he addressed them, and it was back to the formal "Yes, Mr. Secretary-General," and "No, Mr. Secretary-General."

Looking at Hammarskjöld, and trusting to the judgment of my eye, I have estimated that his physique would probably be expressed in the Sheldon rating as 2-3-6. This rating, devised by W. H. Sheldon of Harvard, indicates numerically the participation of the three basic types in any given individual. The first number refers to the Round; the second to the Muscular; the third to the Thin. I have thus judged that Hammarskjöld's fragility is far preponderant, and that his muscular inheritance from his father has a slight edge over the round softness of his mother. Sheldon's description of this physical type strikingly fits that of Hammarskjöld:

> The 2-3-6 is a slender, upright physique, usually tall and when not dysplastic, he has a symmetry and beauty of proportion that is aesthetically of the highest order. It is a lean, clean-cut body throughout, the muscular relief is sharp, but the muscles are long and slender and there is no muscular bunching.
>
> The shoulders are wide and the still rather flat chest is usually well supported above. The abdomen is flat but not

tightly pinched in. Arms and legs are long, but well-propor-
tioned. The fingers and toes are often long and hands and
feet are narrow.*

Similarly, Sheldon's account of the corresponding temperament of such individuals strikingly illuminates the Secretary-
General:

> Temperamentally, 2-3-6 lives under an almost cerebrotic
> strain. He carries the weight of *Weltschmerz* on his slender
> shoulders. In a society built upon a theological certainty he
> would probably be quite happy, for he is tender-minded and
> a born savior, but he is sufficiently intelligent to have real-
> ized the difficulty of determining in just what direction society
> can be best saved, and so he is caught in the position of a
> hen with an egg to lay, but with no nest to lay it.**

Of course, Sheldon's research was based on observation of
Harvard students who were having difficulty in finding perfect
nests. But Hammarskjöld had found his in the United Nations.

> The 2-3-6 temperament is not likely to turn to orthodox
> preaching. Their youth closely resembles what has been
> called the Promethean personality ... The great weakness of
> Prometheus is an inability to compromise.†

This statement is particularly striking in view of the following observation by Arthur Gavshon concerning Hammarskjöld: "In mid-1961, he gave as his favorite motto ... 'to hope
'till Hope creates from its own wreck the thing it contemplates.'

"Perhaps Hammarskjöld found all the power and splendor
of Shelley's poetic drama embodied in that one poignant line.
The symbolism of *Prometheus Unbound* needs no stretching.
Lesser leaders than he may well have identified with the cap-
tive Prometheus, friend of man, chained in the mountain fast-
ness by Zeus."

* W. H. Sheldon, *The Varieties of Human Physique.*
** W. H. Sheldon, *The Varieties of Temperament.*
† *Ibid.*

There is indeed a coincidence between Hammarskjöld's preference for Prometheus, Gavshon's remarks, and Sheldon's diagnosis.

Equally intriguing are Dr. Sheldon's further remarks about this personality-type:

> In an informal study of over one hundred different historical pictures of the Christ we found that about thirty percent of the artists have pictured the Christian central figure as approximately a 2-3-6, and about thirty-five percent of them have made him approximately a 2-3-5.*

This study was made about a quarter of a century before the publication of *Markings* which brought down upon the late Secretary-General's head such bad names as "myth-maker," and "Savior," and "saint."

I am a caricaturist, and it is certainly not my business to make saints of statesmen. But I know that men are as they are made to be, because I can see it; and when a man of a particular personality sees before him an empty chair marked *This is the Siege Perilous,* he will sit on it as if it had been made for him; and from that moment myths cohere to his name of the sort that have been told about such pure souls since this world began.

Here for a start is a Hammarskjöld myth in the ancient manner which has moreover trustworthy eyewitnesses.

Once the Secretary-General visited United Nations Headquarters in Geneva and admired the peacocks strutting on the lawn of the Palais des Nations. "I wish we had some in New York!" he exclaimed.

Shortly after he returned to New York, he received from the Geneva office a gift of four peacocks, which were then housed in the rose garden at Headquarters, next to the children's playground.

One day, Drake McGuffey and José Cura, both working in

* *The Varieties of Human Physique.*

the UN record library, were sitting on a bench in the rose garden, watching the children play and the peacocks strut. Dag Hammarskjöld and Andrew Cordier passed by, followed by Bill Ranallo. When the peacocks saw the Secretary-General, both the male and the female walked over to the pathway, and as Hammarskjöld passed by the male puffed out his chest, lifted his feathers, and greeted the Secretary-General with a wondrous display of tail. Hammarskjöld stopped, smiling at the peacocks, and contemplating the beauty of the fan; and then he passed along. The peacock then folded his tail and trotted back towards the playground.

"Good Heavens!" exclaimed McGuffey, "they've extended bureaucracy to the peacocks!"

Hammarskjöld's favorite contemporary philosopher, Martin Buber, wrote in *I and Thou:*

> Animals, like children, are not seldom able to see through any hypocritical tenderness. But even outside the sphere of taming, a similar contact between men and animals some- times takes place—with men who have in the depths of their being a potential partnership with animals, not predomi- nantly persons of "animal" nature, but rather those whose very nature is spiritual.

Tales of the communion between saints and animals are of course common in Christian hagiology, and these are repeated in the folklore and religious literature of all the peoples of the earth.

Three days after Hammarskjöld departed for Ndola, his male peacock died. There were two days left for the people in the Guide Service—with whom the peacocks administra- tively belonged—to worry about how this news was to be broken to Mr. Hammarskjöld.

An autopsy established that the bird had died of cirrhosis of the liver. I know the story would have been better if the peacock had died of a broken heart, but inscrutable are the ways of God, and it really doesn't matter in Heaven what a peacock dies of.

The surviving peacocks were given to the Bronx Zoo. I asked the Guide Service the reason for this, and a young lady from Pakistan told me, "We got so many letters from delegates demanding the removal of the peacocks, because they bring bad luck."

10

Men Called the Unicorn Abnormal

WHEN on that March day of 1953, Dag Hammarskjöld was designated as Secretary-General, Mat Gordon, a United Nations press officer, stood outside the door of Conference Room 8 and read out some short biographical notes. He intoned Hammarskjöld's official positions: "Chairman of the Board of Governors of the Bank of Sweden, Undersecretary of the Department of Finance, Vice-Chairman of the Swedish delegation to the United Nations..."

A voice from the crowd broke in loudly: "And a fairy!"

This was the pebble that started an avalanche of gossip that continued to roll and grow throughout Hammarskjöld's tenure of office. The rumor became intolerable. A member of his 38th Floor "family" told one of his close friends and trusted collaborators that it had to be stopped. "You've got to tell him about it," he said.

This was a delicate mission even for a friend, and he hesitated for some time but concluding that it was duty to keep the Secretary-General informed in every respect, he broached the subject. Hammarskjöld shrugged his shoulders and was silent; he made no comment at all.

The rumor had followed him from Sweden where those who had watched his splendid career had noted also that he formed no tender attachment to a woman. His friends arranged matches: they hopefully introduced him to a beautiful young woman whose good fortune it was to be both a Doctor of Philosophy and a daughter of a financier. The project went on the rocks at once. Why? His friend, Bertil Ohlin jokingly explained, "Probably she didn't like T. S. Eliot."

Sven Stolpe writes, "He gave up a woman who had attracted him for a while upon noting that a friend of his was also interested in her. He became a loyal friend of the couple—the sacrifice seemed in no way difficult to him. But it was noticeable that each time he met the couple, he addressed himself to the man and not to the woman." *

Another story has it that a certain lady—perhaps the same as above—keeps an evening dress in her closet which she wore on her last date with Hammarskjöld, and that to it an enigmatic label is attached: "The happiest day of my life."

Solomon in all his glory had hardly more opportunity to accumulate romantic reminiscences than this meteoric, well-to-do and handsome young Swede. One evening he returned to his bachelor apartment in Stockholm with a friend to find a girl in his bed. She had gained entrance by telling the superintendent that she was a maid; what she really wanted was a secretarial job and she had devised this means of ingratiating herself with the boss. Hammarskjöld handled the situation by imitation of Christ but not the Christ of the Mary Magdalene episode; he behaved more like Jesus driving the moneylenders from the temple. He pulled the young woman out of his bed, slapped her face, and held her while his friend called the police. The girl was taken to a psychiatric ward, and the next day Hammarskjöld moved out of his sullied apartment.

A while after his arrival in New York, one of his bodyguards made bold to ask a question: "How about the girls, Mr. Secretary-General?"

* Sven Stolpe, *Dag Hammarskjolds Geistiger Weg*, p. 23.

"I'll tell you about it some other time," replied Hammarskjöld.

One week later, his bodyguard was about to revive the subject but before he could open his mouth the Secretary-General cut in: "I know what you are going to ask me. Yes, as a young man, I was interested in a girl, but then I began to study hard and I had no more time for girls."

He had great charm for some women, and there were those in the Secretariat who tried, and tried hard, to draw his amorous attention, but without success. Yet, their feeling was not precisely sexual; it was indirect and occult. "I was attracted by the mystery of him," said one of them to me. "I wished to share his secret." Another said, maternally, "I preferred him when he was tired and his face drawn. He was more human." And still another, "I didn't look at him as a man at all. I sensed his spiritual excellence, his intellectual greatness and remoteness." To these chaste observations, her companion, a plump blonde, snapped, "Nonsense! You know what women want."

Whatever women want, they were not to have it from Hammarskjöld, and most of them, even those who greatly admired him, sensed this neutrality in him. He kept his distance from women. On Staff Day, the annual dance that he himself had established, he danced only twice in all the years of his office, and then with the same woman, Audrey Langston, whom he regarded as a sort of nanny. Even so, she had to bully him into it. Once, she spied him in conversation with a group of men at the edge of the animated dance floor, and she said to him, "Haven't you had enough shop talk. Why aren't you dancing?"

"I was just about to ask you," said Hammarskjöld.

"What kind of a dancer was he?" I enquired.

"Mediocre. He was nervous. He did not have his mind on it. I told him funny stories and he laughed, and we talked all the time. A serious dancer doesn't talk while dancing—it was more like the fulfilling of an obligation to him."

The Secretary-General was known to resent the comparisons sometimes made of him with Lawrence of Arabia, whose homoerotic tendencies are well-known; yet anyone who ventured a comment on the subject of women was quickly silenced. A colleague who blurted that Hammarskjöld might improve his public image if he was occasionally seen with a woman never again broke through the ice that formed on the Secretary-General's demeanor. A most unfortunate journalist from Vietnam got his tongue well twisted at a press conference when he said, "Mr. Secretary-General, there is a rumor that you are going to be married."

"From sensation to sensation!" exclaimed Hammarskjöld.

"This was stated by a friend—"

"It is obviously explained by my general silence," said the Secretary-General, sternly. "You get so little news that you really have to invent something."

The poor Vietnamese tried to wriggle out of his fix by a pirouette: "I will only volunteer to say that if there were a choice ... I would rather see you a bachelor Secretary-General than being married."

And from the Secretary-General he received an odd retort: "That is not a very humane approach."

Perhaps this interchange contained unwitting inhumanity for the Secretary-General. His consciousness that Nature who had gifted him so highly had withheld from him the common gratuity of sexual love is apparent in *Markings*. He buried poignant regret in haikus, but it is there: in his pity for the fabulous unicorn, blessed with supreme beauty, but set apart from animalkind because it was a virgin.

Homo sapiens is generally too lazy to be sapient: instead of thinking he prefers such simple alternatives as: if a man does not make love to girls, then he must make love to boys. It is as simple as that.

However, in the United Nations Secretariat, we have those

whose business it is to know everything about everybody, and so I turned to the Security Officers for an answer to the mystery of Hammarskjöld's sexual life. The possibility exists that they are under orders to know nothing about it; but apart from this reservation, I have no reason to doubt their honesty when they asserted that the rumors had no foundation.

A woman whose husband worked closely with Hammarskjöld said, "My husband was repelled by homosexuals and extremely sensitive on this subject. He travelled widely with Hammarskjöld, knew him as well as anyone could—and not one single incident gave him to believe that Hammarskjöld was a homosexual."

Enquiries of Hammarskjöld's closest friends evoke a prompt denial, or else the reply, "I just don't think so." His detractors have disseminated their belief in his homosexuality in print across the face of the earth, presenting this as a flaw in his character; while those who might wish to defend him of the accusation can only shy from it, perhaps for lack of argument.

Under not much duress, I will confess my belief that the constitution of an individual, of which the external aspect is in the body build, is a good argument upon which to base at least an educated conjecture—especially when he has left a map of his soul against which one's observations may be measured.

On the basis of what I see on Hammarskjöld's physique, I think that some part of him did not weather well those stormy years of adolescence when, in the upheaval of glandular changes, the childish personality collapses, and on its ruins the adult emerges.

Hammarskjöld's photos at the age of puberty show a delicately built, "shot-up" youngster with an overlong neck, sloping shoulders, and broad hips. His legs are spindly, and his hands and feet are too big for his wrists and ankles. The facial skeleton is frail, and his head shows the infantile proportions of a much younger child, the braincase being voluminous, as compared to the small, receding chin. He always looked younger than he was; once, when he was Undersecretary of the Treasury, he presented himself at a tourist hotel in a sports shirt and the clerk directed him to a nearby youth hostel.

Hammarskjöld's interest in sports has led some to write facilely that he was a husky, manly boy, but I can see no evidence of this on his body build. He had sinews and ligaments to be sure, and plenty of nervous energy, but muscles are singularly missing on his teenage photos. He brought home report cards studded with A's but a black B in gymnastics; and he wrote a melancholy haiku in remembrance of the time his schoolmates had laughed at him when he had tried to vault, but had fallen ignominiously.

These signs of juvenile weakness did not diminish or change when he grew. He retained the weak neck, the delicate facial skeleton, the small chin and voluminous cranium. Very often I have noted how his napeline, curving down from the voluminous cranium, was concave, like a child's—I have drawn the same feature, even more pronounced, on Gandhi.

Turning to *Markings,* one learns that Hammarskjöld had a late and prolonged adolescence. The juvenile features of his physique lead me to believe that this juvenility extended, as an integral part of his personality, throughout his life. It shone through the radiant boyish charm of his smile of which he was self-conscious for he knew that it was unconquerably coquettish. It awakened the maternal tenderness of women, and brought forth the avuncularity of bodyguards. It made him unpopular, or at least seem mysterious, enigmatic, remote and aloof to some men of pronounced masculinity. It is, I believe, in Hammarskjöld's juvenility that we must look for an explanation of his sexual nature.

Titian has a painting entitled, "Sacred and Profane Love," which represents two ladies sitting on opposite sides of a fountain in which the child Cupid splashes about. One beldam is respectably dressed and carries under her arm a pot of beans or something on that order; the other, naked, holds up an oil lamp or incense-burner.

At the well of the aspiring lover's soul, when these two ladies don't sit side by side, it spells trouble.

The sex impulse appears in adolescence on two planes: on the psychical plane, as eroticism, that is, a tendency to an ideal, sentimental interest in the opposite sex; and on the physical plane, as sexuality, a desire for intercourse in some form. In normal development, the ideal and the physical love fuse into one, and the adult male or female find in their mates both forms of love united.

In boys and girls of delicate body build, whose maturity is late and prolonged, this perfect union may be long in developing; and it may not develop at all, especially when an exaggerated tenderness and submissiveness to the mother is present, as was so clearly the case of Hammarskjöld. Such a child becomes timid and remains deliberately ignorant about sexual matters. A roadmark in Hammarskjöld's life was the time when seeing the body of some loved person, he averted his eyes, lest it should awaken his lust.

Psychologists seemingly agree on these developmental phases of the normal sex impulses, and so—assuming that their agreement makes it "scientific"—we may look to them for some hint of the problems that besieged the young Dag. From the psychologist Spranger, we learn that in a youth of this sort, "erotic relationships are satisfied with admiration from a distance" and that "desire for physical contact, if it appears, is suppressed relentlessly." There is almost a religious quality to his love, similar to Dante's love for Beatrice, revealed in his *Vita Nuova*, and he is tormented by inner shuddering, deep shyness, and shame, on account of his own insufficiency.

"Auto-eroticism is quite normal for this period," we are

told, and also that "attraction to members of the same sex on an erotic, or idealistic, plane is just as frequent as heterosexual attraction." *

At this age, before the aim of the sexual impulses becomes properly fixed, a normal person may exhibit tendencies that at another period of life would be described as perversions. Here lie the extravagant "schoolgirl crushes," and the "school-boy hero-worship." Here indeed lie the mutual ardors common in boys' and girls' boarding schools. It is normally a transient stage.

But when adolescence is prolonged and these emotions are contingent upon adulthood, the problem becomes ever more acute. Kretschmer describes the dilemma with eloquent pen: "Here stand I, my ethical personality, and over there the sexual impulse as something hostile, as a continually disturbing foreign body. This leads to the most bitter moral conflict between the two irreconcilable aspects of the self—which may affect the person's whole life."

Two solutions are open to a person facing this dilemma: one is to convert it into anxieties and all sorts of aches and pains—this produces the sort of bachelor who is "a proper old maid." The other is to sublimate it or transform primitive impulses into dynamically correlated religious, ethical and artistic values.

The sublimation of sexual energy into religious ardor is a well-observed phenomenon. Monks, vowed to celibacy, undertake systematic spiritual exercises, combining mortification of the flesh with mental training, which ingeniously and methodically sublimate crude impulses into the pure love of God, the contemplation of God, and the ecstatic union with God. Luther called this "climbing up into the majesty of God." Gandhi wrote, "I realize that a vow, far from closing the door to real freedom, opened it ... Every day ... has taken me nearer to the knowledge that in *brahmacharya* (celibacy) lies

* Spranger, *Psychologie Des Jugendalter*, 1926, pp. 110, 121, etc.

the protection of the body, the mind and the soul . . . it was a matter of consolation and joy. Every day revealed the fresh beauty in it."

Hammarskjöld must have been aware of this process in himself. His path of spiritual liberation, evident in his diary, has the flesh following along like a Doppelgänger.

I do not know what Hammarskjöld's early questings may have been when he found himself to be incapable of loving a woman and when on "an unspeakably shabby level" he discovered that he hated normal people who could enjoy what was denied to him. I think that *Markings* makes clear that *agape,* the Greek love, was equally beyond his grasp. In 1951 he wrote of his inward asceticism and anti-feminism; and of a man the inflection of whose voice can bind, his glance unite. But in 1952 he wrote of this love or another, that it had escaped him; and not only his own exclusiveness was to blame. He suggests that his passion was incomplete and at the same time too demanding: the passion, indeed, of youth.

There is no question that Hammarskjöld was a man deeply in love with the fulsome beauty of the physical world. His private diary is full of sensuous images. In spite of the attraction he felt for bleak places such as mountain peaks and tundras, it was in a fat and fertile field near Poughkeepsie that he glimpsed Paradise. He wrote tenderly of the human body, but saw it also in its nakedness, male and female, as simply: Man.

Again and again he transmutes sensuous imagery into something pure and transcendent. I believe that this mirrors the process of his own "spiritual liberation," and that at some time in his life, probably before he became Secretary-General, he resolved his physiological difficulties by becoming celibate. Common sense might have dictated such a solution to a man prominent in public life; but in fact he was behaving in harmony with his constitutional brothers, the gentle, intellectual *leptosomes.*

So far as we know, fragile Spinoza never had a love affair; timid Pascal never dared to confess his love for the sister of his patron; Nietzsche gave up women after one unfortunate essay in a brothel; brittle little Kant, the "Chinaman of Koenigsberg," lived like an old bachelor with his serving-man, Lampe, who never dared to inform his master that he was married. Kierkegaard broke up his one romantic attachment to a beautiful young girl and fled to Berlin to devote all his gifts to the service of God.

Gandhi, who married at the age of thirteen and had four sons, chose chastity at the age of thirty-seven because, he said, "It became my conviction that procreation and the consequent care of children were inconsistent with public service..." Still, Gandhi hoped that no one would believe that sublimation was easy. It was "like walking on the world's edge, and I see every moment the necessity for eternal vigilance." Kierkegaard tamed himself to the celibate's life with "shattered nerves and a bleeding heart."

Certainly, Hammarskjöld suffered the agonies of his chastity: loneliness, rooted in the early suppression of sexual desire, was his hateful adversary. He wrote of his envy of others in their partnerships. The very thought of sexual happiness turned his thoughts to "the real bitterness of death": that one dies, while others go on living.

Evident in Hammarskjöld's relentless summary of himself is his narcissism. It is not surprising to find a man of action who occupies a leading position developing a certain heroic idealization of his own personality; it happened to Hitler, Napoleon, Mussolini, and de Gaulle. Success and admiration is the balmy climate in which this trait blooms.

But Hammarskjöld's narcissism was of a different order from these and it came from a deeper source. Freud believed narcissism to be a normal adolescent stage which generally passes with adulthood; and so this, too, is centered around his permanent juvenile components. Looking inward, he saw excessive self-admiration there, and so he denied it with deliberately modest behavior, dressing neatly in modest colors, and choosing unobtrusive neckties; it is certainly not narcissistic to be camera-shy and to refuse to autograph one's own pictures. He tried to puzzle out the difference between élite persons like himself and the non-élite, and he reminded himself earnestly that his successful actions were performed through God. Praise nauseated him, and yet he could not abide those who failed to recognize his own excellence. While sneering at his sins of pride, he found it necessary to reflect sympathetically upon the entranced Narcissus, just as he had upon the lonely unicorn.

Casting about in my mind for another statesman comparable to Hammarskjöld in whom he might have been expected to find a friend on his own intellectual plane, I asked a person who knew him well how the Secretary-General had liked Nehru. I was told to my surprise—but after pondering the matter, not to my surprise—"He did not like Nehru because he could not endure his narcissism."

These two men had singular resemblances, perhaps too many. To my gaze, Nehru had a greater muscular component, more ruthless strength with which to weather political climate, as well as a readier sense of humor.

Both of these men were handsome, elegant, well-to-do, and educated as highly as possible. They were of exquisite demeanor and as explosive as magnetic mines. Sons of kindly mothers and severe fathers, they looked sternly inward to find principles upon which to found the actions of their lives. Both foreswore sex; Nehru spent years of enforced chastity in prison, and after the early death of his wife, Kamala, became celibate.

Both identified humility as the precious jewel of greatness, and both were conscious of their own superiority and vain of it. At the height of his fame, Nehru wrote an anonymous article for a magazine in which he made mincemeat of Nehru, Hammarskjöld-fashion: "He has all the makings of a dictator in him ... and with all his love of the crowd, he is guilty of intolerance of others and a certain contempt for the weak and insufficient ... his conceit is really formidable. It must be checked. We want no Caesars."

Both were Caesars, but measuring themselves against an inner vision of perfection, they would have a thousand times refused the crown. Quite often in reading *Markings,* one has the sense of *déjà vu* in Nehru.

It is hard to draw a line between narcissism and plain self-esteem, especially in men who are self-aware enough to conceal both. One must look for innocuous symbols. Nehru betrayed his self-admiration by wearing a perpetual rose in his button-hole. Hammarskjöld would not have worn a rose; but when-ever he appeared in the delegates' dining room, fresh roses miraculously bloomed on his table, and on *all* the tables on his side of the room. He shared with Nehru all the narcissistic virtues such as gallantry, courtesy, a craftsman's use of lan-guage, and love of aesthetic exercise.

Adolescence is an age of pathos, and for most of us it is a relief to have it over. But it has its beauties too: it is the awakening of idealism, of philosophical questioning, of meta-physical yearnings. Hammarskjöld was aware of this lyricism. While conscious of his own bitterness toward those who en-joyed the advantages of maturity, he admonished himself, "... why don't you put into the balance the long spring en-joyed by a youth who matured late?"

When the long spring is extended into adulthood and idealism finds a cause, metaphysical yearning a calling, and philosophical questioning an answer, then man is capable of great ethical achievement.

Dag Hammarskjöld did not fail to leave a sly warning to popular psychologists who for good or ill would try to unravel his mysteries. He felt that they were far too sure of themselves, but understood less than nothing.

Perhaps so; but one thing is certain at any rate: it matters as little whether Hammarskjöld was a homosexual as it matters in the case of Michelangelo. What matters greatly is what he did and what he was trying to do.

II

Death Was Always
One of the Party

HAMMARSKJÖLD the mountain-climber saw himself
toiling to dizzy heights between two threatening
chasms. On one side lay the "pleasure-tinged death wish,"
which he recognized was "not without its element of narcissistic masochism"; and on the other lay "fear, arising from the
physical instinct of survival."

Statistics-fanciers will be interested to know that in *Markings*, the words death, die, and dead, come up seventy-four
times, without counting words symbolic of death such as
"sacrifice" or "end." This is, in the American edition, an
average of every third page. Hammarskjöld liked fun, he was
swift to smile, and his close friends knew that he could be
quite a gay blade; but "Death," he wrote in his private diary,
"was always one of the party."

To be sure, every one of us has an inbuilt "pleasure-tinged
death wish." It is like a calculated obsolescence that prevents
us from living indefinitely, similar to the brake mechanisms
of growth that prevent us from growing ten feet tall. So strong
is this death wish in man that occasionally he builds an entire
cultural complex around it, such as that of the old Chinese
who used to sleep next to their own coffins or the ancient
Egyptians who wrote poems such as:

167

Death is before me today
Like the recovery of a sick man
Like going forth in a garden after sickness
Death is before me today.
Like the odor of myrrh
Like sitting under the sail on a windy day
Death is before me today
Like the odor of lotus flowers
Like sitting on the shore of drunkenness
Death is before me today
Like the course of a freshet
Like the return of a man from the war-galley to his home
Death is before me today
As a man longs to see his home
When he had spent years of captivity.*

Freud says that it is man's ambition to return to his mother's womb; but I think that man is preparing for a longer journey —a return to eternity. For the man of delicate, narrow body-build who lives an inward-directed life and who in his heart never lost his sense of belonging to eternity, the membrane that separates the physical and spiritual world is indeed thin. He is acquiescent to death and broods upon it, he falls in love with it. His death wish is pleasure-tinged.

In the case of Hammarskjöld it was consistent with his prolonged adolescence, which carried with it a pathetic idealism, a yearning for a better world, and a desire to sacrifice himself upon the altar of his ideals. Adolescents very frequently commit suicide in order to retrieve in death what beauty they could not find in a crass world. But the Promethean Thin Man, who is secretly motivated by youth's lovely dreams, manufactures with reason and intellect a noble cause, and it is his privilege to involve himself in it, suicidally.

It seems coincidental, but perhaps it was as inevitable as in

* Will Durant. *Our Oriental Heritage*, Simon & Schuster, 1954, pp. 195-196.

a Greek tragedy that one of the most dramatic episodes in Hammarskjöld's tenure of office was a confrontation with a man who was constructed by nature as exactly as Hammarskjöld himself to die for a principle. His name was Povl Bang-Jensen, a Danish member of the Secretariat. The two men had known each other before either of them came to the United Nations, and they customarily addressed each other with the familiar "thou."

Bang-Jensen, like Hammarskjöld, had followed a successful career in the public service of his small nation. A lawyer, during World War I when Denmark was occupied by the Germans, he was attached to the legation in Washington which handled Danish interests abroad. Later, he became *ad interim* chargé d'affaires in a number of Latin-American countries. In 1949, he joined the Secretariat in the department of Political and Security Council affairs.

When in 1956 Janos Kadar refused to permit the United Nations Commission to enter Hungary, the Assembly set up, on Hammarskjöld's recommendation, a Special Committee to investigate the causes and implications of the Hungarian uprising. Mr. W. M. Jordan, an Englishman, was named principal secretary of the Committee, and Bang-Jensen was his deputy. At that time, I was Hungarian broadcaster for the United Nations, and I therefore followed closely the work of this committee and came to know Bang-Jensen well. He was a brittle, sensitive man who walked as if performing a *valse hésitante* upon bubbles. His face was narrow and sparsely bearded: only around his lips was there a blue glimmer, and sometimes an alien smile would wander onto his austere countenance and light it for a moment. His mind was like a lacy fretwork wrought in stone, a Germanic lawyer's mind, that intricately opposes every pro with every con, and lines them all up in unalterable progression towards a conclusion massive as a rock.

Since the Special Committee was banned from Hungary,

the Soviet Union, and from every Warsaw Pact country, it was obliged to reconstruct the history of the uprising by pasting together press clippings, Russian army orders, official Hungarian documents, and reports of foreign legations who were represented in Budapest during the trouble. To these it added the testimony of eyewitnesses.

A total of one hundred and eleven witnesses was heard in New York, London, Geneva, Rome, and Vienna, and it was Bang-Jensen's task to dig up such witnesses and interview them. He kept a list of their names and addresses, giving each of them a solemn promise that the list would never fall into the hands of the Hungarian government which might then have taken vengeance upon their families left behind. Probably many swift-thinkers gave fictitious names; certainly Bang-Jensen would not have been able to investigate them, for he had neither time to do so, nor money.

This list was purely unofficial and it remained in Bang-Jensen's possession alone. His secretary might have kept it for him, but she did not because she was already overworked; the committee was operating on a shoestring. It was really his private memo, an unimportant document about whose existence nobody cared for a long time; but when it came to light, he died for it.

One day a witness happened along who, far from wishing to keep his testimony secret, asked for a certificate showing that he had given evidence before the Committee. Hammarskjöld's permission was needed before such a document could be given out. The Secretary-General had no objection to this; but having noted the existence of the list, his orderly mind was offended by its being kept in the coat pocket of an official of the Committee. He thought that it should be deposited instead with the United Nations for safekeeping.

Bang-Jensen refused to hand over the list of witnesses. He said that it might get into the hands of Russians on the 38th

Floor and eventually wend its way to the Hungarians. Besides, he had given his word to the witnesses that they would remain anonymous.

Hammarskjöld could not, of course, admit that a document entrusted to the safekeeping of the United Nations would not remain safe.

At Headquarters Building there is a special section in which all manner of secret and valuable political documents are kept in great muscle-bound safes, penetrable to the eye of God alone. I have seen these safes: I was once called upon to proof-read the translation of a Hungarian document. I saw there a document signed with the hand of the grand master of my childhood, Emperor Francis Joseph I, of Austria-Hungary.

This circumstance draws my sympathies onto the side of Bang-Jensen. If I can read Francis Joseph's secrets even after a half-century, those safes are not absolutely safe. The battle between Hammarskjöld and Bang-Jensen was an heroic one, involving high principles in the classic manner: bureaucratic insubordination, duty, conscience, and the honor of the United Nations. But part of the tension generated by the story is due to the feeling on the part of the appalled onlooker that a little less principle and more common sense on both sides could have solved the problem before the end of Act I.

At the onset of the conflict, Bang-Jensen asked for a private meeting with the Secretary-General; but Hammarskjöld did not grant it. This refusal on the part of a personal friend struck deep at the sensitive Bang-Jensen who bitterly commented, "We could have settled this affair in twenty minutes. But he is not a man, and he does not dare to meet a real man face to face." And he added, "Such men destroy themselves." However, the initial wound had begun to destroy Bang-Jensen.

The advisers of both men offered counsel heavy with common sense. Hammarskjöld was implored not to turn the case into an administrative issue. Bang-Jensen was beseeched to sit down with the Budapest telephone book and make up a list of one hundred and eleven fictitious names. But this is not the stuff sacrificial lambs are made of. Very soon the affair burgeoned into a *cause célèbre* in the Secretariat and even in the press. The two men met in a clinch of "abuse of principle" and neither of them was constructed to compromise on a principle, once they had gotten their teeth into it.

The tedious, wasteful battle went on for more than a year. The Special Committee on Hungary had operated on a shoe-string, but not the battle of Hammarskjöld versus Bang-Jensen. It involved a Joint Disciplinary Committee and a Special Investigating Committee set up by the Secretary-General; and the Administrative Tribunal. Hammarskjöld engaged the assistance of former United States Ambassador Ernest Gross, and Bang-Jensen that of Undersecretary Adolph Berle, Jr.

The Titans wrestled, and the judgment in the end went against Bang-Jensen. But it did not in itself destroy him. Throughout these months he had been busily destroying himself, gradually losing contact with the world of reality, becoming more depressed and hanging onto his list like a mother clutching to her breast the shoes of her dead child. In the Secretariat, the quip was heard, "It was not without reason that Shakespeare made Hamlet a Dane."

Some people have contended that at the bottom of the deadly argument lay personal animosity between the two men, especially on the part of Bang-Jensen who was envious that a fellow Scandinavian, whose career and qualifications were similar to his own, had received the highest post in his diplomatic world. This view is certainly advanced by the virulence of contemporary Danish criticism against Hammarskjöld. I have noticed also, a remarkable photograph taken on the occasion when Hammarskjöld for the first time took his place on the dais in the First Political Committee. The expression on the faces of people around him is generally joyful—except that of Bang-Jensen who looks straight at Hammarskjöld with an unmistakable glare.

But knowing both men, I believe that any puerile emotions, had they been conscious of them, would have terrified them both. I believe that principles were guilty, but that Bang-Jensen proved to be, in the end, not strong enough to support their weight. Throughout the session of the Gross Committee his colleagues noticed his mental deterioration, and they behaved to him with great kindness. They said that "he was not quite himself." He, on the other hand, accused his colleagues of "sabotage of the Hungarian question," and of "dishonest motives."

The Committee concluded that Bang-Jensen's "allegations were largely childish and without foundation." They noted his irrational behavior when he was formally instructed in writing to abstain from attendance at the Special Committee but refused to comply. They found that he "had given assurances to prospective witnesses which were in excess of his authority, or that he had subsequently made a wrong and unjustified interpretation of such assurances, or both . . ."

The Gross Committee, in its final report, advised the Secretary-General that "the continued employment of Mr. Bang-Jensen would be incompatible with the best interests of the United Nations," and that he had "departed markedly from normal and rational standards of behavior . . . he should undergo medical examination."

Bang-Jensen refused to undergo psychiatric examination. He acquiesced, however, to the final disposal of his precious list. It was decided that it should be placed in a sealed envelope and burned by Bang-Jensen personally in the presence of witnesses, including Ed Begley, Chief Security Officer of the United Nations, on the roof of Headquarters Building.

This might have been enough for a more adaptable man. But Bang-Jensen had been shattered by the affair. So far as is known, he left no diary, like that of Hammarskjöld, to explain the progress of his love affair with death. But one day he was found on a park bench, dead, with a bullet-hole through his head, leaving a widow and children.

An explanation was ready-made, satisfactory to all in the years of the cold war: the Russians did it. There are many who still believe that it was a political murder. But the colleagues who worked most closely with him do not believe that the Russians killed Bang-Jensen—in fact, for some time they had lived in fear that Bang-Jensen would one day shoot Hammarskjöld, or failing Hammarskjöld, his chief, Mr. Jordan; or else himself.

He chose to shoot himself. He was a man of immovable honor who had the misfortune to run head on against another man of immovable honor. When it was over, and he had been "relieved of his duties," he had enough strength left to determine not to kill others, but—to use Hammarskjöld's words in another connection—"to die with decency so that at least decency will survive."

Hammarskjöld, like Bang-Jensen, was a tense, irritable, vulnerable man, but there is no evidence that his death wish ever got the better of his instinct for survival. No indication of manner ever made his close collaborators suspect a "death wish" turned pathologically against himself or anyone else. And yet that some self-destructive worm existed in him is indicated by the fact that the word "loneliness" is mentioned in *Markings* at least as often as death. And this is a key, I think, to the understanding of Hammarskjöld.

The term "loneliness" belongs to lyric poetry. In the medical textbooks a sterner term for it is "melancholia." I am not qualified to make a psychological diagnosis of the late Secretary-General; I can only bring to bear upon him what I have observed in the course of my profession about other men. I remind myself of Aristotle's remark that "Men distinguished in philosophy, politics, poetry, or art, appear to be all of melancholy temperament." Perhaps this is too sweeping a statement to survive unchallenged for two thousand years, but it retains a partial validity.

A modern psychologist, Kretschmer, says, "Premature renunciation of the sexual impulse may lead to melancholia." And another, Bleuler, tells us further, "nearly all melancholics have suicidal impulses and would perish if they were not guarded." Bleuler gives some descriptions of symptoms of melancholics that are startling in their revelation of the man who wrote *Markings*. The melancholics, he tells us, "have sinned . . . against the Holy Ghost which can never be forgiven . . . They hear the scaffold erected on which they are to be executed."

Hammarskjöld too saw clearly an arena, a well, a cross; a place of death for himself.

". . . They must be punished usually in a most terrible way," says Bleuler. And Hammarskjöld sees his naked body enduring the stoning, slit up, and the live heart plucked out.

While one cannot equate sane men precisely with the insane, still the demarcation line between them is often very broad and blurred. We find in these remarks of the psychologists a sort of Triboro Bridge between Hammarskjöld's chastity, his loneliness, and his death wish.

But there is a distinction drawn by psychologists between "melancholics," and those who believe themselves to be "persecuted." The melancholic has somehow blessedly deserved his tortures. "Weep, if you can, weep, but do not complain," writes Hammarskjöld. "The way chose you—and you must be thankful." *

Kraepelin observes that the handwriting of melancholics

* *Markings*, p. 213.

"... shows in its pressure curve weak and greatly prolonged movements." * This is certainly true of the handwriting of Hammarskjöld.

Certain varieties of melancholia are observed. One is the *"depressive melancholia"* which retards the physical and mental processes. Another is quite the contrary; in *melancholia agitata activa* the subjects manifest the desire "... to express or get rid of inner tension through movements ... have no feeling of fatigue and run around continuously and when permitted, take tireless walks." Here, the relentless long walks of Hammarskjöld that Bill Ranallo hated and referred to as "forced marches" come to mind. The desire for physical exercise would seize the Secretary-General at the oddest times. One snowbound Christmas morning, Heinz Wieschhoff's telephone rang and he was heard to say, "Yes, Mr. Secretary-General, I'll pick you up right away."

SEASON'S GREETINGS

It was Hammarskjöld, wanting a stroll. Wieschhoff drove in to New York from Bronxville, picked him up at his apartment, and then brought him back to Bronxville where the two men strolled in one foot of snow along the Bronx River Parkway; eventually Hammarskjöld returned Wieschhoff to the bosom of his family soaking wet and half alive.

Hammarskjöld's constant and sometimes debatably neces-

* Bleuler-Brill, *Textbook of Psychiatry.*

sary travels can be ascribed to a latent pattern of *melancholia agitata activa*. Trygve Lie and U Thant together did not travel as many miles during their terms of office as Hammarskjöld in one year. A mere portion of his schedule gives some idea of the pace he maintained. In January, 1956, he went to Egypt and Israel; between January 26 and February 14, he held nine press conferences in Asia and Australia; in April he was in the Gaza Strip, and again in July when fighting broke out there, he returned to the Middle East; and again in November. In the following year, 1957, he made two trips to the Middle East.

Several figures of history who suffered from *melancholia agitata activa* show surprising similarities with Hammarskjöld. The Empress Elizabeth of Austria was a compulsive traveller, and she was addicted to hectic walks in lonely mountain tops. She wrote many poems with death as a recurrent theme. Kierkegaard, to whom Hammarskjöld has rightly been compared, would run about the streets of Copenhagen on his spindle legs, carrying his inseparable umbrella, drawing grins from passers-by. He tried to look indifferent, but his writings confirm the opinion of the psychologist Bleuler, that melancholics suffer the tortures of the damned. "What is to be roasted alive at a slow fire? Or to be broken on the wheel? Or as they do in warm climates, to be smeared with honey and put at the mercy of insects—what is that in comparison with this torture: to be grinned to death?" *

But Kierkegaard, like Hammarskjöld, felt that his torments were in the nature of a reward. They were bestowed upon him for having fought for the truly Christian life.

The great Swedish naturalist, Linnaeus, was another who drowned his melancholy in agitation, and it is interesting to find that he was a particular hero of Hammarskjöld who greatly admired his long wanderings in nature and his having been permitted "to peer into the secret council chamber of

* *Kierkegaard*, ed. Lee M. Hollander, Doubleday Anchor Books, p. 23.

God." In his presidential address delivered before the Swedish Academy in 1957, he chose Linnaeus as his topic and perhaps not inadvertently drew for us an indirect self-portrait:

- Linnaeus' humility did not exclude a strong self-confidence.
- Until melancholy caught up with him, he was saved by his lively eye for those amusing features which are rarely lacking in even the most somber situation.
- The irony which he showed towards pretentious know-alls did not conceal his sense of superiority.
- His "drastic imagination."

His enumeration of Linnaeus' themes is evocative of his own *Markings:* misfortune breeding misfortune; the vanity of mundane aspirations; fatalistic mysticism. And he quotes a poem wherein he says, Linnaeus' brooding finally gives way to the trust of a grown-up child:

> Thou sawest my happiness
> when I was still lying
> in darkness.
> Thou settest my clock,
> Thou cuttest my bread.
> So why, almighy Hero,
> shouldst Thou forget me now?
> My house I have built
> by the Grace of God.
> Therefore, I sleep unafraid.*

In the same way, Hammarskjöld was to find relief in the "sanctuary of God," and he expressed his sense of serenity in his diary by composing prayers of delicacy and tranquil beauty. He quoted the Fourth Psalm: "I will both lay me down in

* Foote, *Dag Hammarskjöld*, p. 155.

peace and sleep, for thou, Lord, only makest me dwell in safety."

It has been said of Hammarskjöld that he gave no indica-tion in his writings of any belief in a life after death. Anyone whose vision of Heaven has been stage-managed by Dante, or even by Swedenborg, will certainly find no such superpro-duction in *Markings*. But in a Scandinavian whose childhood literature must have included tales of those wraiths of Viking warriors who wandered across dreamlike northern wildernesses in search of Valhalla, the last poem in Hammarskjöld's diary would seem to indicate not only a belief in life after death, but in a life before birth also—in fact the pattern of reincarna-tion. He visualizes a gray mountain landscape with a river and a lake which he had visited twice before, and though the light, the weather and the hour had changed, yet he felt that he knew that land and that by and by he would find a familiar path in it.

In June of the year he died, he again suggested a vision of immortality in a lovely poem about a ship trembling on the horizon's edge in the slanting sunrays, and he says that for a fleet moment he glimpsed the sail of that vessel. Sailing ships have been bearing away the souls of northerly heroes for a long time, not to oblivion, but to the Blessed Isles. A spectral model of such a ship, wrought by the artist Cronbach, was placed by Hammarskjöld upon the north wall of the Meditation Room foyer. Although its proper title is *Ship*, Hammarskjöld always referred to the sculpture as *Viking Ship*, and I hardly think it is a mere decoration, but a Norseman's symbol of infinite continuance.

Anyone who will ever write about Hammarskjöld will dig deep into *Markings*, which is an astounding self-analysis and by no means a banal or naive one; the Secretary-General was precisely aware of the minute workings of many levels of his personality. It is erroneous to suppose that this spiritual diary has no relation to political events; the entries do not record

the result of the voting in the Security Council, yet they report accurately the complex moods of a complex man in the
hours of victory, doubt, disgust, pain, and defeat.

Most curious is the fact that the publication of *Markings*
after his death annulled the two correlated sorrows of his life:
his lack of communication with others and his loneliness. The
diary has touched others on the deep center of being which is
common to all; the liberated spirit has become the companion
of thousands.

In contemplating the lean idealists to whom Hammarskjöld may be endlessly compared in physique, temperament,
behavior, and even eccentricities, it is astonishing to see how
many of them do not simply die, but offer themselves as sacrificial victims on the altar of passionately held principle. If
there is a death wish, after all, then death is a wish fulfillment;
and the Thin Man approaches the threshold of eternity like
a homing pigeon, never swerving from the taut line of magnetic force that draws him there. Gandhi exposed himself to
death all his life long. As a boy he attempted suicide by swal-
lowing poisonous seeds. When he was twenty-seven he faced
a lynch mob singing "Hang old Gandhi on the sour apple
tree." He was attacked with knife and bomb, and the railroad
tracks were dragged out from under his train. Not content
with this, he courted death by fasting time and again. It was
only by a miracle that he lived to be seventy-nine before his
wish was granted him at the hand of a Hindu fanatic.

Nehru too accepted death as his companion of the road.
Woodrow Wilson, fragile in body, tender in feeling and stubborn by nature, shattered his health while crusading for his
cause. Madame Curie, brittle, sensitive and unbending, died
a martyr's death, exposing herself in her research to radiation.
Empress Elizabeth, stubbornly refusing the royal encumbrance
of bodyguards, was assassinated by an anarchist. Lawrence of
Arabia to whom Hammarskjöld is often compared, superior,
humble, and lonely, relentlessly wooed death in Arabia and

finally found it in a motorcycle accident. Trotsky, slender and
wiry, a fiery crusader and brilliant polemist was more than
once offered reconciliation by Stalin, but he preferred to live
in exile in Mexico, where he submissively waited for someone
to murder him for principle's sake, with a pickaxe.

In fact, one has only to visit a museum and look at the portraits of martyrs to find the pinched midface, the narrow chest,
and the upward turned glance, very much the aspect of the
photograph by Yussuf Karsh which Hammarskjöld chose to
be his official United Nations portrait.

When bouncy Trygve Lie was declared nonexistent by the
Russians, he simply put on his hat and bounced out of the
way. Hammarskjöld held fast to the Siege Perilous, like Martin
Luther before the Diet of Worms: "I cannot do otherwise.
God help me. Amen."

As for Patrice Lumumba, he was a lean idealist, too, and
the guest of honor at Hammarskjöld's party.

12

We're About a Tragic Business

I T WAS indeed an ironic tragedy that among the many false
prophets of anticolonialism, Hammarskjöld, who energet-
ically and idealistically had worked for Africa would have
fallen victim to Africa.

The Charter has committed the United Nations to the
furtherance of independence of colonial peoples and the Secretary-General had adopted this as a personal crusade. But his
devotion had deeper roots than mere duty; it was rooted in
the belief he inherited from scholars and clergymen on his
mother's side that "in the very radical sense of the Gospels,
all men are equals as children of God, and should be met and
treated by us as our masters."

As a boy he had greatly admired Albert Schweitzer, whose
"reverence for life" and service to humanity had inspired him.

The Secretary-General therefore had a ready-made vision
of an "African Renaissance" which he expressed in a lecture
before the University Institute of Somalia in January of 1960.
He told Africans, "You can create, and I know you will create,
the African personality as part of the picture of mankind
today."

His adviser in Africa affairs, Dr. Heinz Wieschhoff, had
begun work in the Secretariat in the Trusteeship Division and

was later a high official for Political and Security Council Affairs. Hammarskjöld came to refer to him as "my grey eminence," and together they travelled extensively in Africa where former colonies and trust territories were graduating into new nations.

It was predictable that the transfer of power from rulers to subjects would not always take place decorously and that the black continent might well open up with vacuums large enough to suck the whole world in. The Secretary-General therefore pledged plans on behalf of the new countries: vacuums were to be filled by a "UN Presence" consisting of economic and technical advisers, so long as they were needed, to ensure political stability and continuance of economy.

Nowhere was such personnel more direly needed than in the Congo, a comparative giant among the new nations, and one of the richest regions of the earth, in minerals. Hammarskjöld's special representative in the Congo, Rajeshwar Dayal of India, described the situation thus:

"It would be an understatement to say that no country was less prepared than the Congo to shoulder the responsibilities which came with independence. There were just eleven university graduates, not one Congolese doctor, judge or magistrate, not one trained administrator, customs or financial official, not a single engineer or senior technician, and there was just one lawyer. It takes, however, at least two lawyers to argue a case—but there were no courts which could try criminals..."

Mr. Thomas Kanza, Congolese representative in the Security Council offered a possible explanation of this state of affairs: "Only eight years ago I was the first to leave Congolese territory to go through higher education, and I think you will understand that it was not an easy thing to do then. If I were to write my memoirs, it would not be to praise the Belgians who did not allow us to have a horizon wide enough for us to be able to learn and to study outside the country.

We had to manage somehow, and therefore the Congo today lacks technical assistance, it lacks military officials, it lacks doctors ... I admit that it may be in part the fault of the Congolese, but let us also admit that it is also partly the fault of the Belgians."

When due sympathy has been accorded to the Congolese leaders for disadvantages beyond their control, it must be said that in their hands the Congo situation became a morbid caricature of contemporary diplomacy in action. They wore ribbons and bibbons across their chests, pinned stars and moons to their ribs; they bestowed upon themselves high-sounding titles, gave receptions and bowed and bobbed, "presented their compliments" and had "the honor to refer"; but when it was expedient, their lies were barefaced and their murder was barehanded.

All of their antics were manipulated from behind the scenes by white statesmen of various ideologies who, when they wish to abjure their given word, usually get a spokesman of the foreign office to do it for them; and when they wish to commit murder are accustomed to dividing the responsibility prudently with appropriate government agencies with initials. In other words, they respect diplomatic proprieties in such a way that kid gloves remain clean, and the seamy side of their profession remains invisible.

But Congolese diplomacy was uncouth and it smelled of garlic. It was as candid and menacing as a Mousterian flint implement found amid strewn bones under the cellar of a gilded chancellery.

"It would be a tantalizing subject for a musical comedy writer with a sense of satire," said Dag Hammarskjöld, "if only it were not so tragic."

Mistrusting diplomacy as I do, I too could laugh at the Congo situation in better spirits, if only Hammarskjöld, Wieschhoff and the others had not died of it.

Independence Day in the Congo was June 30, 1960. The

Belgians withdrew abruptly leaving, as a slim prop for the maintenance of order, Belgian officers in command of the Force Publique. But within days of independence, the Congolese had mutinied against these officers. They seized the telephone exchange, the radio station, the airport; they drove Europeans off the street at gunpoint, spitting on them and kicking them; they ransacked hotels, dragged guests from their beds, and they imprisoned in his hotel room Dr. Ralph Bunche who was in Leopoldville for the precise purpose of working out plans with the government for United Nations technical assistance to help the new country towards orderly existence.

Hammarskjöld learned of the Congolese mutiny in Geneva where he had been attending the meetings of ECOSOC, and he left for New York at once. He said—with alarmingly swift perception—"I must do this. God knows where it will lead this Organization and where it will lead me."

Meanwhile, the Belgians were again back in charge in the Congo. Without asking permission of the new government at Leopoldville, they flew in paratroopers, ostensibly to protect the lives and property of Europeans, but also to reestablish a Belgian presence. Their stake in the Congo was enormous, and it is represented by the Union Minière du Haut-Katanga, an enterprise of fabulous wealth which mines the province of Katanga for copper, uranium, cobalt, and other minerals. The company is owned by Belgian, French, and British interests, and it squats in the political center of the tale like a lump of gold around which civilized men dance as ferociously as cannibals around their dinner. A Belgian close to the Congo affair has the opinion that money-diplomacy was mainly responsible for the tragic development of events there. "Belgium's policy was led by businessmen," he said, "and they led it disastrously. They gave independence to the Congolese knowing well that they were unprepared to run their affairs and hoping to continue to run them—cheaper."

The reappearance of the Belgians in their land was vigorously protested by the Congolese government as a violation of its sovereignty; and it was joined by a chorus of newly-independent African nations who felt that if this sort of thing were countenanced there was no telling whose former colonial masters might come dropping out of the skies. To their dismay they were opposed by one of their own kind: Moise Tshombe, political leader of the Katanga province and a Belgian puppet. Not only did he promptly declare Katanga's independence from the rest of the Congo, but he asked for more Belgian troops. He said, "Belgian troops must stay in Katanga, otherwise we will have the anarchy and chaos which is happening in the rest of the Congo Republic."

The following day, rotund Congolese President Joseph Kasavubu and his weedy young premier, Patrice Lumumba, appealed to Dag Hammarskjöld for United Nations military assistance in evicting the returned Belgians and in getting Katanga back into the fold.

Hammarskjöld meanwhile, acting upon the authority granted him by the perilous Article 99, had convened the Security Council and he asked the members to consider what was to be done "with the utmost speed." The eleven gentlemen debated throughout the night of July 13/14; by morning they were carrying their diplomatic pouches under their eyes. At dawn, Mongi Slim of Tunisia pushed through a resolution that called upon "the government of Belgium to withdraw their troops from the Republic of the Congo."

The rest was left to Dag. He was to provide the government of the Republic of the Congo with such military assistance as might be necessary to maintain order. Within three days a United Nations force was assembled and entitled ONUC (Organization des Nations Unies: Congo). It was made up largely of Afro-Asian troops with some from Sweden and Ireland.

On the same day that the Security Council voted military

assistance to the Congo, President Kasavubu and Premier Lumumba appealed for aid also to Moscow. Nikita Khrushchev proved to be a friend in need and in deed. He promised them any assistance over and above that of the United Nations. As a first installment he flew in a shipment of food. Sitting on the sacks of wheat, presumably as a nutrition expert, was "the Soviet's top political adviser on Africa." A Russian presence was now established in the Congo.

One of the main handicaps with which the United Nations contends is that it is something new in the world; even educated populations have an imperfect knowledge of its powers and limitations, indeed about its very nature. The Congolese officials were from beginning to end utterly in error about what the United Nations was doing in the Congo. "The feeling in Leopoldville in July, 1960," said Dr. Ralph Bunche, "seemed to be . . . that the United Nations personnel, military and civilian alike, would be constantly at the bidding of the Congolese government officials, even at times to serve the most petty personal aims. As Mr. Lumumba bluntly stated in his letter . . . to Mr. Hammarskjöld, the Security Council '. . . is to place all its resources at the disposal of my government.'"

In fact, the mandate of the ONUC specified that they should not "be a party to or in any way intervene in or be used to influence the outcome of any internal conflict, constitutional or otherwise." If it came to a clash between the Central Government and the Katanga rebels, the United Nations troops were to stand by and let them fight it out. They were to use their weapons only in self-defense.

ONUC was there to assist and advise the Congo government and to replace the Belgian troops that had returned to the Congo in order to protect lives and property. The trouble was that the real purpose of the Belgians was to protect their interests in the Union Minière, and they had no real intention of allowing themselves to be replaced by ONUC. Unaccountable delays prevented them from effecting the withdrawal and whatever time they gained was used to send more and more troops into Katanga province.

Moise Tshombe warned that any attempt of ONUC to enter Katanga would be met by force.

On July 24, 1960, Patrice Lumumba arrived at New York airport to "establish direct contact with the Secretary-General in order to find a speedy solution to the problems facing our country." Because the Congo Republic was not a member of the organization, United Nations protocol was not at the airport to greet him: only Mr. Quaison-Sackey of Ghana was present in a checkered African toga, and of course the New York police, with revolvers at their side and with bullets, handcuffs, writing pads and ball point pens stuck into their leather belts, who flanked him left and right as if he were being arrested. Hammarskjöld was annoyed by this lack of *politesse* towards Lumumba. He was by no means out of sympathy at first with the young man who had been hand-picked by destiny to play such a pivotal role in his own destruction. Perhaps he felt drawn to the youthfulness of Lumumba and to his idealism. The African sincerely wished to serve the Congolese future and he was personally disinterested. Dr. Bunche judged him to be "not greatly concerned with ideology." He wanted an end to tribalism, and he desired a unified, stable country.

But there was to be no "direct contact" between these men. Although they conferred for two days, no dialogue whatsoever developed between them. They spoke in separate monologues which took place on different levels like a multi-layered chess game. Lumumba wanted Hammarskjöld's imprint on his own political aims, with ONUC forces placed at his disposal. To this Hammarskjöld could not agree—although he promised Lumumba far-reaching technical assistance for his country. The meetings ended without love or animosity; in truth the two had never really met. In their lack of rapport lay the seeds of tragedy for both of them.

A remark attributed to H. E. Timberlake, United States ambassador to the Congo was that "if Lumumba had walked into a gathering of Congolese politicians as a waiter with a tray on his head, he would have come out as Prime Minister." He was forceful, glib, and quick-minded, a born demagogue. But he was not astute. He played politics "by ear" with spears and tommyguns, tom-toms and radio, and he accepted aid from whence it came, impatiently and reckless of consequences, which in fact he probably did not perceive, for he was completely inexperienced. His inexperience compounded his basic instability.

I was in sympathy with Lumumba's political viewpoint, but nothing will induce me to set political sympathies higher than my judgment of a man's face and physique. I saw and drew Lumumba when he appeared, all arms and legs like a jumping spider, at a press conference at Headquarters Building, and I wrote of him for my papers:

> Lumumba has a childish midface in an adult framework. It advertises an extraordinary contrast of force and fragility. No amount of technical assistance can help such underdeveloped faces!
>
> "He is half-baked: inside soft and outside tough. Nothing is more dangerous than power in the hands of a strong weakling. Paranoid explosions will alternate with sudden reversals and indecisions ... Balanced diplomatic procedure will have a hard time keeping in step with such a catch-as-catch-can personality.
>
> Adolescent pathos, idealism, defiance of authority, and a tendency to flirt with self-destruction lies in Lumumba. If I were Lloyds of London, I would not insure his political future.

After his talks with Lumumba, Hammarskjöld flew to Leopoldville in the Congo; Lumumba went on to Washington where he asked for hard cash. The United States had the problem of aiding the Congo, while in no wise offending NATO ally, Belgium, and so Lumumba was told that while assistance would be forthcoming, it would have to be channelled through the United Nations.

From Washington Lumumba flew to Montreal, Canada, and in his hotel room he witnessed a miracle: French-speaking television. In Ottawa he conferred with Prime Minister Diefenbaker who told him that Canada was eager to assist the Congo with food, agricultural machinery, and pharmaceutical products; he need only state which should come first. Lumumba said that television should come first.

Mr. Diefenbaker also told him that all assistance, including television, must be directed through the United Nations.

In Ottawa, Lumumba received a visit from the Soviet ambassador. What they talked about is not known. But he apparently was persuaded that he could reach his political aims quicker with the support of the Soviet government than with the United Nations, because from that time forth he was a changed man. Passing through New York on his way home, he gave a farewell press conference in which he dropped a hint that the Congo would henceforward place its principal reliance on individual countries to provide experts for long-range development. This was an unpleasant surprise, not only for Hammarskjöld, but for Eisenhower and Diefenbaker.

Barely a month had gone by since independence, and already Lumumba, with childish irresponsibility, had widened the Congo vacuum sufficiently to contain a cold war.

On his way back to the Congo, he called on President Bourguiba of Tunisia who sadly noted that Lumumba had "shifted his rifle from one shoulder to the other and became an enemy of the United Nations. Henceforth nothing but words of invective and insult for Mr. Hammarskjöld fell from his lips."

He wrote nevertheless politely enough to the Security Council that "the people and the Republic of the Congo extend a warm welcome to the United Nations troops and to Mr. Hammarskjöld." At the same time he complained that although

ONUC had been in the Congo since July 16—more than two weeks—"not a single Belgian soldier had left Congolese soil." By a strange coincidence, the day Lumumba wrote this letter, *Pravda* accused Hammarskjöld of acting in the Congo on behalf of the United States and other NATO colonial powers.

ONUC was indeed failing in its aim of replacing Belgian troops and this was because of the intransigence of Mr. Tshombe. On August 5, Ralph Bunche flew to Katanga to negotiate with the Katangan leader and arrange for the entry of ONUC into the province. Tshombe assured him that United Nations troops would be received by bullets, and he emphasized this by having Dr. Bunche eased back into his plane with bayonets digging into the small of his back.

Tshombe had at this time no army, but he was busily building a "gendarmerie commanded by Belgian officers, and by other white mercenaries imported from abroad." But, resistance to ONUC would have been made up mainly of civilians. Hammarskjöld had 3,500 ONUC troops in Leopoldville, but he decided, on the advice of Bunche, to avoid bloodshed and not to shoot his way into Katanga.

Lumumba now raised a terrible outcry against the Secretary-General for his failure to move against the recalcitrant province and he was joined by Ghana, Guinea, and the United Arab Republic, who promised that at the drop of a hat they would move in themselves; and by the Soviet Union. All of these nations cried with one voice that Hammarskjöld had capitulated to the pressure of the Belgian, British, and French shareholders of Union Minière.

These events were a fateful roadmark in the life of Hammarskjöld, though we do not find that he noted them on any page. But he defended his decisions in a confrontation with Soviet Deputy Foreign Minister Vasily Kuznetsov: "I do not believe that we help the Congolese people by actions in which Africans kill Africans or Congolese kill Congolese, and that will remain my guiding principle for the future."

Before the Council he blamed the Belgians for their dalliance in the Congo, and the Congolese for their impatience. After another all-night session had taken place, the Council again called on Belgium to withdraw troops, and upon Tshombe to admit ONUC. Once again it was affirmed that the United Nations soldiers were to use force in self-defense only and that they were not to be used to "influence the outcome of any internal conflict, constitutional or otherwise."

Tshombe is a man with the backbone of an eel, especially when he is being advised by Belgians. He at once complied with the resolution: United Nations troops would be permitted to enter Katanga, though on one condition: "that they 'should not' interfere with the operations of the Katanga police ... the arms now in the hands of the Katanga army must remain under the control of the Katanga authorities."

On August 12, 1960, Dag Hammarskjöld, in what he called a "breakthrough" of the Congo deadlock, flew to Elizabethville, the capital of Katanga, in a white Convair. Following him were seven transports containing 240 Swedish troops under his direct command. At Elizabethville the Convair was given permission to land but warned that the planes carrying troops must be turned away. Back came the response from the Secretary-General's plane: unless all land, nobody would land. Tshombe then gave permission for all the planes to land and soon he was shaking hands with Hammarskjöld on the tarmac. A guard of honor was drawn up to receive the Secretary-General, which he then politely reviewed.

Once again the Secretary-General had scored a spectacular triumph and it brought him accolade from the world press. James Reston in *The New York Times* called Hammarskjöld "one of the great natural resources in the world today." The Japanese saw him as the "bridge between the reality of the world situation and the ideal of world peace." Yet it is doubtful if Hammarskjöld was much cheered by all this praise. In Elizabethville he and his troops had been greeted by a mixed crowd of Belgians and Africans with the cry of "Down with the United Nations!"

Although Hammarskjöld's purpose in meeting Tshombe was to bring about a rapprochement between Katanga and the Central Government, his visit to Tshombe enraged Lumumba, especially that he had not ignored Tshombe's honor guard. In three bitter letters to Hammarskjöld he reproached the Secretary-General for not having cleared the visit with him—in fact, Hammarskjöld had cleared it with Lumumba's vice premier, Antoine Gizenga. He accused Hammarskjöld of "unilateral and erroneous interpretation of the Security Council resolution" and said that the government and people of the Congo had lost their confidence in the Secretary-General.

He still did not appear to understand why the United Nations troops had not been put at the disposal of his government with which to fight a civil war.

The sympathies of the Soviets toward Lumumba were now thoroughly aroused: they began to talk ominously about "genuine volunteers" from other African countries and from "countries situated in other continents who were loyal friends of the Congo's independence," who were itching to enter the Congo and throw everybody else out. Lest these public-spirited citizens should find themselves at a disadvantage, Russia sent to Lumumba 100 military trucks, 29 Ilyushin transport planes, and 200 technicians.

Lumumba did not wish all this technical assistance to go to waste. He was speaking eloquently over the radio, inciting his supporters to rise up and fight. Before long his armed forces in the northern provinces fell upon the Baluba tribe and massacred them in an operation the Secretary-General afterwards described as nothing short of genocide.

In order to halt the entry of Russian arms and Lumumba's eloquence, Andrew Cordier in Leopoldville closed the major airports of the Congo to all but United Nations traffic, and ordered the radio station seized. This action by an American was decried by the Russians who now saw Hammarskjöld revealed clearly as a NATO lackey.

Meanwhile Hammarskjöld, in New York, about to face the firing squad of the 15th General Assembly, was receiving from his personal representative in the Congo, Ambassador Dayal, "progress reports," if such they can be called, about a rapidly backsliding situation. On September 5, a series of events were set in motion such as a satirist would hardly dare to invent. On that day, President Kasavubu, alarmed at the unbalanced behavior of his prime minister and at the sudden prominence of Russia in the affairs of the Congo, fired Lumumba. Lumumba promptly turned around and fired the president. The Chamber of Deputies met, and, deploring the attitudes of both the president and prime minister in firing each other in this way, annulled both dismissals. The Senate however convened, and rebuffing Kasavubu, voted full powers to Lumumba.

Thereafter, Kasavubu fired both the Senate and the Chamber of Deputies, saying that as president, his decisions did not require parliamentary approval. He designated former President of the Senate, Joseph Ileo, as his new premier.

There now sprang fully armed into the Congo fray a former sergeant in the Congolese medical corps, Colonel Joseph Mobutu, Kasavubu's chief of staff. For a time he looked to be a beneficent "strong man" of the Congo. He announced that the army would temporarily take over the ruins of government. "This is not a *coup d'état*," he said. He merely wished to superimpose military order on chaos and to "neutralize political personalities." He arrested Lumumba, but later released him.

Mobutu ordered the Soviet, Czech, and "other socialist" embassies and their technicians out of the Congo, and he personally saw them off. Like Alexander the Great, he provided himself with Companions; these were a group of young university students, and Mobutu caused them to be appointed, by presidential ordinance, a "College of Commissioners." He made it clear that they would not act as ministers, nor as substitutes for popularly elected representatives, but *only as technicians.*

He was only twenty-nine years old, and his friends were even younger. They were if anything even more pitifully inadequate than most university students would be if they were suddenly called upon to rule a country. The correspondents on the spot contemptuously referred to their press conferences as "The Children's Hour."

Their presence certainly did not prevent Mr. Lumumba from forming his own rival government which the Russians promptly recognized as the legal one. He felt strong in the Lord by reason of Soviet support and that of some Afro-Asian countries of strong anticolonial persuasion. At the same time, Tshombe was being touted by Belgian, British and French interests as the possible "last bulwark against Communism in Africa."

The United Nations was having a terrible time with these quick changes; it could only "continue its policy of dealing in routine matters with whatever authority it finds in the ministerial chairs." Ambassador Dayal's report to Hammarskjöld gives a vivid notion of the singular difficulties the United Nations was facing: ". . . Each contestant for power has continually attempted to enlist United Nations support to enforce his own particular or factional political solution. The inevitable result has been that almost every significant measure taken by ONUC, in the impartial fulfillment of its mandate, has been interpreted by one faction or another as being directed against itself by the United Nations . . . Indeed, even a decision by ONUC to refrain from a particular measure, in order to preserve its neutrality, has often been interpreted as an act of political collusion . . .

"In the heat of political passion, the same party which has condemned ONUC for 'interference in domestic affairs,' not infrequently calls upon it to intervene against the actions of a rival."

The Congo situation was now this: what had started out as an assistance program to a new country in distress, had wound up as a cold war intrigue. The United States and the USSR had above all to keep each other out of the Congo. Belgium, France, and Britain, determined to cling to the Union Minière, were paying lip service to the United Nations while financing Tshombe to defy the World Organization. Africans, generally, wanted to give Africa back to the Africans, and therefore deplored every concession to Tshombe. Mao watched from a distance, wishing he could give Africa to the Chinese.

Burly Nigerian Foreign Minister, Jaja Wachuku, said rightly: "There are too many fingers in the Congolese pie."

Much later, Ambassador Dayal was to look back upon the events of the summer of 1960, and say: "The Congo was like a ship adrift on mid-ocean, tossing about on the uneasy waters, abandoned by its crew, and full of panicky passengers." Dr. Bunche described the United Nations' dilemma: having "virtually the entire responsibility of holding things together in the Congo, while not trespassing on the authority of the government, when governmental machinery was just about non-existent."

It sounds rather like trying to catch at midnight in a tunnel a black cat that wasn't there.

On September 9, Dag Hammarskjöld made a crucial statement before the Security Council in which he expressed his opinion, that according to the Congo constitution Kasavubu had a legal right to dismiss Premier Lumumba from his cabinet.

He could not foresee the bloody consequences to Lumumba

or himself; but in this way he played his part in throwing Lumumba to the wolves, and to this day there are many who do not forget it.

There now descended upon New York from the East a shining knight, Nikita Khrushchev, and it was his purpose to rescue the giant damsel Africa from her captivity to the capitalist-monopolists, and slay the dragon, Hammarskjöld.

13

Tooth, Fang, and Whiskers

THE greatest asset of a diplomat is flair—or what the Germans call *Fingerspitzengefühl*. Some of us call it hunch. The diplomatic wizard is one who can coordinate his hunches with political reality.

Hunch is the secret weapon of the political analyst who senses the invisible hyphens that lurk between ideas and events. He can sometimes draw far-reaching conclusions from apparent trifles, such as who stands next to whom—or who is missing —on the Kremlin wall, watching the May Day parade.

A caricaturist's hunch dwells in a face. Like a haruspex who divines the future from the entrails of sacrificial animals, I scrutinize the faces of each newcomer on the political scene, for whatever fatal vision is to be read there. The Soviets are particularly transparent. When they send to Washington such an ambassador as "Smiling Mike" Menshikov, it is possible to predict with confidence a warm breath in the cold war; but when they aim at us a dour individual, trouble is bound to come of it.

During the great days of Hammarskjöld's reign at the United Nations, the Russian delegate was the self-effacing, mild-mannered, faintly-smiling Vasily Kuznetsov, whose relationship with Hammarskjöld, in spite of the Congo troubles, was cordial. Shortly before the opening of the 15th General Assembly, he was whisked away, and replaced by Valerian Zorin, a man with a formidable lantern jaw, like a pike. He had a sharp nose and a sardonic grin, and he spoke with the screeching voice of a frustrated witch. His reputation was sinister. It was said that he had engineered the Czechoslovak *coup d'état.* True or not, one look at this man is enough to suggest that he is not sent anywhere to be agreeable.

A Special Emergency Session of the General Assembly was convened on September 17, and Zorin made his debut with a sizzling attack on Hammarskjöld. He said his conduct of the Congo operation was a failure; that indeed, he had obviously acted in connivance with the NATO colonizers. He placed before the Assembly a resolution that noted the failure "of the Secretary-General and the United Nations Command to implement a number of very important . . . resolutions."

On the following day, Hammarskjöld replied: "The representative of the Soviet Union used strong language which, quite frankly, I do not know how to interpret. The General Assembly knows me well enough to realize that I would not wish to serve one day beyond the point at which such continued service would be . . . in the interest of the Organization."

This statement marks the beginning of his agony. Two days later was the formal opening of the Assembly at which it became clear that the lethal Zorin was only a straight-man for Nikita Khrushchev.

This 15th General Assembly in the fall of 1960 brought together the most menacing gathering of tooth, fang, and claw since Noah's Ark. Ten heads of state, eleven prime ministers, twenty-eight foreign ministers and four other cabinet ministers participated in the general debate. Nkrumah of Ghana came wearing an orange-red-green checked Africa-for-the-Africans toga, and he was the leader and chief spokesman of the leftish-leaning Africans. Panther-eyed Nasser was the lodestar of the Arab states, and Khrushchev stood at the helm of a boatload of Warsaw Pact cronies. Fidel Castro led a phalanx of *barbudos*.

With the Headquarters Building teeming with live targets —and not for caricaturists alone—Hammarskjöld personally took charge of security arrangements in and around the UN Building. A couple of days before the opening, he called a sudden meeting of high Security brass in his office on the 38th Floor. It was a Sunday, sultry with summer's leavetaking, and some of them had to be pulled out of the Atlantic Ocean wringing wet. John Cosgrove, straight from the beach, felt embarrassed by his slacks and open shirt, but Hammarskjöld reassured him: "We're all in the same family." He told the meeting, "Security will be of prime importance, above everything else," and he set to work with Col. Alfred Katzin and Ed Begley to map out a strategic program which would ensure the safety of delegates, even those who came with daggers hidden under their cloaks destined for his own breast.

The night before the opening, the Headquarters Building suffered an invasion of sixty Cuban *barbudos* dressed for KP duty and followed by a platoon of twittering blondes, brunettes and redheads. They were led by Fidel Castro and they all rushed upon the elevators, intending to take the Secretary-General's office by storm. The guards closed around them and lured them, with the promise of drinks, into Conference Room 8—the same room where once Hammarskjöld was designated as Secretary-General. Great was the disenchantment of the bearded gentlemen when they found the table set with nothing but dead microphones.

A delegation of ten men was then chosen to go with Castro to the 38th Floor to see Mr. Hammarskjöld. The Secretary-General, however, who was being informed of the proceedings by telephone, sent word that he would receive no more than three. In the end, Fidel went with two companions to the Secretary-General's office where the source of the trouble was at last revealed.

It seemed that the Cubans had been insulted by their hotel, the Shelburne, where the management, upon noting that their distinguished guests were burning cigar-holes in the carpets, pouring rum into the telephone receivers, and plucking chickens in the bathrooms, demanded a bond of $10,000 against damage. Outraged, Castro had led his cohorts from the inhospitable premises of the Shelburne Hotel, and he now demanded that sofas be made available for his sixty men and an appropriate number of ladies in the delegates' lounge. But to be fair, Castro is not an inconsiderate man. Since the night was warm, he offered, if necessary, to sleep in the rose garden.

With private visions of his careful security schemes laid waste, the Secretary-General made a gesture of brotherhood: he invited the Cubans and their ladies to have dinner in the delegates' dining room. But they did not want to eat: they wanted to drink. The party was therefore piloted out of Conference Room 8 and into the bar of the South Lounge. There —since ill winds really do blow somebody good—the bartender placed before them certain bottles of rum and Mexican beer which in all the years since the bar opened, he had been unable to sell. The Cubans apparently had no use for bottle-openers and corkscrews. They simply hit a bottle against the edge of the bar, broke off its neck, and at great risk to their whiskers, drank from the broken bottles. By this time these celebrations were being enjoyed by quite a number of eye-witnesses. They reported that every time Castro went to the men's room, all sixty Cubans went off with him in a flying wedge.

In the meantime, Hammarskjöld had succeeded in securing free room and board for the entire Cuban delegation at the nearby Hotel Commodore. But Castro refused it. His own envoys had already started negotiations with the Hotel Theresa, the Waldorf-Astoria of Harlem, at 125th Street and Seventh Avenue. The Secretary-General had no objection to this, so long as they stayed put while the police checked the hotel for security. Much later that night, the delegation, with oscillating steps, moved into the Hotel Theresa where Castro made a proclamation: "We are all brothers here! I feel as if I am in Cuba!"

He thus turned the foolish episode into a species of victory for Human Rights. For his merits, Khrushchev paid him a visit at the Hotel Theresa and rewarded him with a resounding kiss.

On September 20, the Assembly opened. Ah, that microphone on the rostrum, what a magnet it is for men of power! It is like a light that attracts the night moths and also the birds of prey that feed on them.

Kwame Nkrumah mounted the rostrum dressed in rainbow hues and swishing that symbol of the white man's burden, a ceremonial swagger stick. As he carefully deposited this aggressive instrument upon the awesome altar, I recollected the time Marshal Pilsudski, Dictator of Poland, brought his sword with him to the League of Nations. In a voice like the sound of ack-ack, Nkrumah praised Hammarskjöld's work on behalf of African nations, but he nevertheless made it clear that he supported Lumumba, his "brother."

Sukarno of Indonesia had thought it was necessary to have nine full-fledged colonels standing behind him while he delivered his speech. United Nations protocol had some trouble dissuading him from his display of martial prowess. First they talked him down to six, then to three, and finally dwindled him to one solitary lieutenant colonel, Mohamed Sabur, whose honor it was to stand at attention behind his master on the rostrum. Sukarno was in uniform with his chest covered with self-inflicted decorations, and he read his speech in a grating rattle. As he finished each page, he handed it back to his braided moustached minion who immediately tucked it into a leather portfolio.

When Sukarno finished speaking he bowed to the Assembly

President Boland, and, followed by Lieutenant Colonel Sabur who clutched the precious speech under his arm, he walked down the aisle towards his seat, stopping to shake hands left and right with his admirers whom he favored with a bear-trap grin.

The young King Hussein of Jordan also saw fit to keep a giant warrior with a towel on his head towering over him, but he mustered the strength at least to carry his own pages, though he was a king.

Gamal Abdel Nasser, his green eyes fixed like cat's-eye marbles in a bowl of iodine, complained in a high-pitched voice and with false humility how misjudged his most innocent actions generally were.

I do not know what sort of world leader alarms me more, those who advertise so naïvely and unconsciously their delight in power, or those who take unfair advantage of it. Castro spoke before the Assembly for no less than four and a half hours. He was dressed in an open-necked fatigue uniform, and he turned his oily eyes to heaven like a saint standing in boiling oil. His black beard contrasted with his waxy complexion.

Delicate Nehru spoke, his eternal red rose glowing against his brown achkan; he leaned tiredly over the rostrum, occasionally sweeping his brow with a limp caress, and his elegant speech outhesitated the most hesitant Englishman. Quoting the Buddha, he informed the Assembly that there is no victory unless all men are victorious, and he submitted a resolution in the name of the "noncommitted," such as Nasser, Tito, Nkrumah, Sukarno, and himself, asking the great powers to meet at the summit. But when the Assembly had finished with this resolution, it was so crippled with amendments that Nehru withdrew it, because he said it was "reduced to absurdity."

The British Prime Minister, Macmillan, a Scotsman who has the air of a perfect stage-Englishman, spoke in a voice like a boo in a bucket. He chastised the colonialist-baiting Khru-

shchev. "Where are the former British colonies?" he cried.
"They are here, and here, and here!" And he pointed to the
seats of the Indian, Pakistani and African delegations. "Why
don't you give freedom to East Germany?" he wanted to know.
In reply, Khrushchev, with the glee of a naughty boy, pounded
upon his table.

There is no doubt that the efforts of all these gentlemen
to shine before the Assembly paled beside those of Nikita
Khrushchev.

The passing of Khrushchev has been a loss to caricaturists,
and I mourn his downfall. But I must admit that the descrip-
tive terms hurled at him by his colleagues when they deposed
him were all in evidence at the 15th General Assembly: he
really was "bragging and immature," a "schemer" and a
"phrasemonger." I do take exception though, to their calling
him "hare-brained." He was not that at all.

He made of his seat a rival rostrum from which he heckled
every speaker, banging away at his table with his little fist.
Poor Punchinello-faced Gromyko was obliged to follow suit,
although he did not appear to bang with much conviction.
Not long before, Khrushchev had said of him, "If I tell my
foreign minister to sit on a block of ice and stay there for
months, he will do it without back talk." No doubt Gromyko
considered that a few bangs on his table were still easier than
sitting on ice in Outer Mongolia.

Certainly Comrade Khrushchev made signal contributions
to diplomatic technique in 1960; but historians will have to
wrangle about whether he is to be credited with his famous
shoe maneuver. No film, no still photo, and no kinescope
recording exists to show Khrushchev in the act of taking off
his shoe and banging the table with it. Houlbreque, the ever-
reliable film cameramen of the United Nations, assures me
that while he saw the shoe on Khrushchev's desk, he did not
actually see him banging with it. Gossips state that a record-

ing did exist of the incident and that the United Nations discreetly destroyed it along with other compromising visual documents.

Some weeks later, when Khrushchev returned home to the Soviet Union, he was to explain his ebullient behavior carefully in a speech to the Moscow workers: "It is for the Soviet people to judge how the Soviet delegation fulfilled its mission in the General Assembly. We tried to represent the interests of the Soviet Union with honor and dignity."

Lest they should believe that his actions had been at all unusual, he related with disapproval the shocking case history of Mr. Boland during the debate concerning colonialism: "The United States representative made slanderous attacks on the Socialist countries... Romanian representative Comrade Mezinescu mounted the rostrum and gave the deserved rebuff. He called upon the president of the Assembly, Mr. Boland, not to permit insults. A curious scene followed. The president showed excess of zeal: he did not expect his main instrument—the gavel—to fail him, and he rapped it on the desk with such force that it broke in pieces. Having lost this token of power, the president made haste to declare the meeting closed."

"It is a pity that the meeting was closed..." said Mr. Khrushchev. It is also a pity that Khrushchev's description of the "curious scene" somehow fell short of the truth. Mr. Mezinescu had not exactly "mounted the rostrum." He had leapt from his chair like a madman in the middle of the American speech, and stormed the rostrum, screaming with a noise like a police car. President Boland could no longer hold back the Irish in him, and red in the face, he pounded the desk until his gavel broke. Fellow Irishmen sent him hundreds of gavels and one sent him a shillelagh. An anonymous collector offered five thousand dollars to Mr. Boland's favorite charity for the broken gavel; but it had disappeared without a trace.

Khrushchev's star turn was scheduled for September 23,

when he made his speech in the general debate of the Assembly. He wore the Order of Lenin for the occasion, and two more decorations sparkled upon the lapel of his black coat. His trousers were very tight at the seat, and he toddled up to the rostrum with his entire body agitating around his belly-button, like a child's. He adjusted his eyeglasses, took a sip of Borzhom, the Soviet mineral water which he was plugging as a Soviet export, and began his two-and-a-half-hour talk. He spoke of disarmament and the U-2 incident; without wasting much passion, he called for the seating of Red China; he demanded "for all colonial countries, trusteeship territories and other non-selfgoverning territories complete independence and freedom . . ." He suggested removing the United Nations Headquarters from New York to Geneva or Vienna —even to the Soviet Union. Finally he came to his main objective: that of demolishing Hammarskjöld and the office of Secretary-General.

After accusing Hammarskjöld of having "sided with the colonialists," he suggested that the post of the Secretary-General should be abolished and replaced by a "collective executive body," consisting of three persons, each of whom would represent a certain group of states, the "western powers," the "socialist states," and the "neutralist countries." It was his famous "troika" proposal.

Having placed this time bomb underneath Hammarskjöld's seat, he collected his papers, toddled down the steps of the platform, and rolled back to his seat, grinning amid the rousing applause of Communist countries and the gaping astonishment of westerners and Africans.

A weekend intervened before Hammarskjöld gave his answer. On Monday, September 26, he took the rostrum. He began by assuring the Assembly that the matter before them did not concern his handling of the Congo affair so much as the very principles from which the United Nations had its form and substance.

"It is a question not of a man, but of an institution," he said.

"Use whatever words you like, independence, impartiality, objectivity—they all describe what, without exception must be the attitude of the Secretary-General. Such an attitude ... may at any stage become an obstacle for those who work for certain political aims which would be better served or more easily achieved if the Secretary-General compromised with this attitude. But if he did, how gravely he would then betray the trust of all those for whom the strict maintenance of such an attitude is their best protection in the world-wide fight for power and influence. Thus, if the office of the Secretary-General becomes a stumbling block for anyone, be it an individual, a group or a government ... and if, for that reason, he comes under criticism, such criticism strikes at the very office and the concepts on which it is based.

"I would rather see that office break on strict adherence to the principle of independence, impartiality and objectivity than drift on a basis of compromise."

The bland indirection with which Hammarskjöld had inferred that his office had perhaps become a stumbling block to those with certain political aims without having vouchsafed even the iciest appraisal of the "troika" proposal brought Khrushchev out of his corner in a rage, determined to box with no shadows. In his unforgettable speech of October 3 he placed on display not only the faults with which he was charged upon his downfall, but also his main quality: that he was an exceptionally shrewd and penetrating judge of men and situations. Incredible as it may seem, it was Hammarskjöld's enemy, Khrushchev, who first publicly accused him of being a saint, as positively as if he had been reading a copy of *Markings*.

"There is an old saying," said Chairman Khrushchev, "that there are not and never were any saints on earth. Let those who believe in saints hold their opinion: we do not credit such tales.

"Everyone has heard now how vigorously the imperialist countries defend Mr. Hammarskjöld's position. Is it not clear then, in whose interest he interprets and executes . . . decisions, whose 'saint' he is?

"Mr. Hammarskjöld has always been prejudiced in his attitude towards the socialist countries. He has always upheld the interest of the United States of America and the other monopoly-capitalist countries. The events in the Congo (Leopoldville) where he played a simply deplorable role, were merely the last drop which filled the cup of our patience to overflowing.

"In order to prevent any misinterpretation, I should like to repeat: we do not and cannot place confidence in Mr. Hammarskjöld. If he himself does not muster up enough courage to resign, so to say in a chivalrous manner, then we shall draw the necessary conclusions from the situation obtaining."

Upon the podium, above Khrushchev, Hammarskjöld listened to his ruination, immobile, his eyes cast down upon the pad before him. Sometimes he jotted down a word, or he pretended to do so. No emotion was visible on his face. When Khrushchev collected his papers to walk away, he shot an insolent smile upward toward the Secretary-General, but Hammarskjöld did not return it. Boland shut off his microphone, leaned over towards Hammarskjöld, and advised him not to answer at once.

He wrote his answer over lunch on the 38th Floor, showing it afterwards to Andrew Cordier. Then at 3:00 P.M., when the Assembly reconvened, he was the first speaker. The atmosphere among the members of the Secretariat was extraordinarily tense. He had been for us a fulcrum and yet we had seen him that morning cynically obliterated. None of us had any notion how he would meet his fate.

Hammarskjöld spoke deliberately, leaning on every word and he said: "The General Assembly can rightly expect an immediate reply from my side to a statement so directly addressed to me . . .

"The Assembly has witnessed over the last weeks how historical truth is established: once an allegation has been repeated a few times, it is no longer an allegation, it is an established fact, even if no evidence has been brought out in order to support it.

"However, facts are facts, and the true facts are there for whosoever cares for truth. Those who invoke history will certainly be heard by history. And they will have to accept its verdict as it will be pronounced on the basis of facts by men free of mind and firm in their conviction that only on a scrutiny of truth can a future of peace be built.

"I have no reason to defend myself or my colleagues against the accusations and judgments to which you have listened. Let me say only this, that *you,* all of you, are the judges. No single party can claim that authority. I am sure you will be guided by truth and justice . . . Let those . . . who are not pursuing aims proper only to themselves pass judgment on our actions there.

"Let the countries who have liberated themselves in the last fifteen years speak for themselves.

"I regret that the intervention to which I have found it necessary to reply has again tended to personalize an issue which, as I have said, in my view is not a question of a man but of an institution. The man does not count, the institution does. A weak or nonexistent executive would mean that the United Nations would no longer be able to serve as an effective instrument for active protection of the interests of those many Members who need such protection. The man holding the responsibility as chief executive should leave if he weakens the executive; he should stay if this is necessary for its maintenance. This, and only this, seems to me to be the substantive criterion...

"The statement this morning seems to indicate that the Soviet Union finds it impossible to work with the present Secretary-General. This may seem to provide a strong reason why I should resign. However, the Soviet Union has also made it clear that if the present Secretary-General were to resign now, they would not wish to elect a new incumbent but insist on an arrangement which—and this is my firm conviction, based on broad experience—would make it impossible to maintain an effective executive. By resigning, I would, therefore, at the present difficult and dangerous juncture, throw the Organization to the winds..."

As Hammarskjöld spoke, he would sometimes interlock his fingers, or else rest his hands lightly before him on the desk. Occasionally he folded them in a prayerful gesture. As he reached the point in his speech where a flat statement would be made, he picked up a pencil and began to slide his fingers up and down its length, and these moving fingers were mesmeric.

"It is not the Soviet Union or, indeed, any other big powers who need the United Nations for their protection; it is all the others. In a sense the Organization is first of all *their* Organization, and I deeply believe in the wisdom with which they will be able to use it and guide it.

"I shall remain at my post during the term of my office as a servant of the Organization in the interests of all those other nations, as long as *they* wish me to do so."

As he said the words, "I shall remain at my post," a thunderous applause went up from the Assembly. The small nations of this earth have very little reason to clap their hands, but when they do they can certainly make a racket. Hammarskjöld threw up both hands to calm the clamor, the pencil held daintily upright in his right hand, like a teacher, but it was some minutes before he was permitted to resume his sentence.

When he did, his Swedish sing-song, that sign of rare emotion was very much in evidence, and the hard consonants of his native land sounded through his concluding remarks:

"In this context the representative of the Soviet Union spoke of courage. It is very *eassy* to resign; it is not so *eassy* to stay on. It is very *eassy* to bow to the wish of a big power. It is another matter to resist.

"As is well known to all members of this Assembly, I have done so before on many occasions and in many directions. If it is the wish of those nations who see in the Organization their best protection in the present world, I shall now do so again."

He leaned back in his chair, his eyes sunk into the shadows of his brow. Suddenly a murderous glare shot at the Assembly, and we glimpsed a passion that we had not suspected could exist in the cool and formal person of the Secretary-General.

The drama of the moment exploded into huge applause, not tempered at all by Khrushchev and Gromyko who were trying to compete with the joyful fracas by banging hard upon their desks. Mr. Khrushchev's plans had indeed gone sour. The entire pattern of his behavior at the 15th General Assembly had been a planned bid for the favor of the new nations. From the beginning he had wooed them by taking a strong anticolonialist stand; by suggesting the removal of the Headquarters from the United States "where the Negroes are not regarded as human beings, where they are victims of savage discrimination that goes as far as lynching."

Seeing in them the emergence of a "third force" he had offered them a special plum: their own private Secretary-General, a member of a "troika." To prepare the ground for this, the old United Nations, and Hammarskjöld along with it, had to be discredited. So he applied the pattern of Lenin's Bolsheviks who, in 1917, had disrupted the meetings of the Duma, and that of the Nazis who, in 1930, turned the Reichstag into a bedlam. He had banged and waved his fists, he had termed the Security Council a spittoon, the Philippine delegate a "jerk," and Franco, "the hangman of the Spanish people." Lest all this should escape the attention of faraway Mao, he had even taken off his shoes.

But principally his display was for the benefit of the Africans close by who sat in the Assembly Hall in their best clothes like newly confirmed boys in the pew of a church which they had entered with awe and reverence.

And now what did Khrushchev see with his own eyes but all of Africa on its feet, swaying and flashing their patterned hues as they clapped in an enchantment of enthusiasm for the Secretary-General.

Hammarskjöld had made his compelling integrity so strongly felt that it had cast a spell around the "third force," drawing it away from Khrushchev; he had turned political ruination into a whacking diplomatic victory. So it was thought and so it was widely reported to be.

It is apparent in *Markings* that Hammarskjöld himself suffered no such rosy illusions about the nature of his triumph. For all practical purposes the Assembly's applause was no more than a tidal wave of compassion for the innocently persecuted, a tribute to a *chevalier sans peur et sans reproche*. It was nothing but an elementary outburst of man's deep-seated sense of justice.

On second thought, perhaps it was after all a famous victory.

It need hardly be said that for us in the Secretariat that day of sliding emotions was an unforgettable one. I cannot speak for the gentlemen who retired with their vindicated chief to the 38th Floor, but I can speak for Sven Åhman's cleaning woman. As he wandered back to his office that night, he found her emptying his wastebasket, and she turned to him with worried eyes. "How is Hammarskjöld doing?" she asked. "I hope he's coming through."

Then she heaved a sigh and said, "He's all right."

I can also speak for myself. I went back to my office and

reflected. That fall I had published a book of political satire, entitled *Platypus At Large*. The hero was a duckbilled platypus, my symbol of the international "little man" who was guided through the political jungle by a shrewd and cynical fox. I had earmarked a copy for the Secretary-General, but I had not dared to trouble him with fables in those crowded anxious days.

But after he defied Khrushchev on October 3, I said to myself: "Now he has it off his chest." I therefore wrote a letter recalling Abraham Lincoln whose jokes and quips were much resented during the Civil War and who said, "War is no joking matter. But a good laugh now and then makes it easier to bear." The following day I sent it with my book to the 38th Floor.

To my astonishment, at that very dramatic juncture of his career, the Secretary-General took time to read my book and replied at once, on October 5: "I am glad that the thought of Lincoln's reply brushed aside your hesitation, thereby having given me the opportunity for great enjoyment and appreciation of your 'Platypus At Large.' Although, indeed, 'war is not a joking matter,' the intelligent humor of your book gives a much needed and useful perspective as a balance to the all too frequently prevailing tendency to overdramatization."

I wonder what he meant by "overdramatization"? It seems that Khrushchev had the same philosophy. The day after the confrontation, he sent the Secretary-General an invitation to a reception he gave at the Soviet consulate. Unable to believe the evidence of his eyes, Hammarskjöld checked whether it was an error of protocol. But it was no error, he had actually been invited, and as a matter of protocol, he was obliged to put in an appearance.

Khrushchev met him at the door and gave him a jovial bear hug. Nina Khrushchev looked at him with a flowering smile which on her guileless face can only be interpreted as an expression of maternal tenderness.

Afterwards, Janos Kadar of Hungary is said to have asked Khrushchev why he had behaved so cordially to Hammarskjöld, and Khrushchev is said to have replied: "Do you know the tradition of the mountain people of the Caucasus? When an enemy is inside your home, sharing your bread and salt, you should always treat him with the greatest hospitality. But as soon as he steps outside your door, it is all right to slit his throat."

14

The Lumumba Murder

THE dialogue with Khrushchev continued throughout the session of the Assembly, but it was not the kind that Martin Buber had in mind. Furthermore, ugly cracks were appearing in the Secretary-General's hitherto good relations with his Soviet Secretariat members. That year Georgy Arkadev had become his Soviet Undersecretary heading the Political Affairs Department, and it became obvious that after the Khrushchev fracas, this gentleman considered Hammarskjöld expendable. On New Year's Eve of 1960, upon the urgent request of Cuba—which charged that an American invasion of that country was imminent—he initiated a Council meeting for the following day, without telling Hammarskjöld. Then he took himself off to the Soviet delegation's New Year's party.

Hammarskjöld soon heard of this and he was furious. He had Arkadev whisked out of his party and onto the 38th Floor where he gave him a piece of his mind.

On another occasion, their encounter was less discreet. At a meeting of the Political Committee in Conference Room 4, a whispered argument between them developed into a shouting one. Noting the gaping crowd, the two got up and still arguing moved into one of the adjacent smaller conference rooms, and then into still another one, shouting all the way.

As the cold war entered deep into the heart of the Congo, Hammarskjöld took to excluding Arkadev from the Congo Club, as his closest advisers were then called. He worked directly with Heinz Wieschhoff who was technically Arkadev's deputy. The situation was thereby exacerbated—and so was the Secretary-General. At a press conference he was challenged on the subject: the questioner wanted an explanation of the absence of Mr. Arkadev from the group of Undersecretaries sitting behind him. Hammarskjöld replied, "Mr. Arkadev is a human being and is entitled to his vacation, and he has got his vacation." When the correspondent went on to probe other relations with Soviet members of the Secretariat, Hammarskjöld became irritated and snapped, "You excel in follow-up questions. I think that is not a good technique."

In the first months of 1961, the Secretary-General continued to receive Ambassador Dayal's "progress reports" from the Congo where "the basic conditions prerequisite for some measure of stability . . . are still tragically lacking."

Lumumba had been arrested by Colonel Mobutu's gendarmarie, but he was released for obscure reasons. His life was in grave danger, for many Balubas were employed as soldiers, and they thirsted for his blood. He therefore asked the United Nations for protection, and this was granted him. He also wanted ONUC to intervene on his behalf against Colonel Mobutu, and he threatened that should the United Nations fail to comply, he would "requisition" ONUC's Afro-Asian troops.

On October 10, one week after Hammarskjöld's "I shall stay at my post" address, representatives of Mobutu's Congolese Army appeared at ONUC Headquarters asking United Nations help in arresting Lumumba for having made speeches which incited the population against established authority. This was a crime left over from the colonial regime whose penal code continued in force for lack of any other.

ONUC refused this request as inconsistent with their neutrality. Their reply enraged Mobutu who accused the United Nations of bad faith. The president of the Children's Hour next published an ultimatum threatening that if ONUC failed to arrest Lumumba for them by a set date, the Congolese Army would attack ONUC from all garrisons.

October 24 was United Nations Day. Mr. Dayal issued an appeal for unity which would "lead to stability, integrity, and progress. The path of division would lead only to fratricidal strife, disintegration and chaos . . ."

Moise Tshombe boycotted United Nations Day.

Lumumba was by this time sitting in the center of a concentric three-ring circus. The first ring was his house. The second ring was the guard of ONUC troops which surrounded it. The third was the menacing ring of Congolese soldiers which surrounded ONUC. He lived quite happily there for a while. Ambassador Dayal explained the routine to Hammarskjöld: "Mr. Lumumba was perfectly free to leave if he wanted to; but the Congolese guard was there to prevent him from doing so. Our guard was to prevent unauthorized persons from coming in."

ONUC was protecting Lumumba from violence within his own quarters. They made certain that no one entered the residence carrying "weapons, knives, daggers, bombs, or anything of that kind." They did not, however, check persons leaving the residence. This was in the hands of the Congolese Army who performed their task with zeal.

"On numerous occasions," reported Mr. Dayal, "Mr. Lumumba's servants had been prevented from going to market or his children from attending school . . . The United Nations often had to make representations on humanitarian grounds to facilitate Mr. Lumumba's personal household administration."

The night of November 27/28 was stormy. President Kasavubu had just returned from New York where he had addressed the General Assembly and where his delegation was duly seated as a member of the United Nations. Now he was holding a sumptuous banquet at the presidential palace to which all the UN military and civilian leaders had been invited.

In front of Lumumba's residence the UN Moroccan guard watched a large black car drive up through the heavy rain. They stopped it, as was their duty. But they had often seen this same car pass in with the same driver, and so they waved it on. Shortly afterwards the car departed with three passengers—all men. They did not stop it, and apparently the Congolese Army did not stop it either.

The following afternoon, a search established that Lumumba had left his residence. The first thing President Kasavubu did was to accuse the United Nations of having "assisted in Lumumba's escape and of having been accomplice in it." He then asked them to help him find Lumumba.

Ambassador Dayal issued a clear order: "ONUC will not under any circumstances provide intelligence or assistance to the pursuer or the pursued." When a certain Major Pongo, who was placed in charge of the search, requested that a helicopter be put at his disposal, he was refused.

Lumumba was making northward towards Stanleyville where his friend, Antoine Gizenga, with other followers supported by armed troops loyal to Lumumba, had set up a rival government which the Soviet Union chose to recognize as the legal government of the Congo. He never reached his destination because he was a victim of his own speechmaking. While pausing at the village of Mweka for luncheon, he could not resist the opportunity of exercising his silver tongue. He made a political speech, news of which soon came to the ears of the Congolese Army soldiers who were stalking him. They tracked him down and pounced. By December 2, they had him back in Leopoldville.

Dag Hammarskjöld transmitted to the Security Council Mr.

Dayal's report of his arrival there: "... he was without his glasses and wearing a soiled shirt; his hair was in disorder; he had a blood clot on his cheek and his hands were tied behind his back. He was roughly pushed into an ANC (Congolese Army) truck with rifle butts and driven off."

He was later removed to Thysville where ONUC troops reported: "His head has been shaven and his hands remain tied. He is being kept in a cell under conditions reported to be inhumane ..." There he was joined by two supporters, former Vice-President of the Senate, Mr. Okito, and former Minister of Youth, Mr. Mpolo. They had been arrested in Leopoldville.

Hammarskjöld, upon hearing of the arrest, had immediately addressed two letters to President Kasavubu. The first letter stated that a number of delegations had approached him expressing their grave concern that action might be taken against Lumumba which would be, in the Secretary-General's neat phrases, "contrary to recognized rules of law and order and outside the framework of due process of law." He reminded Kasavubu that the Congo had just become a member of the United Nations and expressed confidence that his "wisdom and fairmindedness," as head of the delegation, would "lead him to regard the principles of the United Nations Charter as the only basis on which fruitful national and international cooperation in our present world can be built." No one can accuse the Secretary-General of talking down to the heads of half-baked nations.

The second letter was more to the point. He mentioned the reports that Lumumba and his detained companions had suffered physical violence and degrading treatment. He suggested that the International Red Cross be called in to supervise the conditions of the detention of the prisoners. He wondered about the legality of the arrest itself, and he called Kasavubu's attention to the requirements that the prisoner be informed within twenty-four hours of the reasons for his arrest;

and that he be given a fair and public hearing with counsel of his own choice.

These communications drew from President Kasavubu a stinging rebuke. "I am somewhat surprised at the importance that a number of African-Asian and East European delegations attach to the arrest of Mr. Lumumba. The fact is that since September he has been under a warrant of arrest ... the reason it was not possible to carry out his arrest ... was that the United Nations troops, acting in what we consider an arbitrary manner, prevented it."

He listed Lumumba's crimes: usurpation of public powers, assaults of individual freedom accompanied by torture, attacks against the security of the State, organization of hostile bands for purposes of devastation, massacre and pillage. He reminded the Secretary-General that he had himself referred to Lumumba's operations against the Baluba tribe as a "crime of genocide."

As for the Secretary-General's sanctimonious references to the United Nations Charter, President Kasavubu, a fast learner, had the correct answer:

"Must we in turn investigate the treatment the members of the opposition in Ghana are receiving, or ascertain what has become of General Naguib in Egypt, or recall the victims of the Hungarian insurrection? You may be assured, Sir, that our country has not acceded to the Charter of the United Nations in vain."

He wound up his remarks by advising Hammarskjöld that public opinion in the Congo had become very sensitive indeed to all outside intervention. In the interests of a tranquil termination of the Lumumba affair, he exhorted the Secretary-General to use his influence with the complaining delegations to persuade them to mind their own business. The same day, December 7, he sent off a telegram to the Secretary-General indignantly denouncing ONUC for having decided to "provide such protection to Mr. Lumumba as virtually to shield him from the prosecution lawfully initiated against him ..." In this he was in flat disagreement with Valerian Zorin who, still on the same day, made known his government's outrage at the "base role" the Secretary-General and the United Nations were playing in the Congo. "When it became known," he said, "that Mobutu's gangs ... had seized the Prime Minister, Mr. Lumumba, the United Nations representatives firmly denied reports that they had tried to prevent the lawless activities of those gangs and to help the Prime Minister. They boasted ... of 'noninterference' in the matter. That served to prove yet again the servile role played by the representatives of the United Nations, or more precisely, the representatives of the colonialists, in the Congo."

The Soviet representative declared in purplest Russian prose that "Colonialism regards poverty, disease, ignorance, brutality, treachery, the bondsman's chains and the hangman's rope as its allies in Africa," and he labeled Hammarskjöld as a lackey of colonialism. By the end of the year, the Secretary-General had written a poem advising himself to forget the fun and conceal the pain.

Zorin's speech started fireworks in the General Assembly and provoked the United States representative, James J. Wadsworth, to defend the Secretary-General. He said that Mr. Zorin had now reached his "zenith of distortion, hypocrisy, and prevarication ... The Soviet Union wants United Nations to fail, while others ... want it to succeed. The Soviet Union wants to destroy the office of the Secretary-General, while others want it to grow and become more influential. The Soviet Union is trying to bankrupt the United Nations, while others want the organization to be sound and healthy ... the United States will continue to give its support to the UN, to the UN action in the Congo, to the Secretary-General ..."

Not long since, Mr. Christian Herter, Secretary of State, had handed to Hammarskjöld a check for five million dollars as a contribution to the Congo operation.

Hammarskjöld's letters to Kasavubu had apparent monitory effect, for the Red Cross was permitted to visit Lumumba and his companions at Thysville and they found his health satisfactory. ONUC Moroccan troops were stationed nearby, keeping an eye on things, and they testified that the prisoners were being treated correctly. The commander of the Congolese garrison was a moderate and reasonable man and on December 25, "in a good Christmas spirit," he invited Lumumba to dinner.

But President Kasavubu, now that he had caught Lumumba, was finding that he did not want him after all. He had two fears: one was that some Baluba tribesman in the Congolese Army would take it into his head to avenge his murdered fellow-tribesmen by assassinating Lumumba and that he, Kasavubu, would be blamed for it; the other was that his persuasive ex-prime minister might subvert his Congolese Army captors to his support. An idea occurred to him for keeping his hands clean: Moise Tshombe, Lumumba's bitterest enemy, must look after Lumumba. He requested Tshombe to take the prisoners off his hands, but Tshombe refused to do so—at least he said later that he had refused.

On January 13, a mutiny flared among the soldiers of the Congolese garrison guarding Lumumba. The reasons for this mutiny did not seem to have anything directly to do with Lumumba, and yet a certain idealism can be discerned in them: the soldiers did not see why other Congolese no better qualified themselves were sleek and slick, wore big titles and owned motorcars, while they existed on vile food and were wanting their back pay.

This mutiny precipitated Lumumba's fate. He, Okito, and Mpolo were removed from the Thysville jail and flown to Elizabethville in Katanga. They were accompanied by a representative of the Congolese Sûreté, and they travelled in a

DC-4 operated by a Belgian crew. The pilot later told a journalist that throughout the flight the three prisoners were tied to one another and suffered beatings, and that the Belgian crew, disgusted, had shut themselves up in the front cabin of the aircraft.

About one hundred Katangese soldiers were at the Luana Airport near Elizabethville to greet Lumumba and to draw a cordon around his plane. It landed in a military area not included in the area patrolled by ONUC's Swedish troops. Nevertheless, six ONUC guards witnessed the scene and their officer later testified: "An armored vehicle, trucks and jeeps drove up to the airplane and surrounded it, after which gendarmes formed a cordon about seventy-five meters around the airplane. A number of gendarmes, about twenty, formed a gauntlet from the airplane to the jeep ... The armored vehicle directed its cannon towards the door of the airplane ...

"First to leave the airplane was a smartly dressed African ... Three other Africans followed the first passenger, blindfolded, and with their hands tied behind their backs. One of them, the first, had a small beard. As they came down the stairs, the police ran to them, kicked them all, beat them with their rifle butts and threw them onto the jeep ... one of the three prisoners yelled loudly ... The jeep then ... drove off ..."

The entire operation took two minutes. The Swedish troops did not intervene—indeed they were powerless to do so.

The transfer of Lumumba into the hands of his bitter enemies stirred the members of the United Nations to general consternation. The president of Mali telegraphed Dag Hammarskjöld stating that the "colonialists and their allies in the Congo are threatening Lumumba and his fellow prisoners with serious personal violence. The government of Mali cannot remain indifferent to these discreditable activities which are a disgrace to humanity and an insult to the freedom of the African peoples."

Valerian Zorin wrote a letter to the president of the Security Council:

> The transfer of Mr. Lumumba, Mr. Okito, and Mr. Mpolo to Katanga territory means nothing more nor less than their direct surrender to the Belgian colonialists... The arbitrary imprisonment of Mr. Lumumba and his colleagues... the recent acts of violence committed against them, were carried out before the eyes of the United Nations command in the Congo. Thus, neither the United Nations command nor the Secretary-General can divest themselves of responsibility for these acts...

Hammarskjöld sent an immediate message to Tshombe pointing out the international concern on Lumumba's behalf, "particularly since it appears to involve further postponement of judicial proceedings to which Mr. Lumumba, after his long period of detention, is entitled under commonly accepted principles of law and human rights..."

He enumerated for Tshombe's benefit the minimum rights generally guaranteed to an accused man, and he expressed confidence that Tshombe would consider how to place Lumumba, with his companions, in a position where he "may be given the benefit of due process... I am sure that, pending a decision in this matter, you will see to it that they receive the humane and fair treatment to which they are entitled."

Tshombe pondered this communication for two weeks. Then he replied to Hammarskjöld, expressing amazement that the United Nations should be concerned about a man whom they recognized as guilty of genocide. He said that since Mr. Lumumba's crimes had been against the Congolese nation, it was the business of the "authorities of the former Belgian Congo alone" to decide the treatment accorded him and what was to be done with him. "In view of the unfortunate repercussions which Mr. Lumumba's inflammatory statements have always had, I consider that for the time being, and in the interests of restoring general calm, there should be no contact between Mr. Lumumba and the outside world."

To this stately exchange, let us respectfully add that there was indeed no contact between Lumumba and the outside world, for he and his companions had been murdered.

General calm, however, had not been restored. In Leopold-ville the rumors of this killing were running riot. The Red Cross was making anxious inquiries after Lumumba's health. A United Nations commission which had arrived in the Congo expressly to effect a reconciliation between the contending Congolese leaders became even more insistent upon seeing Lumumba. ONUC had found out that the office of the Pro-cureur General, in charge of criminal proceedings, had no file on Lumumba, and they were wondering why.

On February 9, Tshombe and his Minister of the Interior, Godefroid Munongo, issued an official denial that Lumumba had been killed. At the same time, they were thinking up further reasons why he could not be put on public display. On February 10, Mr. Munongo broadcast over Radio Katanga that Lumumba and his accomplices had escaped from the farm where they had been in custody. He said that they had over-come their guards, gagged them, seized their rifles and fled in a black Ford car which contained enough gasoline to take them a hundred kilometers. A search was in process by land and air, and roadblocks had been set up. A reward was established of 300,000 Congolese francs for information leading to the recap-ture of Lumumba. Fifty thousand francs each were offered for his two friends.

The news of this "escape" sounded ominous to Hammar-skjöld. He instructed the ONUC representative to "use all his resources in order to verify the stories connected with the escape of Mr. Lumumba and to establish firm information . . . for the purpose of reporting to the Security Council." He was also to remind Tshombe of the importance of according humane treatment to the fugitives.

But Tshombe refused to cooperate with the ONUC representative. He said the Lumumba affair was of an internal nature and did not concern the United Nations.

Further details were, however, forthcoming on the following day, February 11, from Munongo who held a press conference in order to impart them. He said that villagers taking part in the search operation—not because of the reward, but because they were eager to see such a traitor as Lumumba brought to justice—had discovered a car abandoned in a ditch. The ignition key housing in the dashboard had been unscrewed and the car had been started by connecting the dashboard wires. He informed the press that a Commission of Inquiry had been appointed by the Katanga Government to establish the facts of the escape.

Indeed, two days later, this commission came up with some new facts which they published in a communiqué:

> The escape took place on the night of February 9/10, apparently towards midnight. The prisoners made a hole measuring about 35 by 40 centimeters in the rear wall of the house. The hole was made with the aid of spikes used to hold up the curtains. The task was made easier by the fact that the walls were made of mud bricks. An additional factor was that a violent storm was then raging and thus made it harder to hear any noise made by the prisoners.

Having crawled through the hole, the prisoners knocked down their guards with some pieces of firewood, tied them up with the curtains (white cotton ones), requisitioned the Ford car, and made off.

Mr. Munongo found it in his heart to sympathize with the prisoners' plight, for, he said, "they are in an area where the entire population is favorable to the Tshombe government."

This Godefroid Munongo is not at all negroid looking. His lips are rather thin and tight. His broad and obtuse forehead pushes deep against his short beaky nose and in the shadow of his brow sit a pair of cinder black hawk eyes. Some people in Katanga called him the "Bad African" and he looked the part. The dark eyeglasses he habitually wore, completed the sinister image.

His fears for the safety of Lumumba and his colleagues turned out to be justified, for on the very day he had expressed them he was obliged to call a press conference at his private residence. No more than eight or nine correspondents were present. Munongo appeared to be tense and he took some unusual precautions: he had the door closed carefully so that nobody could enter while he spoke, and he requested the journalists to listen very carefully to what he was going to say and to report the news accurately.

Said one correspondent, "If any other politician had spoken to journalists like that, they would have gotten up and walked out." But they sat tight, as tense as Munongo himself, to listen to his words: "I have called you here to announce the death of Lumumba and of his accomplices, Okito and Mpolo.

"Yesterday evening a Katangan from the Kolwezi region— I shall not be more explicit—came to my private residence to inform me that Lumumba, Okito, and Mpolo had been massacred yesterday morning by the inhabitants of a small village situated quite a distance from the place where the vehicle had been discovered, so that we are still wondering how the three fugitives could have got there." He himself had helped to identify the bodies. They were immediately buried, "in a place which we shall not reveal, if only to prevent any pilgrimages from being made to it. Nor shall we disclose the name of the village whose inhabitants put an end to the sorry exploits of Lumumba . . . for we do not want these Katangans . . . to be the object of possible reprisals on the part of Lumumba supporters.

"Nor do we wish to be exposed to pressure to make us bring to trial for murder these Katangans who have perhaps acted somewhat precipitately . . . but whom we cannot honestly blame for having rid Katanga, the Congo, Africa, and the world, of a problem which some persons have unduly magnified and which threatened to be a source of trouble to mankind."

Mr. Munongo did not pretend to be grieved at Lumumba's death; however, he did wish he could have been given a fair trial. He blamed the tragedy on the United Nations whose pro-Lumumba behavior had aroused the indignation of the Katangan peoples to fever-pitch. And then he said, "I am, of course, aware that the United Nations will say that the whole thing was a plot and that we murdered them ourselves. Such an accusation is inevitable. If Lumumba had died in Katanga of sickness, old age, or some other natural cause, we should still have been charged with murder . . . I am going to speak frankly and bluntly, as I usually do. We shall be accused of having murdered them. My reply is: prove it . . ."

One of the journalists present later said, ". . . this was said in a defiant tone, as if it was a kind of challenge. I do not want to attach too much significance to a tone of voice, which is hard to interpret accurately: but to me it meant clearly: 'Believe it or not, as you will, I do not care. I know perfectly well you can prove nothing.' "

On February 21, 1961, Munongo's challenge was taken up by the General Assembly; it was decided to set up a commission to "endeavour to ascertain the events and circumstances relating to and culminating in the death of Mr. Lumumba and his colleagues and to fix responsibility thereof."

This Commission suffered the same fate as had the Special Committee on Hungary some years before when it was refused permission to pursue its aims in Budapest. The Lumumba Commission held sixty-six meetings in New York, Geneva, and Brussels; but it never got to the Congo.

Requests were sent to all member nations to forward relevant information, but only those states that had no relevant information replied. The Belgian government was asked to provide facilities for the interrogation of fifteen persons. Only three were heard. The rest were on holiday, or their addresses were not known, or they did not reply. A request was telegraphed by the Commission to President Kasavubu for authorization to enter the Congo, but somehow it was "never received." When at last, in July of 1961, six months after Lumumba's death, the Commission decided to proceed to the Congo, they met with unexpected resistance from ONUC; for miracle of miracles, Hammarskjöld had by that time succeeded in bringing together the various conflicting parties in the Congo and a new government was being formed under the premiership of Mr. Cyrille Adoula. It was thought that the sudden appearance of the Commission would only exacerbate old wounds.

But after Mr. Adoula's government had been approved by Parliament, the Commission renewed its request to enter the Congo, and it received an amazing statement from the foreign minister: that the United Nations resolution which had set up the Commission in the first place was adopted when the Congo had no constitutionally established government; now that it had, that government considered it "its right and duty to conduct the investigation of this affair with a view to finding and punishing the perpetrators of this crime," and that the arrival of the Commission would be "inopportune and pointless."

Mr. Adoula's foreign minister permitted himself some beautiful language in refusing the Commission's request. He said the murder was "primarily an affair which concerns the Congolese people, who in the person of Mr. Lumumba have lost one of the architects of their independence, the head of their first government, in short, one of their finest sons."

Of course, this sentence was composed some time before the Commission of Inquiry established the responsibility of the Leopoldville government in the murder of one of the Congo's finest sons.

As handicapped as the Commission was, and as studded with "howevers" as their report is, all possible reasonable guesses about how Lumumba met his end are equally horrendous.

He and his companions had been last seen by United Nations personnel descending from an airplane at Luana Airport, preceded by a smartly-dressed African who was possibly Kasavubu's officer of the Sûreté. They were blindfolded and their hands were tied behind their backs. After they were handed over to the Katangese they were driven away from the airport in a truck.

One witness, who asked the Commission not to disclose his name, said that they were driven to a point several kilometers from the airport where Mr. Munongo was awaiting Mr. Lumumba's arrival. Munongo approached Lumumba, and after a few remarks, took a bayonet from the rifle of one of the soldiers and plunged it into Mr. Lumumba's chest. While Mr. Lumumba lay on the ground dying, a certain Captain Ruys, a Belgian mercenary serving in the Katanga Army, ended his suffering by putting a bullet through his head.

The witness said that Tshombe was furious upon hearing of Lumumba's death, but, confronted with a *fait accompli,* he was obliged to devise means of misleading the public. "He had Mr. Lumumba's body taken to a refrigerator at the laboratory of the Union Minière du Haut-Katanga."

A somewhat different version of the story was forthcoming from a British mercenary who had heard it from a Belgian friend named Colonel Huyghe. He said that on a day which he supposed to be the day the prisoners had arrived at Elizabethville, a few men were gathered in a nearby villa garden to "celebrate" Lumumba's arrival. Among them were Munongo and Tshombe and Colonel Huyghe. Huyghe later told the witness that the murder had been planned in advance and was accomplished by himself with the assistance of a Captain Gat.

This account was corroborated by another British mercenary named Roddy, who also knew Huyghe. Huyghe had told

Roddy that Okito and Mpolo had been "brought into a room and were told to pray for their lives, and that they were then shot in the back of the head as they knelt."

The witness continued, "He then mentioned that Lumumba was brought into the room and that he himself personally shot Lumumba. He rather stressed the death of Lumumba by stating that when Lumumba walked into the room he started screaming and crying for his life. He turned to everybody in the room and stated that whatever they wanted as a reward he would give them, if he was not killed. Huyghe's words to me were: 'Pray you bastard!—you had no pity on women or children or nuns of your own faith, so pray!'

"Lumumba, according to Huyghe, fell on the ground and started rolling and screaming for mercy, and Huyghe said he shot him as he rolled on the ground.

"I said, 'Christ, no, Charley,' and he said, 'Yes, Roddy, it is so.'"

But the witness warned the Commission that when this tale was told to him, both he and Huyghe had been drinking and Huyghe "might have been bragging—though I would not personally put it past Huyghe to have carried out this act."

The Commission also heard the statement of a senior officer of the Katangese government who worked closely with Tshombe and his account was gentler, though still bizarre. "According to what I heard," he said, "some of the ministers of the Katanga government are supposed to have paid a visit to Mr. Lumumba on Tuesday evening; it is said that they became rather angry with him and that one of the ministers suddenly struck Mr. Lumumba a hard blow. The latter is said to have fallen on a bidet which it seems was in the room: it is said that he was knocked out and remained unconscious and—it seems—was killed by that blow."

If this was true, Lumumba is the first of the world's martyrs to have died by striking his head on a bidet. But betwixt these various accounts it is difficult to make a choice; except to note that President Kasavubu is not alone culpable, but that various excellencies who now share with him the leadership of the Congo were said to have participated joyfully in Lumumba's murder.

The Commission concluded that Lumumba, Okito, and Mpolo "had been killed on January 17, 1960, after their arrival in a villa not far from Elizabethville, in all probability in the presence of high officials of the government of Katanga province, namely Mr. Tshombe, Mr. Munongo, and Mr. Kibwe; and that the escape story was staged.

"A great deal of suspicion is cast on a certain Colonel Huyghe, a Belgian mercenary, as being the actual perpetrator of Mr. Lumumba's murder which was committed in accordance with a prearranged plan and that a certain Captain Gat, also a Belgian mercenary, was at all times accessory to the crime."

Both of these men avoided appearing before the investigating Commission.

In any mystery story, sooner or later the question pops up: where is the body? This is exactly what Mr. Dayal wanted to know in a letter addressed to Tshombe:

> I urge you to return the remains of Mr. Lumumba, Mr. Mpolo, and Mr. Okito to their families, not only out of considerations of elementary humanity, but having regard to Bantu custom and Christian tradition.

To which, three days later, Mr. Tshombe replied:

> The President of the State of Katanga, while he fully appreciates the humanitarian character of the request, would draw Mr. Dayal's attention to the fact that the Bantu custom to which he refers is in fact opposed to all exhumation, even by the family, in cases where the deceased has died a natural death. Bantu tradition prohibits the uncovering, even for a few minutes, of a body covered by the earth; such action constitutes a serious insult to the memory of the deceased,

whose soul may then haunt the survivors. When a member of the family has been unable to attend the funeral ceremonies, Bantu custom permits him simply to take part in such ceremonies *a posteriori* by holding a religious ceremony over the tomb. It is obvious that a holding of such a ceremony would reveal the identity of the village in which the fugitives have been buried.

This ignorance of Bantu custom, incidentally, provides further evidence of the complete inability of the United Nations to impose its trusteeship on territories with which it is completely unfamiliar.

Poor Mr. Dayal. Here he was, totally unfamiliar with Bantu custom, and being badgered by Bantus, apparently equally unfamiliar with it, who wanted their dead. He replied to Tshombe:

> I, for my part, note your statement that under Bantu custom, with which I am certainly much less familiar than you, families may hold ceremonies over the tombs of their dead. I also note that your attachment to the observance of Bantu custom is not sufficiently strong to interfere with your desire not to reveal the place of burial . . . I am led to conclude that although . . . exhumation is contrary to custom, it would nevertheless be possible to carry it out in order to meet universally recognized humanitarian requirements. I would therefore ask you for the last time . . .

But the wife of Patrice Lumumba, who had once worn diamonds and dresses designed in Paris, following Bantu custom, now bared her breast and led a funeral procession of bare-breasted women in the streets of Leopoldville; and they wailed together, but there were no bodies to wail for. Some say they had been dissolved in phenol in the laboratories of Union Minière.

15

Strapped Fast to the Altar

THREE parties foresaw the implications of the Lumumba murder: the Russians, who pegged their future maneuvers to it; the murderers who at once began to accuse one another of it; and Hammarskjöld.

The immediate effect was a serious weakening of ONUC strength by the withdrawal of various outraged nations. Even before the murder, Mali and Yugoslavia had recalled their troops because of their disagreement with Hammarskjöld's Congo policies. After Lumumba's death, four Afro-Asian nations further depleted the United Nations forces. The influential Nkrumah, who had affected to regard Lumumba as his "brother," did not withdraw his forces, but he loudly demanded that Hammarskjöld should use them to disarm his favorite villain, Mobutu; Kasavubu, on the other hand, was more eager for him to disarm Antoine Gizenga, who was regarded as Lumumba's heir. Tshombe, who had not yet been implicated by the Commission of Investigation in the murder of Lumumba, denounced the United Nations for "bathing the Congo with fire and blood." But he did not cease to reinforce his army with imported mercenaries, who slipped across the Rhodesian border, impeded not at all by the Prime Minister of Rhodesia, Sir Roy Welensky. Since the Katanga copper belt extended into Rhodesia, Sir Roy was proving to be a most useful neighbor to Tshombe.

Telegrams from delegates poured into the Secretary-General's office, all of them declaring themselves against sin. The King of Morocco wrote, "We strongly stigmatize this odious act ... this crime against African nationalism strikes a terrible blow at the prestige of the United Nations." The Brazilian government "in accordance with its Christian tradition and historical formation," expressed horror and repulsion. The Russians bombarded the Secretary-General with their most malevolent jargon: Hammarskjöld was a "sorry lackey" whose actions had placed a "dark stain" on the whole United Nations. In February, Mr. Zorin said: "It is clear to every honest person throughout the world that the blood of Patrice Lumumba is on the hands of this henchman of the colonialists and cannot be removed.

"The Soviet Government," he said, "will not maintain any relations with Hammarskjöld and will not recognize him as an official of the United Nations."

This declaration of Hammarskjöld's nonexistence was echoed by a great thunder from the left. Fast on the heels of Zorin's prediction that the blood of Patrice Lumumba would become a banner in the Congolese struggle for freedom came Czechoslovakia's conviction that the "legacy of Patrice Lumumba and other Congolese martyrs will become a glaring symbol ..." Castro took an especially optimistic view of the murder. He thought that Lumumba's shining sacrifice would serve as "a bulwark and a light and shall point the way. This dead rebel shall not rest until the Congolese people is free, independent and sovereign." He ordered flags in Cuba to be flown at half-mast for three days.

In life this African leader's words had been meretricious and some of his actions foul. His burning idealism and his intellectual gifts had been pathetically misused to serve purely demagogic ends, but now that he was a martyr, masses of people were aroused to Lumumba-worship. He was being canonized. The foundations of Lumumba institutes were laid, Lumumba monuments, parks, shrines, boulevards, and streets were in the making. They rest today in peaceful coexistence with those built for Hammarskjöld. Why not? Both men wanted the same thing: a unified Congo and a good life for the people.

It would be pleasant to record that the forces of colonialism, capitalism, and oppression stood by their lackey when he was at bay, but they did not. At the beginning of 1961, Hammarskjöld's conflict with France over the Tunisian affair was just starting towards its vicious boil. The United States, while publicly supporting the Secretary-General, was privately agitated about what they considered to be his "softness" towards the Lumumba faction; and lest they should not be agitated enough, a lobby financed by the Union Minière was at work to make sure that they should feel more so.

The Americans were polite enough to fix most of the blame on Hammarskjöld's special representative in the Congo, Ambassador Rajeshwar Dayal. Backed by the ghostly voice of Britain and by the loud complaints of Kasavubu, they were demanding Dayal's recall. This Indian diplomat had in fact behaved throughout the Congo affair with discretion and impartiality, and Hammarskjöld therefore resisted these powerful demands for some time; but as the Congo situation increased in gravity and muddle, he was eventually obliged to accept Dayal's resignation.

Behind the American attitude—besides the plots of Union Minière—was an old American dilemma: that of committing themselves to the side of the angels and finding that they must pay for it as well. The Congo vacuum-filling operation was costing the United Nations approximately ten million dollars a month, and a great part of this was coming straight out of the pocket of the United States. The Soviet Union refused to "divert a single kopeck" towards booting themselves out of the Congo. The Belgians took the same view of an operation whose ultimate purpose was to boot the Belgians out of Katanga. The French had formed the habit of not paying for United Nations military operations ever since UNEF had booted them out of the Suez Canal area; and the Latin Americans said they could not pay because they had no money. Now all of these nations are honorable nations, and when they say they are not going to pay, they don't pay.

The only substantial help the United States received in footing the Congo bill was from the United Kingdom. But Britain could afford to be punctilious in money matters; for she is responsible for the foreign policy of Rhodesia, and was therefore able, through Sir Roy Welensky, to badger Hammarskjöld, assist Tshombe, and wreck the United Nations operation, while still paying for it. Politics is the only form of criminal activity at which it is possible to laugh, occasionally.

Kierkegaard, the recluse, had quailed before the grins of strangers. Hammarskjöld, whose spirit was similarly sensitive and morbidly sorrowful now had to endure in public and in private the invective and reproof of the world's leaders, his integrity called in question, his pride and self-esteem bruised. It is no wonder that he saw fit to note in his diary a quotation from St. John Perse about the pain of wearing the shirt of Nessus. Perhaps he suffered what his father had suffered before him. But the elder Hammarskjöld had faced public scorn with all the stiff-necked arrogance of a civil servant who has done his duty according to his lights; it had cost the young Dag ostracism and a beating.

The Secretary-General had his father's unbending will, but far less muscular strength with which to stand up to his ordeal. His "markings" after Lumumba's death become self-pitying and apprehensive, and they do not cease to beseech strength from the elusive divine source. The King James Bible was much consulted, and in its storehouse of ancient woes his own case was noted: He was no longer Phinehas, savior of his people, but a reproach from whom men turned away, shaking their heads.

Anger was his substitute for strength. The vengeful Secretary-General who had glowered at the Assembly after his "I shall remain at my post" speech, never really retreated into the background. He abandoned the diplomatic veil, and proclaimed his naked opinions.

His position in the cold war was directly in the path of two colliding icebergs, and he did not hesitate to glower at both of them.

"Of course, we have been accused of all this and from all sides," he told the Security Council, "although the terminology may have varied. What is more natural? By maintaining our aim and by being faithful to the principles of the United Nations, we are bound to cause disappointment . . .

"It should be a reason for reflection that the very day the Soviet Union repeats its well-known criticism against the Secretary-General, we are under equally heavy criticism from people the Soviet Union . . . characterizes as those to whom we show servile subservience . . .

"We have been accused of servility in relation to the West, of softness in relation to the East . . . of supporting this or that man in the Congo whom one group or another has chosen to make its symbol, or for assisting another man to whom another group has chosen to tie their hopes . . .

"However, this is no excessive price to be paid for avoiding the thing for which no one in my position should be forgiven: to compromise in any political interest with the aims and principles of this Organization . . .

"I can only repeat . . . that I would rather see the office of the Secretary-General break on this principle than drift on compromise."

There was melancholy pride in his tone, too, and plaintiveness, or at least an increase in the plaintive Swedish accent. The press, for a change, was treating him with loving care. At a press conference, a newsman asked him sympathetically, "How do you run a troika without a coachman?" Hammarskjöld replied with a tired smile, "Well, I never tried a troika and I do not think I ever will."

Some relief came the Secretary-General's way when President John F. Kennedy's new government sent as ambassador to the United Nations Adlai Stevenson, whose underlying political beliefs were similar to Hammarskjöld's own. After many hours in conference with the Secretary-General, a reappraisal of United States Congo policies took place. They shifted out of the pockets of the Union Minière and more into line with the moderate "third bloc" of new nations— Hammarskjöld's own chickens. Some of them had staunchly fended off the reproaches that fell on him after the Lumumba murder. Tunisia, grateful for his efforts in her conflict with France, even placed the onus of blame where it belongs: "The murder . . . points up the contempt professed by certain Congolese leaders for the sacred fundamental principles of all states worthy of the name."

Sylvanus Olympio, President of Togo (a politician honest enough to have been assassinated by this time) sent a telegram to the Security Council which must have come to Hammarskjöld like the breath of spring on a frosty night: "All assistance by states members of the United Nations must be channelled through the United Nations, the only body which cannot be accused of political or other designs in the Congo." He called for a drastic decision to put an end to hostilities and to wipe out the mercenaries, for which purpose, he said, "the mandate given to the Secretary-General must be precise and unambiguous."

By this time the situation in the Congo was tragically deteriorating; the Force Publique had broken into factions which then claimed allegiance to one or the other of a hundred or so different leaders, thus providing political or tribal cliques with armed might; what is more, they drifted from leader to leader, under no proper military control and they were turning upon the population. At the same time there was a constant influx of men and arms into the country, tolerated, as the Secretary-General told the Assembly, "by foreign governments"; and sales of arms from private companies were likewise being tolerated as a "time-honored form of military assistance, maintaining a seeming neutrality for the governments most concerned."

He described the quagmire to the delegates in February, and on February 21, the Security Council passed what was nothing less than a show-down resolution, charging the Secretary-General in precise and unambiguous language with enormous responsibilities: the mercenaries were to be driven out of Katanga, civil war was to be forestalled, all military operations halted and clashes prevented. To effect these miracles, ONUC might use force, "if necessary, as a last resort."

All members of the Security Council voted for this resolution except France and the USSR; even they did not vote against it, but abstained. Britain voted for it with a clear conscience, because her diplomats had happily noted its one fateful ambiguity contained in the words, "as a last resort."

Hammarskjöld's first problem was to appeal to member nations for reinforcements for his depleted troops. Nehru, in spite of his irritation over the attacks on Ambassador Dayal, came to his aid with three thousand officers and men. Tunisia and Liberia also contributed forces, and the best news came at the end of March when Uncle Sam offered to pay one half of the costs of the Congo operation.

On Ash Wednesday of 1961, Hammarskjöld made a cool crisp speech to the Assembly in defense of his operation in which he said, "One can blame a mountain climber for his failure to reach the summit when his road has been blocked by an avalanche. But to do so is an irresponsible play upon words."

This avalanche must have taken possession of his mind, for the following day, Maundy Thursday, perhaps in the small hours before he went to bed, in a mood that was far from cool and crisp, he used it again in his diary. But it was no longer a mere blockage in the road. It had become a death-dealer descending on his head and sweeping him away: he saw himself as the hero of Ibsen's play *Brand,* who cries out in anguish against God's rude ways with man.

The answer to the eternal riddle in Ibsen's words and in Hammarskjöld's is "God is love."

God is love, and He made men good; but man has wrought many devices with which to circumvent this inconvenience. When Andrei Gromyko arrived in New York for the reconvening of the 15th General Assembly, he demonstrated one of them: the poker-faced diplomatic kill.

It was the habit, or rather the maddeningly pedantic technique of the Secretary-General, when answering his critics, to recapitulate their accusations before refuting them. On April 5, therefore, Hammarskjöld spoke before the Assembly, meticulously quoting Gromyko's words, which, he said, merited to be put again on record:

"The Soviet Government has already declared that it considers Hammarskjöld to be responsible for the murder of Patrice Lumumba and his comrades. Today we are reiterating this accusation from the rostrum of the United Nations for we cannot reconcile ourselves with this villainy which was perpetrated with the connivance of the International Organization in which our country is a member, perpetrated with the sanctions and assistance of the highest official in the United Nations executive body. We cannot reconcile ourselves with the fact that a prominent post in the United Nations is held by a man who has sullied himself by this murder. It is not only he who wields the knife or revolver that is the murderer—the main criminal is the one who placed the weapon in his hand.

"Later," continued Hammarskjöld with relentless masochism, "the Foreign Minister requested the removal of the present incumbent from the post of Secretary-General, 'as an accomplice and organizer of the slaughter of the leading statesman of the Republic of the Congo ... Mr. Hammarskjöld has lost all confidence and has brought upon himself the condemnation and contempt of all decent human beings.'"

In his refutation, Hammarskjöld tried to avoid commenting on these accusations in personal terms; but he brought up an important aspect of United Nations procedure, which remains unresolved to this day.

"Members of the Assembly will have noted that these accusations, couched in the most general and condemning terms, were put forward without attempts to give them credence by the indication of any single substantive fact on which they might be based ...

"Where, in any parliament, jealous about its democratic traditions, its integrity, and its respect for the human person, could such allegations be made without those making them trying to justify their case or, especially, without the parliamentary body requesting them to do so? The United Nations General Assembly has been called the parliament of nations. Are there other laws for such a parliament than for a national parliament? Are the peoples of the world less jealous about the integrity of the General Assembly than the members of a nation are of the integrity of its democratic institutions?"

This reply of the Secretary-General's was a very proper one, for more unwarranted and irresponsible accusations are permitted at the United Nations than anywhere in the world outside of a conclave of baboons.

Gromyko's further observations however were rather harder

to deal with, for the Soviet Foreign Minister was shrewd enough to formulate fears that were not only those of Hammarskjöld's enemies, but of some of Hammarskjöld's friends.

"Having without any legitimate grounds taken the whole affair into his own hands," Gromyko had said, "Hammarskjöld began to decide on his own what should and what should not be done ... He began to determine on his own choice which countries should send their troops to the Congo and in what quantities; he placed those troops under his own command and became, indeed, some sort of United Nations Field Marshal ...

"Hammarskjöld, taking advantage of his Office of Secretary-General, is usurping the prerogatives of its bodies, one after another, and in some cases has acted for these bodies, trying to supplant them by his own person ... If Hammarskjöld is allowed to follow this course, he may assume himself to be Prime Minister of a World Government."

Once Khrushchev had identified Hammarskjöld as a saint; now here was Gromyko pointing him out as Satan. There is no question that Gromyko had put his finger on the sensitive truth. The Secretary-General envisioned a dynamic World Organization capable of growing, whose decisions would have weight; and for sometime he had been training the General Assembly to present him with villainous "Leave It to Dag" resolutions. The projection of this into the far future would have been a powerful Organization, perhaps a World Government, and such a transcendental political notion was consistent with his mysticism as it was with Nehru's and Gandhi's —as, for that matter, with the Soviet International's. But talk of World Government causes fright and consternation among modern ambassadors who receive their credentials and expense accounts from sovereign nations, and it is no wonder that Hammarskjöld responded to this body-blow "with some hesitation."

"I believe that every member of this Assembly knows why over the years . . . the Security Council or the General Assembly have found it convenient to entrust in very general terms, executive action on highly explosive problems to the Secretary-General," said Hammarskjöld. Carefully he recapitulated the Congo crisis: how he had been instructed on July 14, 1960, to "take the necessary steps," and had been given "general authorization" to do so.

"In the early morning hours of July 14 . . . I had to go ahead on the basis of the authorization without the privilege of any prior consultation."

Then, when he had the Assembly glumly contemplating its own fatal decisions, he suddenly spiralled clear out of trouble: "If the Soviet Union regrets its participation in these decisions, it is their right, but is it their opinion now that the Secretary-General, in anticipation of their own afterthoughts, should have refused to respond to requests for which they themselves had voted?"

Of course, he was being unfair. He knew quite well that a General Assembly resolution, resolved upon in the abstract in New York, is not worth the paper of a press release once the concrete situation in the theater of mischief has changed. Krishna Menon once said, "Changing situations may call in a change of reactions." This truth was Hammarskjöld's real trap. The Council and Assembly would adopt a resolution requesting the Secretary-General to take "the necessary steps." But while he took them, the situation changed. Furthermore, some interested members, while voting for the resolution, would continue to play their own political game, taking private measures running counter to the resolution. When the Secretary-General's "necessary steps" trod on their toes, they could always accuse him of clumsiness, excessive ambition, servility, softness, murder. Hammarskjöld inhabited a Crazy House designed by Niccolo Machiavelli.

In winding up his rebuttal of Gromyko, he made a complex point. First he reiterated his refusal to resign "because I have been requested to do so by a big power and its likeminded supporters. On the other hand, I regard the will of the General Assembly in this respect as my law, and the General Assembly may thus consider itself as seized with a standing offer of resignation, were it to find it to be in the best interests of the Organization that I leave."

Then he pointed out the danger "that a big power, by withdrawing its cooperation at any time should be able to break the term of office of the Secretary-General—thus *de facto* extending its right of veto from the election . . . to his conduct of business through the whole of his established term of office . . .

"The question does arise in a very pointed form if the reasons for withdrawal of confidence are found to be of partisan nature."

In this way, Hammarskjöld transferred the horns of Satan from his own brow onto that of the Russian foreign minister. It was said of Hammarskjöld that he could split a hair finer than anyone to prove that he was right, and in his public response to Russian diatribes, he stood on his position with sure-footed argumentation, using all the elusive shrewdness that I had noted the first time I saw him clearly expressed on his midface. The General Assembly never did find itself seized of a decision to oust Hammarskjöld.

But perhaps the strangest aspect of this tragic and destructive dialogue between Hammarskjöld and the Soviet Union is the suspicion that lingers that the Russian sound and fury were merely stage noises signifying nothing except Khrushchev's desire to establish his *poltergeist* diplomacy in the affairs of Africa. Lash, in his biography of Hammarskjöld, records the rumor that one of the Secretary-General's 38th Floor Russians had actually found it in his heart to warn him in 1960 that a storm was on its way and had advised him to "ride it out."

Andrew Cordier, in response to my question whether there had been any hope of Hammarskjöld's survival as Secretary-General, replied surprisingly, "Yes. A fragment of hope."

Looking back, it nevertheless does not seem to me that the fragment of hope existed, because beyond the politics, personalities were at work.

First there was the personality of Hammarskjöld, a sensitive and righteous man whose very soul was being scorched and maimed by his ordeal. Once a Tibetan scholar, of the worldly order of Red monks, said, "To fashion stars out of dog-dung: that is the great work." Hammarskjöld was a worldly monk, and he had set himself this amazing ambition: to impose from the highest possible vantage point one man's moral political viewpoint upon world affairs, which are ruled not by morality, but by principalities and powers.

This was the challenge to which he had answered "yes" in 1953 when he had taken up "the most difficult job in the world." But on Whitsunday, May 21, 1961, he marked down the realization that the "Yes," had really been answered to a question without words, posed by "Someone—or Something," that had no other name. By this affirmation he had placed himself on a Way that led to a "triumph which is a catastrophe and to a catastrophe which is a triumph." And he recognized that reproach and humiliation were the price of daring to set foot upon this Way.

He compared his lot quite consciously to that of Christ, and this, after the publication of his private diary, led some critics to cry Blasphemy! Delusions of grandeur! Madness! It is curious that none of the critics who denounce him is of a particularly religious turn of mind. None has explained why, since it is urged upon mankind to imitate Christ's life, an imitation of Christ's death should be blasphemous.

Either the story of Christ's passion, his human shrinking from his fate and his godly strength in meeting it, is a fairy tale or else it is a significant key that is to be used as a guide in human dilemma. Men of principle will face death or worldly ruin for their beliefs. Their fate is analogous to that of Christ not because they make it so; Christ did.

Christ the Man prayed that "the cup might pass from him," and so did Hammarskjöld. More practically, he tried to re-frame his policy, and find some way out of the Congo, espe-cially when various nations withdrew their troops from ONUC —in order "not to soil themselves," they said. And only a few weeks before his death we find a far from godly Hammarskjöld thundering a Biblical curse upon his enemies whom he sees as mountain-climbers like himself, but in grave difficulties upon slippery declivities from which they shall be cast down and destroyed. The last writings of Hammarskjöld are not free of self-pity or of the gruesome imaginative powers that afflict the melancholic.

But the most grandiose adventure of the human soul is to grasp its own significance and act upon it. Hammarskjöld's last poems are a remarkable documentary of the noble deter-minations of a leader who knew himself to be a catalyst and an inspirer. They state not only a mystic's faith in God, but reaffirm God's unlimited faith in the man fashioned in spirit, as well as in body, in His own image.

Opposed to the personality of Hammarskjöld which, by a conspiracy of every fortunate accident, had been honed and carved into a shape as "civilized" as the modern mind con-ceives, there was ranged "the Congo personality," that product of unfortunate accidents: Belgian neglect, missionary squab-bles, tribal ferocity, and political ambition. The Congolese leaders could not properly understand what was said to them, nor did they hold fast to anything they said. To deal with such men was like playing chess with melting wax figures. They baffled the Russian adviser, the Hindu trader, the American Quaker, and they baffle a Hungarian caricaturist. How could they fail to baffle an unbending Swede?

Once Hammarskjöld was invited in Leopoldville to a dinner given in his honor at which Antoine Gizenga made a speech denouncing him and the Communists distributed literature opposed to the United Nations operation among the guests. The Secretary-General said to his aide: "Well, at least one thing is dependable about them: they are undependable."

Faces, however, whatever their color, carry some message for me, and I have observed that revolution and times of stress throw into prominence men with alarming faces. I noted in those days and wrote about Tshombe's pronounced streak of femininity expressed in his girlish expression, in his tame forehead, his light, elastic, "dancey" way of walking, like a conceited prima ballerina, and I suspected that his fundamental inadequacies might lead him to be unexpectedly brash, irritatingly hard-headed, and astonishingly compromising; and that he would overglaze his innate instability with grandseigneurial gestures and high-flown pathos.

In April, he declared war on the United Nations, and Swedish troops of ONUC were attacked in the streets of Elizabethville. Some weeks later, he attended the Coquilhatville Conference which was called to bring the feuding provincial leaders into one government, but becoming displeased with the way things were going, he suddenly quit it. He was promptly arrested by Kasavubu's troops, and the Congo government announced its intention of trying him, among other things, for "high treason" and for the assassination of Lumumba. He was in jail for two months.

ONUC in the meanwhile was trying its best to replace mercenaries and Belgian officers who evaded them very simply by disappearing into the bush or skipping over the Rhodesian border for a quiet holiday in the domain of Sir Roy Welensky.

The cost of the operation was bringing the United Nations to the verge of bankruptcy, and the Congo's costs in resisting it were doing exactly the same for the Congo. Hammarskjöld was obliged to transfer to the Congo eighteen million dollars from the United Nations Fund to keep things going.

But his diplomatic prowess had not deserted him and there is no question that in the last months of his life the purity of his motives and his personal integrity were beginning to make itself felt among the Congolese leaders. His diplomats in Leopoldville were successful in effecting a reconciliation between the Central Government, Antoine Gizenga, and other leaders. Tshombe was released from jail on condition that he would agree to meet with all parties in a convening of parliament. He signed a paper indicating a relaxation of his secessionist policies and promising other amicable gestures. It took him exactly two days to get back to his capital at Elizabethville and repudiate every promise he had made.

On July 27, the Congolese Parliament held its first formal session in more than ten months and a government was formed on a broad base with Kasavubu as president, Cyrille Adoula as premier, and Gizenga as vice-premier. At long last, unity was in the making in the Congo.

In Katanga, on August 28, ONUC forces assumed control of the airport and radio stations and peacefully proceeded to round up Belgian and foreign mercenaries. President Tshombe made a pleasant speech thanking the mercenaries for their services, but stating that henceforward, the Katangese would command their own armed forces on all levels. However, by the following week, the United Nations Headquarters at Elizabethville were being stoned, and Tshombe was accusing the United Nations of planning to invade Katanga, suspend its government, and disarm its gendarmerie.

Nobody can tell me that people do not act as they look.

The 16th General Assembly of the United Nations was scheduled to open in New York on September 19, 1961.

The Secretary-General took advantage of an invitation from Premier Adoula to visit Leopoldville to discuss United Nations "aid and support" to the Central Government.

But his real purpose was to meet with Tshombe and obtain from him firm commitments toward final unity; in effect, to obtain Tshombe's hide and bring it home to the General Assembly.

16

Naked Against the Night

WE attach special meanings to "last times." Perhaps it is because we do not know what time really is, only that a small portion of it belongs to us. And so, when a good friend or outstanding person whose piece of time we have shared dies, we remember with a mystic tremor the last time we saw him, the point when through him, our time impinged upon eternity.

A great many people in the Secretariat remember with singular clarity the last time they saw Hammarskjöld. For most of them it was September 8, 1961, on Staff Day. This event always took place shortly before the opening of the annual Assembly, and it had been originated by Hammarskjöld when he first took office for the purpose of encouraging camaraderie among the staff members, differing in race, language, religion and ideology, and by reason of the vast grievances which separate those who live their lives on the graduated steps of a great bureaucratic pyramid.

On Staff Day the women turned out in exotic splendor and the men in black tie. Hammarskjöld addressed the members of the Secretariat midafternoon in the General Assembly Hall, and in the evening there was an entertainment, the Secretary-General acting as Master of Ceremonies. In various years we saw Marlon Brando playing drums, Victor Borge falling off a piano stool, Danny Kaye jumping over the speaker's rostrum, and Marian Anderson singing *He Has the Whole World In His Hand*. Then the dance-orchestras took over, and under the outstretched arm of the naked Zeus that dominates the huge public lobby, everyone whirled to the tunes of Jenö Bartal; and lemonade flowed in torrents.

I usually witnessed these festivities from the television control room where they were recorded on kinescope for our archives, but the last time I saw Hammarskjöld, I was one of the crowd. There was no entertainment that year, no dancing, no lemonade, no glitter. This austerity was ordained because of the serious Congo troubles where ONUC soldiers were losing their lives. But the staff was gathered, nevertheless, in the General Assembly Hall to hear the Secretary-General's speech, and he spoke simply and gravely.

"Those who serve the Organization can take pride in what it has done already in many, many cases. I know what I am talking about if I say, for example, that short of the heavy work in which each of you has had his or her part, the Congo would by now have been torn to pieces in a fight which in all likelihood would not have been limited to that territory, but spread far around, involving directly or indirectly many or all of the countries from which you come.

"I also know what the activities of the Organization in the economic and social fields have meant for the betterment of the life of millions, and for the creation of a basis for a happier future....

"Let us work in the conviction that our work *has* a meaning beyond the narrow individual one and *has* meant something for man...."

When he had done he received an ovation such as none of our Staff Day stars had ever received. Everyone rose to his feet in a delirium of applause, and the young woman next to me seemed to be having a laughing fit. "I can't stop!" she told me and laughed with the tears streaming down her face. Our aloof and aristocratic boss who never danced with anyone, who expertly avoided eyes and never shook an unnecessary hand, had achieved an unbelievable degree of I-and-Thouness with his Secretariat.

Within the next two days, the Secretary-General visited the Meditation Room for the last time and ordered the black plaque which hangs to this day on the west wall commemorating those who give their lives for peace. His associates say that the ONUC men were continually on his mind during these days.

On September 10, about 7:30 in the evening Grace Barbey of UNICEF saw Hammarskjöld for the last time, just as he was leaving the Secretariat Building with Bill Ranallo and was about to step into his car. She walked up to him and said, "Mr. Secretary-General, you are going on a mission of great importance. You must know that we in the Secretariat are behind you all the way."

"Yes, I do know," answered the Secretary-General, "and it is one of the strengths I carry with me."

Grace turned to Ranallo and said, "Bill, take good care of him!"

Bill replied, "I will. And we'll take with us your wonderful smile."

The same evening Hammarskjöld dined with some friends: Carl Nordenfalk, director of the National Gallery of Stockholm, and his wife, and Ben Shahn the artist, who had been commissioned by Nordenfalk to paint Hammarskjöld's portrait. He showed them a set of photographs he took of Mt. Everest. The conversation touched upon the Congo. He spoke of the situation there with confidence. The worst was now over, he told his guests.

The following day, he went to Idlewild airport where Victor Noble, a UN Security Guard saw him for the last time. Noble had accompanied the Secretary-General when he had flown the Swedish troops into Katanga, and he said, "Mr. Secretary-General, promise me you won't go to Elizabethville." "I won't," promised Hammarskjöld. And he kept this promise, although Tshombe invited him.

Several members of the "Congo Club," were gathered in a little waiting room to see him off: Andrew Cordier, Ralph Bunche, and General Rikhye. Mrs. Wieschhoff was there sitting next to her husband, Heinz, who was going to accompany Hammarskjöld to the Congo. She folded her arms discreetly, but with one hidden hand she was trying to finger her husband's coat sleeve, as it turned out, for the last time.

The plane took off. While it was in flight, the situation in Katanga crumbled. In Jadotville, one of the most infamous episodes of the entire UN operation took place. At the request of the Belgian consul—who made it clear that the United Nations would be held responsible for any incidents involving Europeans in Katanga—the UN command had sent an Irish company of ONUC to that town to protect the lives and property of resident Europeans. There, at the instigation of those same European residents, the Irish company was surrounded by Congolese gendarmerie led by white mercenaries. They were put under fire and their food and water supply was cut off.

At the same time, fighting broke out in Elizabethville, following the arrival from the Central Government in Leopoldville of a warrant for the arrest of Mr. Munongo and other trouble makers. An attempt of ONUC to round up mercenaries met with stiff resistance, and arms were being distributed to the Katangese gendarmerie with advice to shoot at UN personnel. The skies contained a Fouga jet operated by a Belgian named Delin, which floated about the scene of operations dropping bombs wherever it saw a fragment of UN blue.

When Hammarskjöld landed in Leopoldville on September 13, he was greeted with the news of these events. He immediately instructed his representative in Elizabethville,

Dr. Conor Cruise O'Brien, to negotiate a cease-fire with Tshombe. According to O'Brien, who spoke to Tshombe by telephone to arrange a meeting, Tshombe was amenable to a cease-fire. But Tshombe lived in a tail-wags-dog sort of symbiosis with his advisers, and one could never be sure when he was being the tail and when the dog. In this case the tails had it, because during the night, Tshombe slipped away from O'Brien. He hid himself in a manner perfected by Voltaire in a border village with one foot in Rhodesia where, in case Hammarskjöld wanted to negotiate with him, or the Central Government to arrest him, or his friend Munongo to assassinate him, he could retreat into the sheltering arms of Sir Roy Welensky. From this effective fortress, he now had to be lured by Hammarskjöld.

Mr. Munongo and the mercenaries were feeling themselves equally menaced by the arrival of Hammarskjöld. A most embarrassing hitch had occurred at Jadotville. The black gendarmerie did not really have their hearts in killing the ONUC men. Whether out of love for the United Nations or hatred for their white officers, they had begun to fraternize with the Irish boys. On September 15 the Mayor of Jadotville asked for a cease-fire and promised that food and water would be restored. The situation would have gotten completely out of hand had not Mr. Munongo quickly rushed in fresh troops to arrest the "mutineers" and shoot them, and to make certain that no Irishman ate or drank in Jadotville.

The unpopular white officers were, of course, the mercenaries, *"les affreux,"* as they were called—the frightfuls. Hammarskjöld called them the scum of the earth, but he was too harsh. It is true that their profession attracts the riff-raff of many nations whose joys seem limited to murder. Still, many of Tshombe's mercenaries had (and still have) polished finger nails, being none other than the French officers from Algeria who had unsuccessfully plotted against de Gaulle and who were now debarred from going home to France. Not only had they good jobs protecting the advisers who advised Tshombe to protect the mining interests, but they did not even have to learn another language. Three powerful nations, Britain, France, and Belgium wanted them in Katanga, and they were being paid by the Union Minière which, unlike the Congo and the United Nations, had been operating at a profit since Independence Day and was far from bankrupt.

The Secretary-General was after the bread and butter of these gentlemen.

Godefroid Munongo, the "bad African," was their man much more than Tshombe. He was not precisely a spare dog, but he was certainly that portion of the dog closest to its tail. And the United Nations had the temerity to wish to arrest him.

Now here was the Secretary-General in person with his formidable persuasive powers who had made himself the voice of inarticulate nations and whose integrity had swayed the tough Nkrumah and other African leaders. It was by no means beyond the bounds of imagination that he might sway Tshombe, the most swayable man in the world, if only he could meet him face to face.

In order to forestall any such catastrophe, Mr. Munongo had made himself the heart and soul of a propaganda campaign accusing ONUC forces of perpetrating horrible atrocities against the Katangese population; with great eloquence and imaginative power he spoke over the radio, urging every patriotic countryman of his to kill his Swede, his Irishman, and his Indian. Far and wide across the face of the earth, with the eager cooperation of the Belgian, the British, and the French press, the salacious and bloody stories were spread. Conor Cruise O'Brien speaks bitterly of how the news was distorted in this crisis, even when the newspapermen on the spot were honest reporters sympathetic to the UN operation.

It is hard to say whether Munongo really deceived anybody, in fact the suspicion is unavoidable that he deceived nobody among responsible officials of the former colonial powers. But public opinion was deceived and this was made the most of by interested politicians. In the House of Lords the UN operation was called "thuggery," and the House of Commons called O'Brien a "bloodthirsty Dublin corner boy." Sir Roy Welensky spoke of "wanton and naked aggression against a simple people," and he sent his troops and bombers to the Katanga border, apparently to show how opposed he was to aggression.

A few remarks ought to be made about the simple people of Katanga, although Heaven knows that people in general only serve to confuse clear political issues. According to Conor Cruise O'Brien, they applauded every move the United Nations made to deprive them of their white mercenary protectors. Many of them were fleeing the province; and 45,000 of them had thrown themselves upon UN protection and were living lives of great misery in hastily constructed camps where food was scarce except among those tribes who did not mind making a meal out of chance passers-by.

All of these matters were being studied by Hammarskjöld in Leopoldville. He was as annoyed as he could be about the fighting that had broken out in Elizabethville at the very moment when he was on his way to talk about peace with Tshombe. It is not quite certain how this untimely fighting began; it seems evident that a "Leave it to Me" spirit had infected certain United Nations personnel on the spot and that someone among them had wished to present their chief upon his arrival with a fine bouquet of disarmed mercenaries and arrested Katanga leaders. However that may be, a situation had been brought about that conflicted disastrously with Hammarskjöld's diplomatic aims, and this would have been true even if ONUC had not been getting the worst of it. For Hammarskjöld had made of himself the personification of an article of faith: that international conflicts could be solved by means of persuasion and conciliation. Matters had arrived at a point where his failure in the Katanga affair would amount to the failure of the United Nations as it had evolved under his leadership.

In short, one of Krishna Menon's "changing situations" had occurred with a vengeance. The resolution of February 21 had directed the United Nations to use force "as a last resort." But with the mercenaries determined to protect their bread and butter, with snipers stationed in the windows of public buildings, with eager gendarmes wanting to get their Swede, their Irishman, and their Indian, with the Fouga jet roaming the skies and keeping a sharp eye out for fun, and Rhodesian troops concentrated on the border, any UN action whatsoever to carry out its mandate made the use of force a "first resort," and an atrocity into the bargain.

It would be difficult to match in history an event where one man has faced a situation of such complexity and with the stakes so high: in which victory by force of arms could be afforded even less than diplomatic defeat. It was a very frosty Hammarskjöld indeed who kept his subordinates working around the clock while he waited for O'Brien to flush Tshombe out of his hiding place.

During these few days, various ONUC garrisons had been surrounded by the Katanga gendarmerie, controlled by mercenaries, and they were suffering fire not only from the ground but from the Fouga. This lone bomber also found time to keep Elizabethville airport under control in order to prevent United Nations reinforcements from arriving.

On September 14, Lord Landsdowne, Joint Parliamentary Undersecretary for Foreign Affairs, left London for Leopoldville "with instructions to acquaint myself with the facts ... and to impress upon Mr. Hammarskjöld that Her Majesty's government were shocked at the outbreak of fighting in Katanga and to urge upon him the necessity of bringing the fighting to a close ..."

Hammarskjöld had already faced an unpleasant interview with the British ambassador in Leopoldville, Derek Riches, on the subject of the UN atrocities. He had been told that if matters were not immediately brought under control, Britain, in all humanity, would feel obliged to withdraw her support from the UN operation. Lord Landsdowne now brought him a similar billet doux direct from the Foreign Office.

What was actually said in the private conversation that took place between the two men is not known; but those accustomed to the language of diplomacy may infer from Landsdowne's comment that the Secretary-General had expressed himself "with absolute frankness," that to his own sharp remarks he had received from Hammarskjöld a very sharp reply.

The Secretary-General's last diplomatic triumph was that he was apparently able to convince both Riches and Lord Landsdowne of the mendacity of the atrocity reports. Landsdowne later admitted in the House of Lords that "many of the apparently more outrageous aspects of the UN action as we had seen them from London were innacurate or exaggerated." Yet it is difficult to believe that these Englishmen were at any time unaware of whose money oiled the Katanga propaganda mill or what role their own government had played in keeping that mill at work.

The days passed and Tshombe remained in hiding. The General Assembly was at hand, but Hammarskjöld was determined to have his talks with Tshombe. For these talks he had not a card in his hand.

He had, however, a card up his sleeve, and this was confidence in his own shrewd abilities. A certain technique is observable in the Secretary-General's handling of extremely delicate situations; one might call it his "naked to mine enemies" ploy. He had stripped himself of authority in order to deal with the Chinese; he had exposed himself to humiliation in Tunisia. His fantasy-figure of himself as a naked or helpless target shows up repeatedly in *Markings*, as does his identification of humiliation with triumph.

All of his last moves seem designed to ensure that his position descended from weak to dramatically weak. These moves stunned and shocked Dr. O'Brien in Katanga. I think they were deliberate on Hammarskjöld's part. At night in Leopoldville, he was reading Thomas à Kempis' *Imitation of Christ*.

On Saturday, September 16, midnight, Tshombe showed signs of life. Through Mr. Dunnett, the British Consul in Elizabethville, he communicated to O'Brien his wish to meet with him, and he designated Bancroft, Northern Rhodesia, as the place of meeting. O'Brien disapproved absolutely of meeting with Tshombe anywhere in the domain of Sir Roy Welensky, and he urged this viewpoint upon Hammarskjöld. To his amazement he received from Hammarskjöld a lengthy message to be transmitted to Tshombe in which his advice was completely ignored. The message was a succinct summary of the entire Katanga situation, glossing over all points of difference and spotlighting every congenial sentiment Tshombe had ever uttered in favor of peace, reconciliation, and the United Nations. It requested an immediate order for ceasefire; and it contained the paragraph: "I suggest that I should try to meet you personally so that together we can try to find peaceful methods of resolving the present conflict, thus opening the way to a resolution of the Katanga problem within the framework of the Congo."

The place of meeting was to be Ndola, Northern Rhodesia.

It has not been established who first suggested this fateful site; some say that Lord Landsdowne did so, but he has vigorously denied this implication that he might have sent Hammarskjöld to his death. Whoever it was, I believe that Hammarskjöld himself chose to grant this advantage to his adversary. It was in his nature to do so.

O'Brien disliked this plan. He tried to insist upon seeing Hammarskjöld, of apprising him of the situation in Elizabethville, and of dissuading him from going to Rhodesia. But O'Brien was in disgrace, for he was being held responsible for the Katanga fighting. He received from Hammarskjöld a "polite and cool" brushoff. The Secretary-General said that he wished to deal with Tshombe "outside the framework of ONUC." Again, it seems clear that he wished nothing to disturb Tshombe's sense of victory.

Tshombe was already basking in the role of Moise the Great; he replied with a conditional acceptance of the Secretary-General's cease-fire proposals. His conditions were that United Nations troops were to be confined to their camps and the sending of reinforcements were to stop. Hammarskjöld could not agree to this; he replied that since ONUC soldiers were firing only in self-defense, a cease-fire on Tshombe's part would automatically stop the fighting. He insisted also on maintaining the positions of the military groups in their status quo; he owed this stand to ONUC.

No reply was received to this message. He was told, through Mr. Dunnett, that Tshombe had already made his plans to go to Ndola. And so, the Secretary-General relinquished his stand. He seemed intent upon walking out naked to meet Tshombe. Some remarks made later reveal the pitch of his determination. His aide in Leopoldville, Sture Linner, said, "He was anxious first of all to arrive at Ndola as soon as possible—there was no other thought in the Secretary-General's head." Lord Landsdowne said, "He was determined to go to Ndola, and put himself at the disposal of Mr. Tshombe for the talks which he regarded as so important ... So far as I am concerned, this was a plan that the Secretary-General had made and that he was determined to carry out."

I have lived long enough to become amazed, whenever some disaster occurs, to observe with what pedantic exactitude Fate plans the course of events. Inefficient at all other times, when tragedy is ahead, this supernal bureaucrat takes his feet off his desk, sits up alert and snatches the most unlikely materials as building blocks for the bridge between life and death.

C. C. O'Brien has already described the appalling series of seemingly irrational events, starring the British Consul, Mr.

Dunnett, that prevented a cease-fire being negotiated with Tshombe several days earlier, over a few drinks. We may also ask ourselves the ancient question, "What would have happened if...?" Hammarskjöld had granted O'Brien's desire to meet with Tshombe as preliminary to his talks with the Katangan leader.

There now occurred a series of decisions, any one of which, had they been decided otherwise, might have saved Hammarskjöld's life and those of his companions. It was suggested to begin with that Lord Landsdowne should accompany Hammarskjöld to Ndola. At first the Secretary-General agreed to this but he then changed his mind. Perhaps the friendly relations between the two gentlemen had not returned to their status quo, after their sharp exchange; or perhaps one who wished to walk naked, did not choose to cover himself with the Union Jack.

According to Mr. Andrew Cordier the Secretary-General was exceedingly circumspect about the planes on which he travelled. He preferred United Nations planes to commercial planes, and commercial planes to government planes. "He did not wish to travel to Ndola under British aegis," said Dean Cordier. No, and on this occasion it seems that he did not even want to travel under United Nations aegis, for a Belgian DC-4 with United Nations markings which was available in Leopoldville, was placed at the disposal of Lord Landsdowne who travelled on it to Ndola by direct route. His role, by agreement with Hammarskjöld, was to make certain that all arrangements for the meeting had been made, and then, without talking to Tshombe, make himself absent, travelling onward on his DC-4 to Salisbury, the capital of Rhodesia. Hammarskjöld was most anxious that Landsdowne should have left Ndola before he arrived himself.

The Secretary-General chose to ride on a commercial plane, a DC-6 belonging to the Swedish company, Transair. Ordinarily it was used by the ONUC force Commander, General

McKeown. But that same morning, after spending several gruelling and sleepless nights being catechized by Hammarskjöld, McKeown had at last been released, and in a state of utter exhaustion had flown back to the comparative peace of Elizabethville, from where he sent his plane back to Leopoldville in case the Secretary-General should need it. On its take-off for the return journey, the plane had been fired upon, and therefore, when it arrived in Leopoldville it was immediately put under repair. The repair crew worked on it for some hours, and when they had finished left it alone and unguarded on the airfield.

Had the plane not needed repair, and had Lord Landsdowne—who had agreed to leave before Hammarskjöld—not taken so long over his lunch, the Secretary-General would have left Leopoldville much earlier in the day, and have avoided a night journey.

However, the Secretary-General himself was seemingly not anxious to avoid a night journey, otherwise he would not have taken such a circuitous route to Ndola. Lord Landsdowne flew like a crow to his destination; Hammarskjöld went by an indirect route. He had no protective escort, because the United Nations had no fighter planes in the Congo.

The indirect route was probably taken in order to give Landsdowne time to arrive at Ndola and leave there; and also to avoid the usual area of activities of Tshombe's Fouga Magister. If a cease-fire had been arranged before Hammarskjöld took to the air, this plane would have been grounded. It normally operated from an airstrip at Kolwezi, two hundred and thirty miles from Hammarskjöld's route. Its operation range was a hundred and fifty miles. But that Fouga knew the area like the palm of its hand, and it had been known to take off from unpaved tracks.

The flight plan was kept secret. It was not communicated to ONUC officials. Indeed, even the fact that the flight was taking place was not officially communicated to ONUC. The

Secretary-General was indeed acting "outside the framework of ONUC."

Radio silence was kept throughout most of the trip, so that to this day the exact route of the Secretary-General's plane is not known. It is assumed that it flew due east until it passed the Congo border at Lake Tanganyika, and then turned southward towards Ndola. While it was over Lake Tanganyika, the radio silence was broken with a message to Salisbury Flight Information Center. The Secretary-General wanted to know if Lord Landsdowne had yet arrived in Ndola; and why this matter should have been of such importance to him has not been divulged by the British.

Lord Landsdowne did not in fact leave Ndola until after he had seen the Secretary-General's plane fly over Ndola, and then fly westward preparatory to making its procedure turn onto the Ndola runway.

When the plane did not return, as expected, for a landing, Lord Landsdowne was given clearance to leave for Salisbury. He climbed back into his DC-4 and took off. No doubt wishing to report to Hammarskjöld on his activities in Ndola (and to offer his apologies for having talked to Tshombe when he had promised not to do so), he instructed his pilot to make contact with the Secretary-General's plane. When this effort was met by silence, both Lord Landsdowne and his pilot became dismayed and apprehensive. But, when upon his arrival in Salisbury, Lord Landsdowne voiced to officials there his apprehensions, they were greeted with British phlegm.

When the Secretary-General's plane was sighted overhead, Lord Alport, the British High Commissioner in Rhodesia was waiting on the Ndola airfield as part of the reception committee. Tshombe was not with him, because Tshombe had begun to feel tired and he had gone away somewhere to sleep. When the Secretary-General's plane did not reappear after its procedure turn, Lord Alport was not at all apprehensive. He said that Hammarskjöld had probably changed his mind about meeting Tshombe and had gone back to Leopoldville or somewhere else. It did not seem to him odd that the Secretary-General should fly to the heart of darkest Africa and then without a word, change his mind, leaving important personages such as High Commissioners standing about on the airfield. By and by Lord Alport climbed into his private plane and went to sleep.

Mr. Williams, the Airport Manager, appears to have been infected by Lord Alport's phelgm. A member of the Commission of Inquiry which later found it necessary to deplore the fact that "impressions of political nature were allowed to influence the actions of aviation officials," explained the situation to me: "That's the British for you. When a lord says something, that's the end of it."

Mr. Williams went back to his hotel and to bed. Shortly afterwards, the Air Traffic Controller on duty at Ndola closed the tower, and went home to bed. A communicator was left on duty, and very soon he received a communication from two policemen that a light had seared the sky. The communicator sent the policemen with this news to Mr. Williams. Mr. Williams came downstairs in his night clothes, said that nothing could be done before first light, and went upstairs to bed again. He should not be blamed too severely, because he was really supposed to be on vacation, and he had only resumed his responsibilities that night as a favor to world peace.

The behavior of Mr. Williams, and that of all the Rhodesians at Salisbury as well as at Ndola, is described most elegantly in the report of the Commission of Inquiry as "an attitude of mind." More crudely defined, it was this: since the Secretary-General had not seen fit to inform them in detail about his flight plans, then the Secretary-General's plane could take care of itself, especially in an area accessible to a hostile Fouga Magister jet bomber.

And so, while all these gentlemen were enjoying their rest, nine miles away, close to a jungle track negotiable by day or night, a man whom some believed to have been one of the world's most valuable natural resources, was crawling away from his plane, clutching the grass; and perhaps he lived a while to be aware of his companions' fate and of the ordeal of the living Julien. By and by some Rhodesians came to the site. But they had not come to help, only to loot.

The Swedish doctors were to find that Hammarskjöld was too severely injured to have survived; but if fate had not plotted so carefully the attitude of mind of the Rhodesian officials and authorities and help could have been brought, his survival period "could have been somewhat lengthened." And as for Sergeant Julien, had he not suffered "further from exposure and sunburn in the course of the sixteen hours that he remained on the crash site ... his chances of survival would have been infinitely better."

Ten months before his death, the Secretary-General wrote a poem in his diary which reads as if some vision of his end had brushed him: he finds himself in a forest on a mystic night under the moon, fearful and yet submissive to God's will, calling out to those who cannot hear; and knowing well that he stood at the dawn of Judgment Day when the love he had fostered in his heart for others would have its weighing.

Contrary to Mr. Williams' determinations, no air search for the missing plane or investigation of the fire in the night was undertaken with first light, although eighteen aircraft were stationed in Ndola which their commanding officer testified could have been sent up on one hour's notice. Not until 10:00 A.M. local time did the search get under way. The Commission of Inquiry made every attempt to find out the reasons for these delays, but in the end could only deplore that they had happened. The most reasonable explanation lies in the realm of gossip: that when the Rhodesian authorities were forced to conjecture that a world personality with whom they entertained strained relations had met his death on their territory, they suffered *désarroi de l'esprit;* they hesitated to look for what they feared to find. Nor were they at all certain that one of their own RRAF pilots had not taken it into his head to shoot down the Secretary-General's plane.

Early in the afternoon the wreckage was sighted. Forty-five minutes later, rescuers came upon it lying at one end of a cruel swathe of scorched and crippled trees. The plane must have had five tons of fuel in its tanks, and this had spilled over the last three hundred to five hundred feet of its journey. The fire that engulfed the wreckage had flashed back along the petrol trail. The intense heat had melted most of the fuselage, had exploded the ammunition and the magnesium flares, and it burned the passengers, many of them in their seats. Only the Secretary-General and Sergeant Julien lay outside the charred area.

From the moment the site was discovered, the Rhodesian authorities began to behave with macabre efficiency. They cordoned off the area and took possession of all surviving documents including the Secretary-General's brief case in which were found a shirt, a toothbrush, and twelve pages of his translation into Swedish of Martin Buber's *I and Thou*. They prepared a document of merciless accuracy showing the location of every small piece of rubber, fiberglass, and wing skin, every dead man's shoe, every blanket, armrest and first aid kit. There was a burned camera that might have been the Secretary-General's. They measured the height of nearby ant-hills and found that they were nine, twelve, and twenty-two feet high. The nose cone of the plane had broken off, and they recorded that it was found on top of an anthill measuring twelve feet.

After the wreckage had been removed, the area was raked over and the earth put through quarter-inch sieves. In this way "further pieces of aircraft ... coins and small items of personal property" were recovered. This raked-up residue of people's lives was taken to the airport to be set beside all the other collected facts, with the catechisms of witnesses and the evidence of experts; all of which was put through the fine sieve of three Commissions of Inquiry which endeavored to answer the question that was being asked around the world: what caused the crash?

The Commissions of Inquiry arrived at no satisfactory answer. The Rhodesian Commissions set out to prove, and they proved it very well, that whatever happened to Hammarskjöld's plane, the Federation of Rhodesia and Nyasaland had nothing to do with it. The United Nations Commission arrived at conclusions that can only be likened to a fishtail.

• They said that no evidence of sabotage had come to its attention; but that the possibility could not be excluded.

• They found it improbable that the plane could have been under attack; nevertheless they did not exclude attack as a possible cause of the crash.

• They found no evidence of material failure of the aircraft, but "this possibility cannot be excluded, mainly because of the destruction of a major part of the aircraft by fire."

In fact no particle of evidence showed up to militate against the Rhodesian Inquiry's unhelpful conclusion that pilot error was at the bottom of it: "Descent of a fully controllable aircraft into the trees due to (a) some misunderstanding of the aerodrome altitude or (b) some sudden incapacitation of the three pilots on board or (c) some misreading of the aircraft's altimeters or (d) some incorrect altitude indication on at least one of the aircraft's three altimeters, or some combination of (a) to (d)."

A member of the United Nations Commission gave me a plausible explanation of how these three experienced pilots could have erred. When at night the Secretary-General's plane flew over the Ndola airport preliminary to its landing by instrument, its procedure turn over the Ndola forest took it into a "black hole." This, in aviation lingo, is a point where the pilot is out of contact with signals from the airfield. "Two or three seconds later, the pilot would have been able to judge by the perspective of the lights alongside the runway that he was flying too low and could have avoided the crash."

The Commission came to the end of its fishtail with the statement that it had examined the various rumors that had come to its attention concerning the cause of the crash and had found no evidence in their support.

But it was exactly the Commission's "now you see it, now you don't" conclusions that opened the door to a hurricane of rumors, and they are by no means laid at rest. Conor Cruise O'Brien (in *To Katanga and Back*) wrote, "In Elizabethville I do not think there was anyone who believed that his death was an accident." With the reservation that "my opinion, obviously, has no value," he absolves Tshombe, Sir Roy Welensky, and the British government of murder. "Tshombe had no more reason to murder Hammarskjöld on the way to Ndola than Hitler had to murder Chamberlain on the way to Munich . . . I may add that I do not believe Tshombe or Sir Roy Welensky or even Mr. Macmillan to be murderous by disposition. But that is a less telling argument in favor of their innocence than the fact that such a crime was not in their interests . . .

"Munongo's was the one group in Katanga which would have been capable of such an act . . . The men principally concerned were the OAS officers . . . They were, and are, fascists, and they had scores other than the Congo to settle with Hammarskjöld. Algeria, Suez, Tunisia . . . There is no doubt that they were experienced in political assassination and that they would have regarded the murder of Hammarskjöld as a virtuous act."

Arthur Gavshon, in his detailed study of the events leading to the plane crash is also convinced of the mercenaries' guilt. He quotes a Pole serving with the Katanga mercenaries who was asked how he and his companions had taken the news of Hammarskjöld's death. He replied, "We were delighted." Mr. Tshombe himself might have formulated some private suspicions, for the afternoon after the wreckage had been found, quite of his own accord, he ordered his Fouga Magister grounded. The plane had spent the morning in Elizabethville trying to blow Mr. O'Brien and some *Life* people out of existence.

Mr. Andrew Cordier told me, "If I had had to shoot down Hammarskjöld's plane I should have done it exactly where it was done." Another high official of the United Nations said, "I'll tell you what I think in ten years." And still another, who was in Ndola during the investigation said, "A lot has not been told." A persistent rumor that keeps swaying back and forth over the grapevine is that a certain man acquainted with a mercenary visited Knut Hammarskjöld, nephew of the Secretary-General, with the information that the mercenaries had been able to get onto the wave length of the Secretary-General's plane and gave wrong landing instructions. The possibility that this could have been done was, as you might expect, not excluded by the Commission of Inquiry.

These are only opinions, and the opinion of a caricaturist is perhaps as wayward as any. But I feel that the charcoal burners' evidence ought not to have been so readily dismissed on the grounds that they were primitive people. They were literate, they could read newspapers and keep diaries; they rode bicycles, owned radios, over which they listened to world news, and, living next to an airport, they were familiar with the sight and sound of aircraft. I do not see why a man who wants "nothing to do with anything Federal," should automatically be suspected of suffering from aeronautical hallucinations. It seems unlikely to me that people who hide behind anthills lest anyone accuse them of having caused a plane to crash should, when finally yanked before the Commission of Inquiry, invent fables on purpose to get themselves in trouble with the Federal Government. I do not think the misplaced poeticism of Mr. Buleni who said, "It is easy for one to see aeroplanes flying at night because of the buzz of the engines," should have persuaded the Rhodesian enquirers that he could not possibly have seen a fire coming from a small plane and falling on the roof of a big plane.

To be sure, many witnesses saw the great light in the sky without observing any other aircraft than the Secretary-General's. The fact remains, that some people said they did. But because some of the charcoal burners were intimidated or hostile, and suspected of engaging in "imaginative reconstruction," their evidence was not considered in the Commissions' conclusions. It was never established whether Landrovers containing white passengers really did dash to the scene of the crash directly after it happened; or if the lights at the airport were ever turned out.

The most sensational rumor that emerged from the fatal crash was that the late Secretary-General committed suicide, taking with him into death fifteen companions; and that the tragedy was the culmination of carefully thought out plans. We are told that directly before leaving for the Congo Hammarskjöld made a will and that he left the manuscript of *Markings* neatly typed on his desk in his New York apartment with a note to his friend, Leif Belfrage, suggesting in diffident language that it might possibly be published. It is noted too that in his bedroom at Leopoldville, he left behind his checkbook and his wallet, which contained some secret documents; and on the bedside table his copy of the *Imitation of Christ* marked with a bookmark on which was inscribed the oath of office of the Secretary-General of the United Nations.

All of this is said to have been plotted to make of himself a martyr and a myth; and as punctuation, his dead body was found with an Ace of Spades clutched in his hand.

However, much of this is simply not true. Hammarskjöld

had made his will years before his death, and he did not change it before he left for the Congo. He did, indeed, two weeks before his death, ask his friend Per Lind to take charge of his papers, but Mr. Lind did not find *Markings* prominently displayed. He found it in a drawer inside a portfolio contained in a manila envelope to which the note to Leif Belfrage was attached with a paper clip. He had mentioned this diary to Leif Belfrage in 1956, only once and never again.

For a methodical man who was constantly making journeys by plane to war-torn areas, these arrangements do not seem melodramatic. Most businessmen who travel constantly by plane take the ordinary precaution of leaving their private papers in order.

Again those who pin their hopes to the abandoned wallet and checkbook do not satisfactorily explain why the Secretary-General saw fit to take with him to Ndola homework in the form of his translation of *I and Thou*, still less his toothbrush and a clean shirt, items not useful in the after-life, I hope.

Of course, Hammarskjöld might have committed suicide. Our private inquiry into this matter can only end in a fishtail: in default of being on the plane, we cannot exclude such a possibility. The investigators have mentioned as a possible cause of the crash, a sudden distraction of the attention of the pilot, or the incapacitation of all three of them. If the Secretary-General had shot himself or them, this action would certainly fill the bill. Yet, it seems unacceptable to logic that this sensitive man, whose life's meaning was built on the principle that human life has value, should condemn to death the passengers on his plane. Certainly, there is such a thing as "family suicide," when some gentle, melancholy, and loving soul takes his own life and a number of others, too, "in order to spare them further misery on earth." But this explanation would lie in the realm of insanity, and Hammarskjöld in his dealings before leaving New York for the Congo and his behavior before flying to Ndola gave no indication of being irrational. His only strong feeling reportedly was a "determination" to speak with Tshombe.

Moreover, no material evidence exists to show that any weapon of lethal nature was used on the plane, or any infernal machine laid on it. Bullets were found in the bodies of two Swedish soldiers, but they were located close to the skin, and ballistics examinations revealed that they had not passed through a gun barrel. They appear to have been those which the soldiers carried, and they were exploded by the intense heat of the fire. A Swiss expert remelted and examined all the blocks of aluminum and light alloys that had been fused in the fires without finding any indication of a time bomb on board the plane or that any explosion had occurred before the crash.

It has been maintained that a bullet was found in the Secretary-General's head or neck, but if so, all available autopsy reports made by Rhodesian and Swedish doctors omit to mention it. In the absence of any reliable evidence, we can only assume that there was no bullet hole. The same reasoning must apply to the mysterious tape recorder which was said to have been placed near Sergeant Julien's bedside while he lived and talked deliriously, later to be spirited away by the Rhodesian authorities because of the interesting revelations it contained. Although a large number of doctors and nurses would have been aware of the presence of such a tape recorder, no suspicion of its existence reached the Commissions' official reports. A member of the United Nations Commission explained this, "... because there was no tape recorder. Even the airport at Ndola did not possess a tape recorder, and it is highly unlikely that one was available at the hospital." What is known for certain about Julien's revelations is that Hammarskjöld had said "Go back!" These are perhaps unworthy last words of the Secretary-General, but they do not indicate a suicide.

As for the tabloid touch that an Ace of Spades was found in Hammarskjöld's dead hand, this too is absent from any official report, and I can scarcely imagine that the Secretary-General would have been purposefully guilty of such tragi-comic vulgarity. What was found in his hand was a clump of grass, indicating that far from committing suicide on the plane, he actually lived longer than any of his companions except Julien.

Indeed, if Hammarskjöld had wished to make a myth of himself, surely he would not have chosen to commit suicide on a prosaic procedure turn into Ndola. Surely he would have preferred to join the undines in Lake Tanganyika, poetically, like his drowning suicides in *Markings,* and without a trace.

Another major support of the suicide squad is the notion that Hammarskjöld, by ambition and power-hunger, had maneuvered himself into a political dead end from which the only way out was death. One cannot minimize his vaulting ambition or need to play a pivotal role in his milieu; nor his recent harassment, nervous strain or spiritual stresses. But it does not seem that he thought he had reached a political dead end. Among his last remarks to dinner companions the night before he left New York was that in the Congo "the worst was over." Certainly upon his arrival at Leopoldville, he found the situation worsened, but he did not then return to New York to place *Markings* in a prominent spot. Instead he worked day and night with his usual astonishing energy to retrieve his chestnuts from the fire.

In Leopoldville there was a general mood of national reconciliation. The country had a parliament and a recognized government. Adoula and Gizenga were walking about arm in arm, and Kasavubu was giving parties in the Secretary-General's honor. The scene was bright, and at the heart of it lay Hammarskjöld's efforts and those of his people in the Congo.

Only Tshombe was adrift, and Tshombe was nibbling. He had expressed a wish to come to terms with O'Brien; and he hurried to Ndola to meet Hammarskjöld, although he was warned that the talks would not be limited to a cease-fire, but would include talks about the unification of Katanga with the rest of the Congo. In fact, two days after Hammarskjöld's death, Tshombe signed an armistice with the United Nations, and ultimately, after a little *douce violence* from President Kennedy, he made his peace also with Kasavubu.

Hammarskjöld believed in possibilities, and persuading Tshombe to these good ends was within his possibilities. All of his actions prior to the meeting "outside the framework of ONUC," and of the British government, indicate that he wished this to be a personal diplomatic triumph, a spectacular demonstration of the advantages of leaving it to Dag.

And so, if we insist that Hammarskjöld committed suicide, our only really tempting evidence is "the pleasure-tinged death wish" that emerges time and again in *Markings*. Searching this private diary for clues to a fell purpose is a good parlor game, but it is nothing but a parlor game. Leaving their literary quality aside, I find that these poems and aphorisms of Hammarskjöld's, with their prophetic gloom and mystic grue, do not differ from the writings of other persons whose minds are shadowed by overconsciousness of doom. But notes made long before he became Secretary-General identify him as one of the melancholy brotherhood, who live in the shadow of impending catastrophe, and, on the whole, are quite well pleased to feel "chosen" as sacrificial lamb. His familial resemblance to Kierkegaard and Pascal is obvious; but these men did not commit suicide.

Not often do we see an individual soul so exposed. Not many people dare to search the deep crevasses that plunge into the center of being, still less articulate, examine, and meditate upon what they find there. But I venture to say that anyone who did would first have to call himself shabby, petty, false, furtive; and then blessed. Hammarskjöld looked inward in sheer loneliness, desiring to find the center which is common to all; not the everyday porridge that binds families, villages, and cultures together, but the deep "collective consciousness" that is a bridge between a Swedish aristocrat and the men of modern Congo.

Looking there, perhaps he found the idea that one man's life yielded willingly has the specific gravity of all. It was an ancient notion even when the Secretary-General's ancestors, wearing Thor's hammer on their shields, performed human sacrifice at Uppsala. It has been expressed in religious contexts, both crudely and nobly, among Congo cannibals, Greek philosophers, and Judaic sages. It is part of the pattern of human action, and perhaps unselfish dedication to others, and willing sacrifice in everyday life is not so rare after all.

But some radiant or weighty lives acquire significance beyond the ordinary, so that when they travel, as they usually do, towards conflict and disaster, they become unforgettable. They become our teachers who miraculously resolve for us the puzzle propounded by *I and Thou.*

Enmeshed in the facts, the opinions, and the rumors of the late Secretary-General's death are the feelings about him. I asked a young woman of the Secretariat who she thought killed Hammarskjöld, and although she comes from behind the Iron Curtain, she replied with great bitterness: "Everybody killed him."

17

Why?

THE bodies of the victims were placed in caskets and laid in Saint Andrew's United Church in Ndola beneath a simple cross—nothing but two bars. Some bureaucratically minded individual was moved to place Hammarskjöld's coffin separated from the others as if it were a captain of the cohort of the dead. A pious person was heard to say, "I wonder what God is going to think of that?"

Tshombe came to the church and set a wreath of lilies on the coffin of Hammarskjöld. He muttered, *"C'est triste,"* bowed, and walked away.

It was a strange journey that took those lost ones back to their homelands, a United Nations funeral, with a plane flying halfway around the globe, dropping coffins here and there. It started on September 26 at Salisbury airport where a ceremonial parade and a religious service took place in the presence of the Governor-General of Rhodesia and Nyasaland, Lord Dalhousie; and of Sir Roy Welensky who, after having sent so many acerbic messages to Hammarskjöld, now sent flowers. The coffins were then flown to Leopoldville where at the airport from which nine days before the Secretary-General and his party had flown to Ndola, soldiers of the Congolese army formed a guard of honor. An ONUC bugler sounded the

Last Post and President Kasavubu and Prime Minister Adoula stood with bowed heads.

The following day more than two thousand people waited at the Cointrin Airport in Geneva for the blue and white United Nations plane to arrive from Africa, accompanied by Knut Hammarskjöld, nephew of the late Secretary-General, and Pier Spinelli, Director of the United Nations European office. A military band played *J'avais un camarade,* and all afternoon the townspeople of Geneva and people from over the French border filed silently past the catafalque with small bunches of flowers. In Geneva the body of Vladimir Fabry, the legal counsel of ONUC who had been taken to Ndola because he had been "working himself to a standstill" and he "deserved the honor and experience," was handed over to his mother and sister.

At 3:00 A.M. now with 15 coffins aboard, the blue-white plane took off from Cointrin to Sweden. Silently the plane descended from the grey September sky and touched down at Malmö. The propellors slowed and stopped, a tractor was shackled to the nose of the plane and in slow motion the winged hearse was drawn between rows of Swedish soldiers standing at attention in white boots and helmets, and black bands around their arms. The Swedish flag, decked in long black streamers, dipped in salute. The bodies of the Swedish victims had come home: Captain Per Hallonquist, pilot in command and his two co-pilots, Captain Nils-Eric Aahreus and First Officer Lars Litton; Nils Goran Wilhelmsson, the flight engineer, and Karl Erik Rosen, the radio operator, who was one of the Swedish military contingent and had been chosen for the Ndola trip especially because he was able to send morse code in Swedish, as was his colleague A. P. Harald Noork. Warrant Officer S. O. Hjelte and Private P. E. Persson were ONUC infantrymen who were taken along as guards.

In Malmö the coffins of the pilot and five crew-members were given to their families, and with ten left the plane proceeded to Stockholm. There, on Bromma airfield, Bo and Sten Hammarskjöld stood side by side carrying a wreath, and they received the coffin of their brother.

The plane then flew to Ireland where at Dublin airport Francis Eivers was awaited by a band of the Irish Police Force to which he had once belonged. There was a memorial ceremony, after which his former colleagues took their burden upon their shoulders and carried it away.

With five coffins remaining, the plane landed in Dorval airport at Montreal. There the honor guard of the Regiment de Joliette and government officials waited for the body of Alice Lalande, the only woman member of the Ndola expedition. Alice had once been the secretary of Count Folke Bernadotte, killed in Palestine.

Finally, the sorrowful plane came down at Idlewild, New York, with the last four coffins aboard. The United Nations Security Force formed a guard of honor in front of the hangar. The great doors were rolled back and four United Nations guards slowly brought the coffins from the hangar into the sunshine: those of Heinz Wieschhoff, the German-born ethnographer who had become an American citizen; Bill Ranallo, Serge Barrau, and Harry Julien of United Nations Security. There were flowers and ribbons and four United Nations flags; three American flags and one flag of Haiti for Barrau were draped over the coffins.

A minute of silence was observed. The journey had ended where it had begun.

Meanwhile at the Marine Terminal of LaGuardia Airport in New York, a party boarded a small United Nations plane. Among them were Andrew Cordier, Adlai Stevenson, Mme. Agda Russel, Sweden's permanent representative to the United Nations, Nathan Barnes of Liberia, President of the Security Council, and Raphael Klein of the UN Staff Council who was representing the members of the Secretariat. They were on their way to Washington to board one of the two presidential planes that would take them to Sweden to attend the funeral of Dag Hammarskjöld. Vice-President Lyndon B. Johnson was to represent President Kennedy at the funeral.

The 707 presidential jet on which these people travelled had only two berths. One was assigned to Johnson and the other to Stevenson. Stevenson, naturally, relinquished his berth to Mme. Russel. The party spent the night sitting around tables for four. At bedtime, Vice-President Johnson, dressed in fancy Pinnocchio-style pajamas stepped out of his berth and, good Texas vote-getter as he is, went from table to table, shaking hands with everybody.

The party landed at noon in Stockholm. The funeral was to be held the next day in Uppsala, some thirty miles away.

On September 29, 1961, in the cathedral at Uppsala, named after St. Eric, Sweden's patron saint, the coffin of Dag Hammarskjöld, draped in the flag of Sweden, was enthroned in a mass of flowers, white lilies and larkspur, characteristic of the countryside of Löderup and of Lapland where he loved to wander. Six burning candles shone above it, and students of the university at Uppsala and United Nations soldiers stood guard.

All the shop windows in Uppsala displayed pictures of Hammarskjöld draped in black crepe and all the flags were at half mast. At three o'clock in the afternoon all the bells began to ring. In the cathedral the congregation arose. King Gustav Adolf and Queen Louise, three princes and three princesses were coming down the aisle. They took their places on the right side of the coffin. The places on the left were allocated to the family of Hammarskjöld.

In the general congregation were seated visitors who had come from all parts of the world and members of the diplomatic corps including the Russian ambassador. There was Tage Erlander, the Swedish prime minister, and Östen Unden, who had advised the young economist to take the post of Secretary-General; and Trygve Lie, who warned that it was the hardest job in the world. His aides, Andrew Cordier and Ralph Bunche, were there; and Gibson Parker, who had accompanied him on his visit to Pope Pius XII, was narrating this scene over the United Nations radio.

There were Israelis and Arabs, Congolese and Belgians, Laotians, Frenchmen, Tunisians, men of all the nations whose affairs he had mediated, arbitrated and conciliated. Mrs. Roosevelt was there; Lord Kilmuir had come from Britain and Mme. Pandit from India; Frederick Boland, who had broken the gavel, was there. Sture Linner had come from the Congo. It was to him that Hammarskjöld had said his last "Adjö."

The Boy's Choir of St. Eric's Cathedral sang the *Agnus Dei*, and the congregration sang Hymn 29 of the Church of Sweden: "when man's mind penetrates the profoundest depths to seek the meaning of life, it will find creative will: the love of God."

Nobody knew at that time of the existence of the manuscript we know as *Markings.*

The service was conducted by the 81-year-old Archbishop Erling Eidem. Seven years ago he had buried Hjalmar Hammarskjöld.

> Öster, väster, norr och söder
> korsets armar överskygga
> alla äro våra bröder,
> som på jorden bo och bygga ...

"East, west, north and south, the arms of the Cross stretch bridging. All who dwell on earth and build, they are brothers."

The slanted northern vowels reverberated and the hard r's crashed like rocks; but the ancient message does not pour smooth in any language.

"The Lord is our consolation ... we are not alone, neither in life nor in death." So Hammarskjöld had realized in a moment of rare joy. "... His Cross is our hope, our victory. Grant us Thy grace forever to have before our eyes."

The congregation stood and the archbishop turned towards the coffin. "In the name of God, the gracious and merciful, take now the corruptible body of Dag Hammarskjöld, hallowed to rest in the grave." And the Swedish voices said a hard "Am-men."

Three times during the prayers the Archbishop sprinkled earth over the coffin. The voice of the Swedish soprano, Elizabeth Söderstrom rose to the vaulted arches: "I know that my Redeemer liveth." The king placed a wreath upon the coffin. Four guards raised four flags: two Swedish flags, the flag of Uppsala, and the United Nations flag. His Majesty offered condolences to the Hammarskjöld family. The pallbearers removed the many wreaths from around the coffin, leaving only the Hammarskjöld family wreath on top. They shouldered it and moved slowly down the center aisle towards the door; outside it was placed on a gun-carriage drawn by four horses from the royal stables. It traveled through the narrow streets of Uppsala, passed the library and the university, and the silent crowds and white-capped university students. It came to the seventeenth century cemetery.

At the open grave the archbishop said his last prayers and stood beside the Hammarskjöld family. The students sang Venerable Father, Noble Shadows: the bells tolled. Four men in top hats, dressed in black, silently let down the coffin with its single wreath into the grave beneath a granite slab on which is inscribed

HJALMAR
HAMMARSKJÖLD
FAMILJEGRAV

Thus, Agnes Hammarskjöld's son returned to his elders. She would have had no reason to feel dissatisfied with the number of people world wide who were weeping for her son. And the authoritarian Hjalmar would surely have felt glad

ADDRESS GIVEN BY THE SECRETARY-GENERAL ON THE OCCASION OF THE UNITED NATIONS DAY CONCERT, 24 OCTOBER, 1960

IT IS THE TRADITION that the Organization marks United Nations Day with a concert including the final movement of Beethoven's Ninth Symphony. Today we shall, for the first time in this hall, listen to the symphony in its entirety.

It is difficult to say anything, knowing that the words spoken will be followed by this enormous confession of faith in the victorious human spirit and in human brotherhood, a confession valid for all times and with a depth and wealth of expression never surpassed.

When the Ninth Symphony opens we enter a drama full of harsh conflict and dark threats. But the composer leads us on, and in the beginning of the last movement we hear again the various themes repeated, now as a bridge toward a final synthesis. A moment of silence and a new theme is introduced, the theme of reconciliation and joy in reconciliation. A human voice is raised in rejection of all that has preceded and we enter the dreamt kingdom of peace. New voices join the first and mix in a jubilant assertion of life and all that it gives us when we meet it, joined in faith and human solidarity.

On his road from conflict and emotion to reconciliation in this final hymn of praise, Beethoven has given us a confession and a credo which we, who work within and for this Organization, may well make our own. We take part in the continuous fight between conflicting interests and ideologies which so far has marked the history of mankind, but we may never lose our faith that the first movements one day will be followed by the fourth movement. In that faith we strive to bring order and purity into chaos and anarchy. Inspired by that faith we try to impose the laws of the human mind and of the integrity of the human will on the dramatic evolution in which we are all engaged and in which we all carry our responsibility.

The road of Beethoven in his Ninth Symphony is also the road followed by the authors of the Preamble of the Charter. It begins with the recognition of the threat under which we all live, speaking as it does of the need to save succeeding generations from the scourge of war which has brought untold sorrow to mankind. It moves on to a reaffirmation of faith in the dignity and worth of the human person, and it ends with the promise to practice tolerance and live together in peace with one another as good neighbours and to unite our strength to maintain peace.

This year, the fifteenth in the life of the Organization, is putting it to new tests. Experience has shown how far we are from the end which inspired the Charter. We are indeed still in the first movements. But no matter how deep the shadows may be, how sharp the conflicts, how tense the mistrust reflected in what is said and done in our world of today as reflected in this hall and in this house, we are not permitted to forget that we have too much in common, too great a sharing of interests and too much that we might lose together, for ourselves and for succeeding generations, ever to weaken in our efforts to surmount the difficulties and not to turn the simple human values, which are our common heritage, into the firm foundation on which we may unite our strength and live together in peace.

in front of the orchestra from which he spoke was empty. Instead, we sat in the shadows and listened to a rebroadcast of his last address.

"When the Ninth Symphony opens we enter a drama full of harsh conflict and dark threats. But the composer leads us on, and in the beginning of the last movement we hear again the various themes repeated, now as a bridge towards a final synthesis. A moment of silence and a new theme is introduced, the theme of reconciliation and joy in reconciliation. A human voice is raised in rejection of all that has preceded and we enter the dreamt kingdom of peace. New voices join the first and mix in a jubilant assertion of life and all that it gives us when we meet it, joined in faith and human solidarity ...

"No matter how deep the shadows may be, how sharp the conflicts, how tense the mistrust reflected in what is said and done in our world of today as reflected in this hall and in this house, we are not permitted to forget that we have too much in common, too great a sharing of interests and too much that we might lose together, for ourselves and for succeeding generations, ever to weaken in our efforts to surmount the difficulties and not to turn the simple human values, which are our common heritage, into the firm foundation in which we may unite our strength and live together in peace."

Our programs bore an inserted sheet saying, "There will be no applause during the Memorial Ceremony." But there was no need to tell us that. We sat like stone.

Four years later, in May of 1965, the United Nations Singers toured Sweden, and they visited Backåckra, Hammarskjöld's country house. He had acquired it in 1957, a low farmhouse with stables framing a cobblestone courtyard, at Löderup in Southern Sweden. He meant it for his "retreat" when his years of duty were over, but he never saw the place completely restored. The last time he had visited it was in 1959.

He had cleaned it out himself, with the help of Bill Ranallo.

But one day when they had first moved in, Bill had walked over to Bo Beskow's house nearby, complaining bitterly: "You know what he's doing instead of sweeping the floor? Picking flowers."

In his will, Hammarskjöld left Backåckra to the Swedish Touring Club of which he was president for a number of years. The will specified that for two months in the summer, the Swedish Academy, of which Hammarskjöld was a member, should have the use of the farmhouse for holiday purposes. The Assembly room was to be used for "meetings of associations formed to promote the preservation of nature, of culture, or for meetings arranged on the initiative of the United Nations or any person with the object of furthering its aim."

It was here that all his treasures were gathered together. On the walls of Backåckra hangs the original painting Bo Beskow made for the mural in the Meditation Room. Tenzing Norkay's icepick has found a permanent home over the fireplace. There is a Barbara Hepworth sculpture that had stood by his desk on the 38th Floor; and his menorah from Israel; and his vase from Chou En-lai.

The singers put on their many national costumes and stood in the cobbled courtyard and sang the songs of nations.

They also visited his grave. They placed twelve red roses on it, and stading in a semi-circle sang a Swedish song, *Gladjens Blomster*, The Flowers of Joy. This is known to have been Hammarskjöld's favorite folk song. In 1958 the Staff had given him a surprise party and the Singers had sung this song for him. In his speech of thanks, he said, "The melody . . . I think is very beautiful. The words are perhaps a little bit on the sad side. If I may translate the first line of the song? It runs like this: 'Will the flowers of joy ever grow?' "

But the sad flowers that were buried with him, the ones that formed the Hammarskjöld family wreath, asked a more practical question, though it is one even more difficult to answer. A single word was written on the wreath: *Why?*

The word again recalls a moment of Hammarskjöld's life when he addressed Stamford University in 1955. He quoted some bitter lines of W. H. Auden's *Epitaph On An Unknown Soldier:*

To save your world, you asked this man to die
Would this man, could he see you now ask why?

18

The Legacy

ELEVEN days after the funeral of Hammarskjöld in Uppsala, Mr. Jaja Wachuku, foreign minister of Nigeria, delivered before the Assembly a maiden speech which was far from maidenly. He began with the suggestion—afterwards followed—that the new United Nations Library should be dedicated to the memory of Hammarskjöld; he thought also that a memorial ought to be erected in Leopoldville as a reminder to travellers, in the hypothetically peaceful future, of the man who lost his life in Africa in quest of peace.

Then he turned to the great powers.

"I think the time has come when the question of the definition of 'greatness' in this Assembly must be considered.

"What is true greatness? Is it because one produces a rocket and because one has weapons for destruction—is that greatness? That you have been able to produce a thing which should be used for the good of humanity and for everyone, and that you turn against yourselves. Is that not insanity? Should insanity be equated with greatness? My answer is NO!

"I am losing confidence in the great powers," Mr. Wachuku went on. "... We expect leadership from them; they give us destruction. We expect wisdom from them; they give us lack of knowledge. We expect objectivity from them; they present us with blurred vision. How do you expect me to follow such leadership?"

It should not be imagined that by this time the representatives of the great powers were casting looks of guilt and confusion at one another. On the contrary, they were amused, even gratified, that a new foreign minister from a new country should come to New York and tell them what they already knew: that the emperor has no clothes.

The United Nations *is* what the great powers wanted it to be: this is what Trygve Lie told John McVane of ABC-TV in an interview. He knew what he was talking about. He had been a delegate at the San Francisco Conference in 1945 where the United Nations was born and where the great powers installed themselves in a Security Council, as guardians of the peace. Also present at that conference was a tall and craggy man named Ely Culbertson who had the loudest voice in the press bar. I had no idea what he was doing at such a poker game as an international conference, especially when I was told that he was a bridge champion.

But one day I heard Culbertson toll out some words that struck my mind: "They want to set up an Organization of cats among mice!"

Exactly so. The Five Big Cats set up an Organization to keep the Mice out of mischief. And when those Cats began to fight among themselves, it was woe to Mice as well as Cats; but where is the Mouse who dares to tell Cats what to do?

This is the Organization of which Dag Hammarskjöld became Secretary-General.

In the summer before he died, he wrote his usual annual report on the work of the Organization which he was to deliver before the Assembly when it met in the fall. He died the day before the Assembly opened. But the *Introduction to the Annual Report of the Secretary-General, 16 June, 1960–15 June, 1961,* may be regarded as Hammarskjöld's political testament.

In it he discussed two differing prevailing concepts of the character of the United Nations.

"Certain members conceive of the Organization," he wrote, "as a static conference machinery for resolving conflicts of interest and ideologies with a view to peaceful coexistence ... served by a Secretariat which is to be regarded not as fully internationalized, but as representing within its ranks those very interests and ideologies...."

Other members conceive of the Organization primarily "as a dynamic instrument of governments through which they jointly ... should seek such reconciliation, but through which they should also try to develop forms of executive action undertaken on behalf of all members ..."

The latter group sees the Organization as "served by a Secretariat of which it is required that whatever the background and view of its individual members, their action be guided solely by the principles of the Charter, the decisions of the main organs, and the interest of the Organization itself."

In plain cartoon language, some members want a Debating Society, with the Secretary-General and his staff making certain that the water-jugs on the conference tables are full. Others desire a Dynamic Organization which makes decisions that stick, and with a Secretary-General empowered to get things done.

It is not hard to guess who wants which. Cats want to caterwaul, and Mice want somebody to do something for them.

Hammarskjöld made it clear what sort of Organization he thought necessary for the modern world.

"The first concept can refer to history and to the traditions of national policies of the past. The second can point to the needs of the present and of the future in a world of ever-closer international interdependence where nations have at their disposal armaments of hitherto unknown destructive strength.

"The first one is firmly anchored in the time-honored philosophy of sovereign national States in armed competition, of which the most that may be expected in the international field is that they achieve a peaceful coexistence.

"The second one envisages possibilities of intergovernmental action overriding such a philosophy, and opens the road towards more developed and increasingly effective forms of constructive international cooperation."

This division of concept threads through the entire fabric of the United Nations, dividing the members against themselves. It is at the bottom of conflicting views about the mandatory force of United Nations resolutions; or direct aid for needy countries as opposed to aid channeled through the United Nations. In his "testament" the Secretary-General took up these issues.

"For those who maintain the conference concept of the Organization," he wrote, "it is natural to sidestep the mandatory nature of the decisions in the Security Council. For those who take a different view, it is equally natural and essential to work for full and general acceptance of the Charter rules.

"With the conference approach . . . a choice is made also in favor of bilateral assistance, while the alternative approach opens the door to a development under which international assistance, in implementation of the principle of equal economic opportunities for all, would be channelled through the Organization or its related agencies . . ."

A tragic case of the dangers of direct, bilateral aid is that of the Congo. Assistance to that country in its time of need was not limited to sacks of wheat. It covered "advisers," "volunteers," and the murder weapons delivered to Tshombists by the Belgians, French, and Rhodesians, and to Lumumbists by the Soviets and the United Arab Republic. It covered all the stage machinery necessary for a Spanish-style civil war.

Hammarskjöld explained how his own troubles had arisen from the "lack of balance" between the two concepts in the Charter itself, as it was framed in San Francisco.

"While too much attention is given to the principles and

purposes, and considerable space is devoted to an elaboration of what may be called the parliamentary aspect of the Organization, little is said about executive arrangements.

"When the Charter was written . . . the conference approach still was predominant . . . The need for executive action . . . had not yet attracted attention."

And so, when the need for executive action in the Near East, Laos, Cambodia, and the Congo arose, and neither the Security Council nor the General Assembly was equipped to perform the administrative functions, they entrusted the Secretary-General with "the necessary steps for implementation of the action decided upon." This was "Leaving it to Dag."

". . . In carrying out his functions, the Secretary-General has found himself forced also to interpret the decision in the light of the Charter, United Nations precedents, and the aims and intentions expressed by the members. When that has been the case, the Secretary-General has been under the obligation to seek guidance, to all possible extent, from the main organs; but when such guidance has not been forthcoming, developments have sometimes led to situations in which he has had to shoulder responsibility for certain limited political functions."

This was "filling the vacuum."

"This whole development has lately become a matter of controversy, natural, and indeed, unavoidable in the light of differences of approach to the role of the Organization . . . While the development is welcomed by member nations which feel the need of growth . . . it is rejected by those who maintain the conference concept of the Organization."

And he interpolated a grave reminder: "Those whose reactions to the work of the Organization hamper its development or reduce its possibilities of effective action may have to shoulder the responsibility for a return to a state of affairs which governments had already found too dangerous after the First World War."

This political testament of Hammarskjöld's is written in undramatic language, but it tells the procedural background of his calvary; and more than that. Held beside the entries in *Markings,* it shows how the "road to holiness" passed into the "world of action."

Such understanding as I have comes from what I see. I look at a face and see a pair of eyes, a nose and a mouth across, a forehead topping the whole with two ears sticking out. But the face adds up to something beyond the sum of its physical parts. You may call it the "character" of the face and say that it belongs to Joe or Mike; and give it a Social Security Number. Yet, these are only labels, and there is something still beyond. It is the essence of the face, the miracle of Mike, the limitless mystery of his spirit that existed long before he was born and will exist long after his widow has collected her Social Security benefits.

Just so, the United Nations is not the sum total of its member nations, great or small, any more than Christianity or Judaism are the sum total of churches, temples, priests, and faithful. There is an elusive spirit buried in it that was born when the first man was born complete with an instinct to unify, to share, to serve, to sacrifice, to live in peace with his neighbor. We call it the "UN ideal," or the "UN spirit," or the "UN philosophy"; but whatever label we put on it, we are dealing with something extramundane that can be felt or expressed in a symbol, but never fully comprehended, for it reaches beyond the temporal order into the eternal order.

For this reason the United Nations, this rather radical political concept, is joyfully accepted and supported by all religious faiths on earth, while other radical political concepts for the betterment of mankind are certainly not. And this is why Hammarskjöld never forgot that Pope Pius XII had said to him, *"Vous êtes mon homologue laïque,"* and why he took full seriously his exalted mission as lay pope, isolating in his mind and serving with uncompromising devotion the principles that exalted it.

No political failure could possibly have wounded him more than did the Russian's impugning of his impartiality, that necessary virtue so carefully nurtured, treasured, tended in the difficult soil of the spirit. It is perhaps inevitable that a people whose education contains great doses of ideology should refuse to admit the existence of an unindentured mind. Khrushchev told Walter Lippman in an interview in 1961, "While there are neutral countries, there are no neutral men." Mikoyan had propounded this view to Hammarskjöld when the Secretary-General visited Khrushchev's villa on the Black Sea. Marxist theory does not recognize such an entity as a disinterested person, Mikoyan explained. "Everybody is an agent, even if he comes from Sweden."

In reply, Hammarskjöld compared himself to the Russian sputnik: "True, I was launched in Sweden, but once in orbit I do not come close to any country."

Some westerners share the Russian conviction: an international civil servant must be guided by what he thinks is right, and his idea of what is right is historically and culturally formed, by nationality, social class, education, upbringing, all that shaped the mind, and "he can no more escape from them than he can escape from his skeleton," says Conor Cruise O'Brien.

However, it is on this stark skeleton that I will place my bets.

Nationality, class, upbringing are environmental factors, but a man's personality emerges from their interaction with the organism which is hereditary. Why overlook the organism? Surely it is as erroneous to overlook an hereditary factor as an environmental one.

Organism includes, besides the physical functions of the organs, deep-seated psychic functions, feelings, reflexes, im-

pulses; the temperament a man is born with; primary knowledge, collective subconscious. Deep in the organism lies a sense
of good and evil and the instinct to define them; and the sub-
liminal forces that take frightful Vikings and manufacture
out of them Pacificatory Swedes. Here is the center common
to all men, the skeleton from which we cannot escape. We can
slough off all the rest, or at least we can, if we will it, keep
our environment—as Hammarskjöld suggested in his speech
before Congregation at Oxford—for private, personal enjoyment.

Besides, when Khrushchev raised the question of neutral
men, he ought to have specified, "neutral in what?"

Neutrality is a relative term. Artists, philosophers, mystics
and the like achieve a certain neutrality as they extend their
passion from the specific to the general, from the material to
the spiritual. Becoming neutral in matters that are specific
and material, they stop shaving, cease to wash themselves, and
wear disreputable garments. But in matters that are general
and spiritual, they are fanatically partisan.

When Gandhi became totally absorbed in *brahmacharya*,
ahimsa, and Free India, he ceased to care for his family,
although environmentally this would have been his first duty
as a Hindu. But he callously handed the burden over to his
brother. Christ explained such egoism when, upon being told,
"Behold, thy mother and thy brethren without seek for thee,"
he replied, "Who is my mother or my brethren?" Then he
pointed to the multitude which sat about him and said,
"Behold my mother and my brethren! For whosoever shall do
the will of God, the same is my brother and my sister and
mother."

Hammarskjöld differed very greatly from Gandhi and
Christ, both of whom were far from lonely and able in life
to communicate with homely simplicity to their multitude of
brothers, sisters, and mothers. Christ was not at a loss for words
in the company of women and children. Gandhi would never

have fumbled with Hammarskjöld's moral dilemma betwixt
ends and means or have wondered whether concealment of
truth can ever help truth to victory.

Hammarskjöld was a man of affairs who walked about in a
well-pressed suit. But secretly he sought the skeleton, the core.
He applied himself to the strait gate and the narrow path
along which no man travels unless he leaves his flesh outside.
Receiving his instructions from this strict source, he proclaimed them from the rostrum of the United Nations. All
the insults and the invective he had suffered, he declared,
"were no excessive price to be paid for avoiding the thing
for which no one in my position should be forgiven: to compromise . . . with the aims and principles of this Organization!"

When you consider that the "aims and principles of this
Organization" are precisely that everybody on earth is supposed to be ready to compromise with his specific interest for
the sake of the general interest, you see spectacularly the
smashing partisanship of the man of principle. Material compromise is desirable. Spiritual compromise is unthinkable.

Therefore, one must end by agreeing with Messrs. Mikoyan
and Khrushchev: everybody is an agent of something. One is
an agent of a party, a nation, or some intrigue or interest.
Another is an agent of some lofty principle that concerns the
entire human race. But neither of them is neutral.

Hammarskjöld himself wrestled with the vast egoism of
utter selflessness. On November 12, 1955, he wrote to his
artist friend, Bo Beskow: "Where is human warmth? Everywhere and nowhere. In my situation it is, I suppose, part of
the price of what one does that you can only give yourself as
unreservedly as is possible if, in doing so, you do not steal
even the tiniest part from anyone else: in order to be able
really to 'die'—in the evangelical sense . . . you need the para-
doxical egoism (who is my mother and my brother, etc.?)." *

Again and again in his political testament, Hammarskjöld

* Söderberg, *Pictorial Biography.*

extended—though hopelessly—the strict geometry of the spirit into the no-man's-land of international politics. He wrote:

"The Charter lays down some basic rules of international ethics . . . by which all Member States have committed themselves to be guided. To the large extent, the rules reflect standards accepted as binding for life within States.

". . . By projecting these rules into the international arena . . . the Charter takes the first step in the direction of an organized international community . . ."

While recognizing that great variations of traditions, social development, and character of national institutions exist within the states, ". . . it is not too difficult to recognize the common elements behind those differences. It is therefore not surprising that such principles of national application could be transposed into an agreed basis for international behavior and cooperation."

Yes, but people cherish their old ways, even though obsolete, before trying new ways, even though imperative. The day foreseen by Woodrow Wilson when "a man would be as ashamed of failing in his duty to humanity as he now is if he failed in his duty to his country" is not yet at hand.

Hammarskjöld urged the substitution of right for might. "The Charter," he wrote, "gives expression to another basic democratic principle, that of the rule of law.

"As in national life the principle of justice must be considered applicable in international matters . . . with one measure and one standard valid for the strong as well as for the weak."

Law, even today, is not very popular within the national states, and it was even less so when it was introduced as a new invention. Some memorable words from the motion picture *High Noon* express the state of affairs: "It seems like people need some time to talk themselves into law and order. Maybe they just don't care enough." Certainly that forsaken sheriff-hero commanded no less affection among outlaws and decent citizens alike than a Secretary-General who talked about law and ethics to modern states. UNEF and ONUC are but Hammarskjöld's Vigilantes of the nuclear age, volunteers with obliquely defined authority and inadequate means. Whatever they do is bound to be a sort of atrocity against someone.

The man who takes the Siege Perilous is necessarily a pure and gentle knight, but he strikes terror into comfortable hearts. Hammarskjöld disturbed the ideologists and the hurrah-patriots, the paramount chiefs of power and their money-magicians. He acted—and he continually reminded himself to act—in mercy, and they feared him for it. "In spite of this—and because of it," he wrote, "—Gethsemane."

Was Hammarskjöld a genius? W. H. Auden to whom English readers are indebted for his translation of *Markings* says that he was not a genius, "not, that is to say, a person with a single overwhelming talent and passion for some particular activity—be it poetry or physics or birdwatching . . ."

The Oxford Dictionary has a less parochial view of genius which it defines as "native intellectual power of an exalted type; extraordinary capacity for imaginative creation, original thought, invention, or discovery."

Schopenhauer offers us: "Genius holds up to us the magic glass in which all that is essential and significant appears to us collected and placed in the clearest light and what is accidental and foreign is left out."

Here we are close to Hammarskjöld, and we come closer still with Kierkegaard who tells us, "Genius can be ranked according to the opposition it arouses." He insists that genius must "bring something new." My favorite psychologist, Kretschmer, compromises on the "new" and ranks among geniuses Raphael and Bach, no upsetters of tradition, but perfectors of a style handed down to them. "The essential thing in their genius is much more the creation and lifting up from the stream of everyday professional traditional practice of a special purely personal note which is still recognizable to the expert after the lapse of centuries."

By most of these definitions, Hammarskjöld was a genius; and even by Mr. Auden's. For after all, Dag Hammarskjöld had a perfect talent and passion for being Secretary-General of the United Nations.

I dare say that in the twenty years of the United Nations' existence, its most remarkable achievement was that it produced Hammarskjöld. His ideas were akin to those of Wilson and Lord Cecil; but neither of these was granted an office that enabled them to give new dimensions to these ideas or to improvise new solutions.

After he was gone, those of us who had watched him breathe life into the timid Charter and lend his own volume to the tentative Organization, saw his work quite simply squeezed out of existence.

The Soviet Union and France headed the demolition squad. The Russians refused to divert a single kopek or France a single sou towards the continuation of his peace-keeping operations. Behind the gigantic battle of bookkeepers lurked the fear that a majority of small nations—Hammarskjöld's chickens —in the Assembly might circumcise the great power privilege of veto. Exercising the terrific might of debtors, France and Russia, therefore, forced the United Nations from the Dynamic Organization position to the "conference concept" in which the will of the great powers is certain to preponderate.

We are back to Culbertson's Cats.

But can the dial of human thought be turned back and Dag Hammarskjöld be rendered null and void? If he fought for a lost cause, we might well ponder Chesterton's words that "the lost causes are exactly those which might have saved the world."

I do not think he fought for a lost cause. The Swedes struck a medal in silver to his memory which bears the inscription *Vir vixit, opus vivit*—the man has lived, his work lives on. His work lives in the words he spoke before United Nations gatherings, press conferences, academies. A study of them shows no deviation, sidestepping or backsliding. They formed a taut, narrow, and safe bridge which led us the first few steps from Wilson's age into the nuclear age, but it stretches far beyond into the future.

I think mankind will be using Hammarskjöld's bridge for a long time to come.

Bibliography

Bleuler, Eugen & A. A. Brill, *Textbook of Psychiatry,* The Macmillan Company, New York, 1924.

Boyd, Andrew, *United Nations Piety, Myth, and Truth,* Pelican Books, Baltimore, Md., 1962, 1964.

Buber, Martin, *I and Thou,* Charles Scribner's Sons, New York, 1958.

Dag Hammarskjöld, En Minnesbok, Bonniers, Stockholm, 1961.

Darwin, Charles, *Expressions of the Emotions in Man and Animal,* Philosophical Library, New York.

Durant, Will, *The Story of Philosophy,* Simon & Schuster, New York, 1953.

Foote, Wilder, Editor, *Dag Hammarskjöld, Servant of Peace,* Harper & Row, New York, 1962.

Gandhi, M. K., *Autobiography,* Public Affairs Press, Washington, D.C., 1948.

Gavshon, Arthur L., *The Mysterious Death of Dag Hammarskjöld,* Walker & Co., New York, 1962.

Hammarskjöld, Dag, *Markings,* A. A. Knopf, Inc., New York, 1964.

Jung, C. G., *The Development of Personality,* Bollingen Series, 20, Pantheon Books, New York, 1954.

Kierkegaard, *Selections,* Edited by Lee M. Hollander, Anchor Books, Doubleday & Co., Inc., Garden City, 1960.

BIBLIOGRAPHY : 308

Kretschmer, Ernst, *Physique and Character*, Routledge & Kegan Paul Ltd., London, 1949.

—— *The Psychology of Men of Genius*, Harcourt Brace & Co., New York, London, 1931.

—— *Textbook of Medical Psychology*, The Hogarth Press, London, 1952.

Lash, Joseph P., *Dag Hammarskjöld*, Doubleday & Company, Inc., Garden City, New York, 1961.

Mezerik, A. G., *International Review Service, United Nations Bureau*, Room 301, New York.

O'Brien, Conor Cruise, *To Katanga and Back*, Simon & Schuster, New York, 1962.

Okumu, Washington, *Lumumba's Congo*, Ivan Obolensky, Inc., New York, 1963.

Pascal, Blaise, *Pensées*.

Sheldon, W. H., *The Varieties of Human Physique*, Harper & Brothers, New York, 1940.

—— *The Varieties of Temperament*, Harper & Brothers, New York, 1952.

Söderberg, Sten, *Hammarskjöld, A Pictorial Biography*, A Studio Book, The Viking Press, New York, 1962.

Stockard, Charles R., *The Physical Basis of Personality*, W. W. Norton & Co., New York, 1931.

Stolpe, Sven, *Dag Hammarskjölds Geistiger Weg*, Joseph Knecht, Frankfurt-am-Main, 1964.

Willemse, W. A., *Constitutional Types in Delinquency*, Kegan Paul, Trench, Trubner & Co., London, 1932.

Winn, Ralph B., *Dictionary of Existentialism*, Philosophical Library, New York, 1960.

Official United Nations documents, radio and television scripts, transcripts of press conferences, speeches, etc.

Barbara Fraser Archives.

I am especially indebted to Wilder Foote's *Dag Hammarskjöld, Servant of Peace;* and to A. G. Mezerik's *International Review Service* which was of invaluable assistance to me.

Index

Gaza Strip, 34, 69, 77, 84, 88
Gizenga, Antoine, 194, 220, 237, 251, 252, 278
Glarner, Fritz, 143
Goethe, 107
Goldmann, Nahum, 71
Gordon, Mat, 153
Graham, Billy, 119
Gray, Kay, 142
Green, Sheldon, 118
Gromyko, Andrei, 205, 212, 244, 245, 246, 248
Gross Committee, 173
Gross, Ernest A., Ambassador, 172
Guinzbourg, Victor de, 76
Gustav Adolf, King of Sweden, 284

Hailsham, Viscount, 78
Hallonquist, Per, 24, 282
Halsman, Philippe, 123
Hammarskjöld, Agnes, 25, 29, 31, 36, 37, 38, 39, 286
Hammarskjöld, Åke, 26, 34, 35, 36, 37
Hammarskjöld, Bo, 34, 36, 42, 283
Hammarskjöld, Dag, family background 29-38; early career, 36, 37, Undersecretary of the Treasury, 37, 39ff., Vice-Minister of Foreign Affairs, 44ff., elected Secretary-General, 25-29; diplomatic techniques, 41-42, 64, 71, 84, 263ff.; work habits, 39-40, 79-80, 90-91.
Travels, 84, 129, 176-177; Elizabethville, 193; Leopoldville, 253, 258ff., 261; to Ndola, 266ff.; Near East, 70-72; Peking, 54-65; Rome, 109-110; Tunis, 103-105.

and Castro, 201-203; Lumumba, 188, 189, 191-192, 194, 221-222, 237ff.; Ben Gurion, 71; Bang-Jensen, 169-174; De Gaulle, 100, 105; Khrushchev, 207, 209, 214-215; Laymen, 112ff.; Nasser, 70; Pope Pius XII, 109-110, 298; press, 121ff., 131ff., 134, press conferences, 126-131, 241; Secretariat, 49ff., 54, 63, 88, 145, 217-218, 257, close collaborators, 85-88, 89-90, 145.
and Africa, 183-184; Britain, 262-263; Congo, 252-253; France, 100, 104-106, 239; Hungary, 92-95; Soviet Union, 61, 63, 95, 199-200, 217-218, 223, 238, 244ff., 248, 299; Tunisian crisis, 100-105; United States, 96, 223, 239.
appearance, 30, 49-50, 54, 137ff., 146, 148-50, juvenility, 157, 158, 163, 164.
character, 35, 37, 42, 46, 49-50, 53ff., 57, 89-90, 99, 126, 137ff., 146, 148-150, 168ff., 240-241, 249; death-wish, 167ff., 180, 279; melancholia, 174ff., narcissism, 147, 152-164, sexual life, 30, 153ff., 156-157, 159ff., women, 147, 153-156.
as mountaineer, 40, 47, 61-62, 167, 243-244; taste in art, 56, 61, 115ff., 143; in literature, 58-59, 143-144; New York apartment, 56-57.
religious beliefs, 107-109, 179, 183; see also Meditation Room.

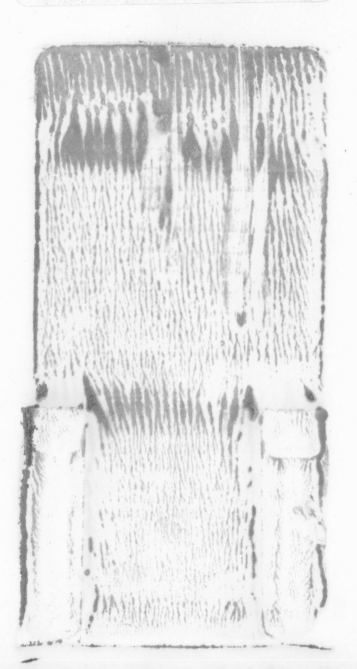